Pete Georgiady's

WOOD SHAFTED GOLF CLUB VALUE GUIDE

5th Edition

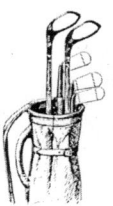

AIRLIE HALL PRESS
KERNERSVILLE
NORTH CAROLINA

2002

Fifth Edition
First Printing
Copyright September, 2002

Peter Georgiady

All Rights Reserved

All photographs copyright Peter Georgiady
except where specifically noted

No part of this book may be reproduced without written consent
of the author and publisher

ISBN 1-886752-16-8

Layout by AHP Services
Manufactured in the United States of America
Printed by Battleground Printing and Publishing Company

Published and distributed by:

**Airlie Hall Press
PO Box 981
Kernersville, NC 27285-0981**

Cover art work:
Long blade putter by Tom Stewart
computer rendered by master draftsman
Curt Fredrixon, Renton, WA

To my wife Kay, son Bryan
and to the memory of Doug Glassey,
the old Dundonian who pointed me in this direction

Special thanks to **Rand Jerris, Patty Moran** *and the staff of the library and museum of the United States Golf Association in Far Hills, New Jersey whose cooperation and support is so greatly appreciated;*

to **Roger Hill** *and* **Ralph Livingston III** *of Grand Rapids, Michigan whose photographic assistance has been invaluable over many years;*

and to the large number of golf collecting friends who helped in many different ways: **Dan Bagdade, Brendan Casey, Andrew Crewe, Randy Crow, Dick Durran, Chuck Furjanic, John Gates, Bob Georgiade, Bryan Georgiady, Tony Harman, Bob Lucas, Ron Lyons, Kevin McGrath, Chuck McMullin, Bill Nelson, Chris Ream, L.R. Rhett, John Sherwood, Allen Wallach, Gary Wyckoff** *as well as CAD cover art director* **Curt Fredrixon**.

Other books for golf collectors available from

Airlie Hall Press

Collecting Antique Golf Clubs

Compendium of British Club Makers

North American Club Makers

North American Club and Course Index

Views and Reviews: Golf Clubs in the Trade Press

Cleek Marks and Trademarks on Antique Golf Clubs

For further information, contact:

Airlie Hall Press
PO Box 981
Kernersville, NC 27285-0981
(336) 996-7836
airliehall@earthlink.net

INTRODUCTION

The Philosophy Behind the Value Guide:

"Value," not necessarily "Price"

To make this guide book meaningful, one must understand the concept of **VALUE VERSUS PRICE**. Simply, price is what you pay and value is what the item is worth in relative terms. Those last few words are very important because value is truly relative depending on the individual's point of view.

For collectors of golf clubs, the range of relativity is still broad owing to individual criteria like specialty interests, re-marketablilty, degree of knowledge and amount of discretionary income. In more meaningful terms, there are serious and casual buyers, pure collectors and dealers, affluent and budget minded spenders and to each permutation club values may differ significantly.

The most important idea is that in golf clubs, like many other types of collectibles, there exist many different levels of market. At the economy end are flea markets, garage and estate sales and cleaning out grandma's attic. Expectations here are that things will not cost very much. The other end of the spectrum might include auction sales, dealer catalogs and upscale antique shows where a more knowledgeable, discerning buying public is usually in attendance. Values there are reflected in higher prices.

Today's antique golf club market includes flea markets, collectors' "swap" meetings, public auctions and dealer sales each of which has its own level of value expectations and subsequent prices. Nothing is precise and at any one of these market institutions one can easily over pay just as one can find bargains. Merging the individual characteristics of each buyer with the array of different market place opportunities creates a very complex economic network, one which would be virtually impossible to document with any authority.

Understanding that, the philosophy of this book is elementary. It is to provide a relative market value rather than give a price expectation for a given club at one or more of the various market levels. The relative market value used here is deemed to be somewhere in the middle of the road; greater than a garage sale value but less than a what might be expected in a transaction at the upper end. The relativity issues are to understand which clubs are in $50 tier, the $250 range or the $2,000 neighborhood as well as realizing that a $50 club might only cost $25 at an outdoor market but might sell for $75 among knowledgeable collectors. There are also clubs so populous in their numbers that established collectors rarely are interested. They may sell readily to novice collectors but almost never to experienced collectors--any price. Let this book be your guide, not your absolute price list.

Variance in Highly Valued Clubs

Another rule to observe is that as the relative value of clubs increase, the variance in their actual selling price broadens. Periodically we see a given club sell for one price one day and for another price, drastically different, a day, a month or a year later. Scarcity of supply causes a perception of greater value but greater price often causes a significantly smaller number of potential buyers. The smaller the available supply is, the far less *predictable* price realized will be.

For that reason, more caution should be exercised in transactions involving clubs of greater value. Within this guide, clubs in the upper price range are valued conservatively or a value spread is provided. Again, the real principle is to understand what clubs belong in the upper value bracket and to become more educated as to their standing in the market and their collector value.

Condition as a Function of Value

More than any other principle, condition plays a role in determining the price of an old golf club. An important premise of clubs listed in this guide is that they are in **"very good"** condition, not damaged, distressed, restored or mint. This takes into consideration that golf clubs were meant to be used with a certain amount of force, in outdoor conditions and that wood shafted clubs are at a minimum 70 years old if not older.

Clubs should look old and used but not damaged or abused. The worst case of condition is a club that is damaged and not fully restorable. Clubs with irreparable damage should be avoided and only retained to fill an important void in a collection. A club needing restoration, which can be spruced up without major repair work, is a better club to acquire. Clubs existing today in "as found" condition that need little repair and usually just a light cleaning are very desirable and the closest match to the values provided here. Those rare exceptions, clubs in excellent or hardly used condition, are few and far between. They generally deserve some degree of upward valuation.

Similarly, overzealous restoration of an antique golf club can render it as worthless as one that has been damaged through abuse. The most often followed philosophy on restoration is to leave the club as closely as possible to its original state. Dirt and rust should be carefully removed, original grips and whipping should be stabilized or, if missing, carefully replaced.

Other Characteristics and Their Affect on Value

There are several other attributes that may or may not alter value. In some cases these are purely of subjective value to the individual collector.

For instance, most collectors are right-handed and tend to avoid collecting left-handed clubs. Some feel they are worth something less than their right-handed club counterparts. Yet there are left-handed collectors that prize the much rarer left-handed clubs and assiduously seek them out.

Some collectors feel that a lady's club holds a lesser value than the corresponding man's model. Just as in the above example, there are lady collectors to whom lady's clubs are very important. In my opinion, the value behind the club is the absolute terms of what it represents and by whom it was made. Theoretically, a man's club and the similar lady's from the same maker should have the same intrinsic value but the perception of the individual buyer also plays an important role, regardless of the validity of accepted valuation rationale.

The vast majority of wood shafted clubs were produced with shafts of hickory grown in America. Every once in a while, a club turns up with a shaft made from another species of wood. Exotic wood shafts made from greenheart, lemonheart, purpleheart, danga wood, lancewood, beef wood, texa ash and bamboo commanded a slight premium for clubs when they were made a century ago. Similarly, they should be viewed as slightly more valuable today.

There are some other variables such as the style and condition of grip and relative straightness of shaft that play a minor part in valuation but in general terms they are not big issues.

The Importance of a Matched Set of Clubs

Since it is almost impossible to buy modern-made clubs singly in the 1990s, we contemporary golfers have a 'set of clubs' mentality. The opposite was true a century ago when clubs were purchased one at a time without regard to how they related to the others in the bag. Matched sets were an innovation available only during the last ten years of the wood shafted era (roughly 1925-35). Related or matched sets marked the industry's turn toward more "manufactured" goods and away from the hand made, individualistic quality of older clubs.

In several places in this guide, the existence of certain club models available to collectors as matched sets is shown. In a few cases, values are given for matched sets of clubs. It should be strongly noted that a "set" of clubs could have been between 6 and 11 in number so collectors should know what they are buying. The historical significance of sets is not great and they do not occupy as important a position in golf collecting as do some other classes of clubs. A full set does make for an impressive display, though, and as collectors move into the 21st century interest in and the value of full sets is rising.

Associating Values

Millions of wood shafted clubs were produced from 1850 to 1935. The former year marks the advent of the guttie ball which made the sport more affordable and induced more people to play; the latter year being roughly the year that steel shafted clubs finally won out over wood shafts, once and for all and most manufacturers ceased to offer them for sale. The sheer number of clubs in existence, the individualistic, handcrafted nature of the product and a shortage of space prevent every club ever made from being listed in this guide. We are trying to cover as many bases as possible without reaching a level of detail so confusing the average collector becomes frustrated.

Associating value from a club listed in this guide to another similar club not listed serves to expand the range of club values for the collector. If you have a *mid iron* in a certain model or by a certain maker and there is only a *mashie* of similar form listed, it's fair to say that those two clubs are closely associated and will probably hold similar values.

There are always exceptions to everything but some good rules of thumb to understand are:

- A putter is generally worth more than comparable iron clubs (mid iron, mashie, etc.) of the same age, series or set;

- The same is true for wood clubs; woods are usually worth more than irons of the same age, series or set. They are less common;

- Within a group of irons, specialty irons like jiggers, sammies and spade mashies are typically more scarce and worth more than mid irons and mashies;

- Smooth face irons are generally worth more than those with line or dot scored faces;

Wood Shafted Golf Club Value Guide

- Splice head woods are older and more scarce than comparable socket head woods.

Use these generally observed conventions when extrapolating a value to a club which is not listed but where a similar counterpart may be shown.

HOW TO READ THE ENTRIES

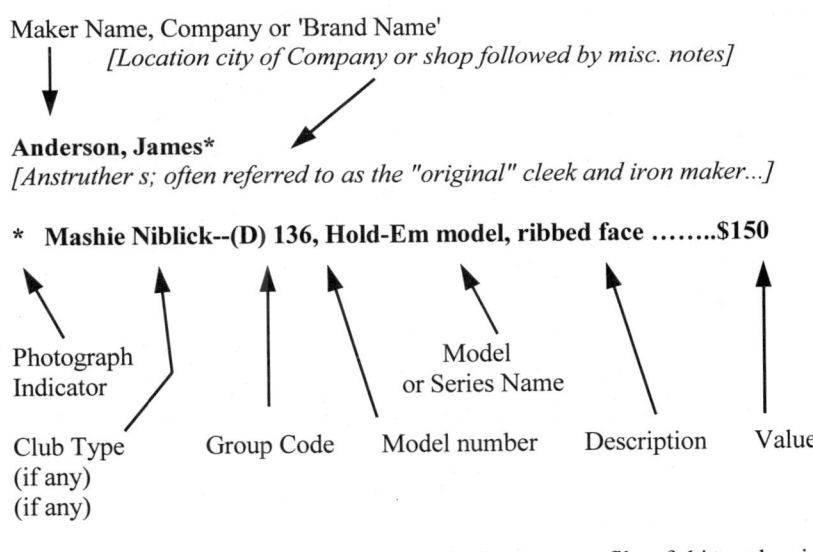

* an asterisk behind maker name indicates a profile of this maker is included in the <u>Compendium of British Club Makers</u>
+ a plus sign behind maker name indicates a profile of this maker is included in the book <u>North American Club Makers</u>

Group Code: Certain clubs have one salient characteristic that categorizes them into a commonality group. The groups used are
      (A) Aluminum headed clubs, drivers, fairway clubs and putters (aluminum clubs are also listed by model/maker name in their own cross reference section)

(B) Clubs awarded a British patent or design registration

(D) Deep Groove clubs, most of which were also patented

(L) Long nose style clubs including many 19th century woods and certain aluminum head replicas

(S) Semi-long nose style clubs including many 19th century woods and aluminum head replicas

(U) Clubs awarded a United States patent or design registration.

Note: Clubs patented in both the US and Britain are designated by (B) or (U), whichever best reflects the nationality of the patentee or manufacturer.

Club makers who have worked in several cities or locations will usually have the primary venue of their work listed followed with *"et.al."* More complete lists of their working locations can be found in the books <u>Compendium of British Club Makers</u> and <u>North American Club Makers.</u>

Club types within maker which have no other delimiter of age or style are group-sorted in the following manner:

Woods--Drivers first followed by Brassies, Spoons, other clubs and 19th century wood putters.
Iron clubs--Listed individually by club type or grouped as **"Iron clubs," Named Irons, Numbered Irons** and **Sets** where the value between types is fairly consistent,
followed by
Putters. The category 'Iron clubs' refers to clubs from driving iron to niblick.

Location listings: The city (cities) or club (clubs) where the maker worked is followed by a country code:

e	England
s	Scotland
w	Wales
i	Ireland

American cities are followed by their two letter state Post Office abbreviation (NY, PA, MA)

Wood Shafted Golf Club Value Guide

Canadian cities are followed by a three letter province abbreviation (ONT)

Select cities which need no further definition are followed by no code (London, St. Andrews, New York)

A single star (*) indicates a photo of the club is shown on that page or an adjascent page. A double star (**) in the left hand margin indicates a photo of this club appears in the color section.

Model or series name: There is no absolute division between these two terms as they relate to golf clubs but I have observed a general differentiation. Model is usually used where the name is applied to one particular club or pattern, like a singular (Schenectady) putter or (Cran) cleek, or a small group of similar clubs, like Gibson's Genii irons. Series is used when a name is applied across a broad range of clubs or within the context of a set, like Spalding's Kro-Flite irons.

Named Irons: gives a general value for most common irons with names like mid iron, mashie or niblick.
Numbered Irons: gives a value for clubs with numbers (4-iron or 6-iron, etc.). A 4-iron may be listed but values are similar for other numbers within the set or series
Iron clubs: can mean any metal headed club with the characteristics within the model/series listed

CM: when used in the description field means Cleek Mark. A true cleek mark was only found on iron headed clubs but in the context of this guide CM refers to any cleek mark, brand mark, model mark, maker's mark or trade mark found on a wood or iron headed club.

Explanation of Terminology

Listed here are most of the terms used in the club descriptions in this guide. Some are contemporary with the clubs themselves while others are names current collectors have chosen to use.

Complete golf club collecting terminology is contained in ***Col-***

lecting Antique Golf Clubs, an excellent accompaniment to this book.

WOOD HEADED CLUBS

Backweight--Most wood clubs have a lead weight nested in the back of the club. Some later models featured backweights of other materials fixed with screws.

Bulldog head--A design like the **Short** or **Compact** head but with a slight thickening of the toe. It was found mostly in brassies and spoons.

Long nose--Most wood headed clubs made prior to 1890 fit into this category as well as a few made after 1890. They are characterized by long thin heads and always **spliced** to the shaft. They may also be called **Long Headed**. In the guide these clubs are designated with (L).

Semi-long nose--Around the time of the invention of the bulger, shorter headed woods became more fashionable for play. One style, the Bulger head tended to be shorter and broader while the type we call **Transitional** today was narrower, more of a shortened **Long Nose** head. These two forms were also **spliced** to the shaft though after the turn of the century semi-long nose style putters were made with **Socket** heads. In the guide these clubs are designated with (S).

Short head or Compact head--As clubs became more modern wood heads became less long. Many were made very small and can be called short to differentiate them from the more elongated heads popular around 1900.

Socket head--Supplanting the use of the splice head was the practice of socketing where a tapered hole was drilled into the neck of the wood head and end of the round shaft inserted and glued.

Splice head--The original method of joining the wood head to the shaft was to plane a side of each flat, glue the two together and wrap with **Whipping**. This method continued into the first decade of the 20th century.

Stripe top--Popular in the late teens and through the 1920s, the crown of the club was given a two-tone stain or paint treatment with a contrasting colored stripe. The maker's name was generally stamped in the stripe.

FACINGS FOR WOOD HEADED CLUBS

Fancy Face--In the 1920s, multi-part fiber faces were made in geometric designs or with images inlaid (like the Spalding Kro-Flite crow).

Fiber-- Sometimes called **Vulcanite**, it first appeared in black and later in the 1900s was available in colors. Fiber was a man made composite of carbon and textile fibers.

Ivorine--A white plastic substance resembling ivory. Also called **Ivor** or **Ivora**. Genuine **Ivory** was also used in premium quality clubs though it tended to crack with use and age.

Leather--The use of the guttie ball on wooden clubs caused damage to the club face; most 19th century clubs with face inserts used leather tacked in place with small cobbler's nails.

Metal faces included **Steel**, **Aluminum** and **Brass**

Plugs-- Some **Fancy Face** inserts included circular fiber studs to secure them in place. Sometimes referred to as **pegs**. Actual wooden pegs were used on older face inserts.

IRON HEADED CLUBS

Some Common Design Styles or Characteristics of Iron Clubs

Beveled--Some of the mass on the back of the head has been removed at an angle. Most common are clubs with **Beveled Heel and Toe** or **Beveled Top Edge**.

Blade--Also called **Regular** in the old days, this is a simple flat bar shaped head. This term is also commonly used for the simple putter head.

Carruthers hosel--The first use of a through-bore hosel designed by Thomas Carruthers in 1890 and imitated by many other makers.

Concentric back--Also called **Centraject** or **Concentrated**, has the weight concentrated behind the sweet spot and tapering to the top edge and heel and toe.

Diamond back--A back coming to a point behind the sweet spot resembling the facets of a gemstone.

Fairlie model--This **"anti-shank"** patent featured the front edge of the club head set ahead of the hosel.

Flange sole--Having a flat, broadened sole for extra bottom weight.

Foulis--A style of mashie niblick with an oval head, flat sole and concave face patented by James Foulis and imitated by other makers.

Hollow back--Has weighting top and bottom or at the sides leaving the area behind the sweet spot thinnest.

Maxwell Pattern--A design incorporating holes drilled in the hosel and a flange sole.

Monel--Also called Monel metal, it is a nickel-bronze allow which proved to be non-rustable.

Musselback--Has a weighted portion on the bottom edge of the club back emulating the shape of a type of sea shell.

Round back--A barrel shaped club back rounded top to bottom. **Convex back** is a similar variation.

Smith model--One of the two major **"anti-shank"** patents, it featured a hosel with a large offset bend. True Smith irons also had extra heel and toe weighting in a **Hollow Back** design.

IRON CLUB FACE PATTERNS

Concave face--The club face is "dished" or scooped.

Dash face--Similar to **Line Face** but using dashed or hyphenated lines instead of continuous lines.

Diamond face--A pattern of diagonal lines creating a diamond shaped design. Sometimes a dot was struck in each diamond creating a **Diamond/dot** face.

Dot face--Most common among old clubs was to punch dot shaped indentations in the club face to help grab the ball. Normally these dots were arranged in rows though circular and other shaped patterns also exist.

Line face--The other most common face scoring was to cut horizontal lines.

Smooth face--Until about 1900, virtually all clubs were without face scoring.

Stagdot--This name refers specifically to a pattern of alternating dots and dashes created by MacGregor and imitated by other makers.

** Many additional combinations of Dashes, Diamonds, Dots and Lines exist.

About 1915, deeply grooved club faces, designed to impart backspin to the ball, were in wide use. They were declared illegal in 1922 and not manufactured after that date. Many designs were created and the primary ones are given here. In the guide, all deep groove clubs are designated with the (D) code.

Ball face--Used primarily by Kroydon and Robert Simpson, the face scoring is in a circular "ball" shaped pattern.

Brick face--Vertical and horizontal grooves resembling brick work.

Corrugated face--Another name for **Ribbed**.

Grooved face--Extra wide, deep grooves machined into the club face, usually numbering 4 to 6; another name for **Slotted.**

Rainbow face--Used by Wilson in its Walker Cup series, these concentric semi-circular lines resembled a rainbow.

Ribangled face--The standard **Ribbed** face with thinner diagonal grooves added.

Ribbed face--Wide, deep grooves, usually numbering 8 to 15 on the club face. The most commonly used deep groove pattern.

Rotary face--A variation of **Waffle** used by Burke.

Slotted face--Another name for **Grooved**.

Waffle face--Deep vertical and horizontal grooves in a grid pattern, like a waffle iron.

Waterfall face--Used by Spalding and Wright & Ditson, the horizontal deep grooves curved downward toward the toe resembling a waterfall.

PUTTERS

Because more attention was given to putter design than all

other clubs combined, many terms are used to describe putters. A few of the more prominent ones are listed here.

Bent Blade--A straight hosel with the blade bent back behind the hosel.

Bent Neck-- Like the **Park** model, the hosel is bent slightly backward.

Blade--The name for the simplest style of putter: a straight flat blade with no offset from the line of the shaft.

Gem--A **Concentric** shaped blade with the thickest portion of the blade behind the sweet spot.

Gooseneck--With greater bend than the **Bent Neck**.

Mallet--Usually in aluminum, this head resembles the shape of a wooden driver head.

Offset--Only a slight bend at the bottom of the hosel offsetting the blade from the shaft line. Found in some later irons as well.

Park--Named for Willie Park, Jr., the originator of the bent hosel putter. Also called **Bent Neck** or wry neck.

Ray--A model of aluminum mallet head designed by Ted Ray for the Standard Golf Company. It featured two flat tiers on its crown.

Schenectady--Named for the city where its creator, A.F. Knight resided, this club is the original center shafted mallet putter, later copied by many companies in aluminum or wood.

Note: A more complete glossary of terminology of golf club construction, attributes, form and shape can be found in <u>Collecting Antique Golf Clubs</u>, Airlie Hall Press.

100 COLLECTIBLE CLUBS

Within the listings in this volume, 100 clubs are noted with a **"100"** at the left hand page margin. They represent some of the most popular clubs golf collectors actively seek. The list is purely arbitrary and based on input from many collectors. It comprises a range of clubs that include:

- clubs made by the most famous and historic club makers as examples of their craft
- clubs that played prominent roles in the history of the game
- clubs that have proved to be popular with collectors by the nature of their appearance

Some are quite pricey, like the Philp playclub or the Spalding Lard shaft iron. Others are quite affordable and easily obtainable like the Mills Ray putter or any of the Ampco metal clubs. The assortment covers the many extremes found in antique golf clubs and, if assembled, would make a most interesting collection.

Collectors will find certain clubs become more or less fashionable over time. In a few more years, clubs on this list might be replaced by new entries that collectors find intriguing.

(**100*,** *where an asterisk is shown with 100, signifies any club of that sort or maker, i.e. any of the Ampco metal clubs or any old iron by John Gray or F.& A. Carrick, not necessarily one particular club).*

Pete Georgiady's

Old Irons

Many old iron clubs, especially those dating from before 1880, have no markings and are impossible to identify by maker. Because of their singular nature, there are very few included in this book. Describing and valuating them is highly subjective and does not easily lend itself to a book like this. They are generally one of a kind.

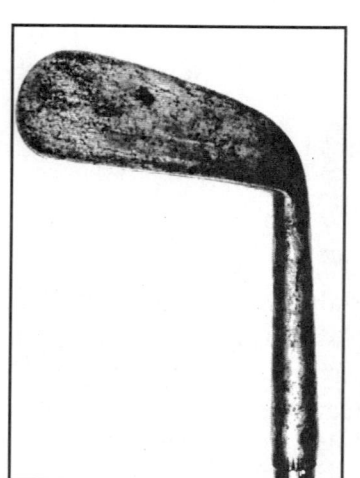
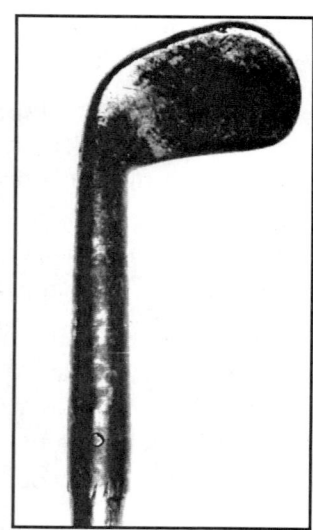
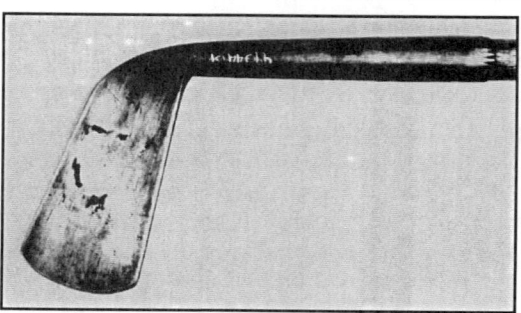

Wood Shafted Golf Club Value Guide

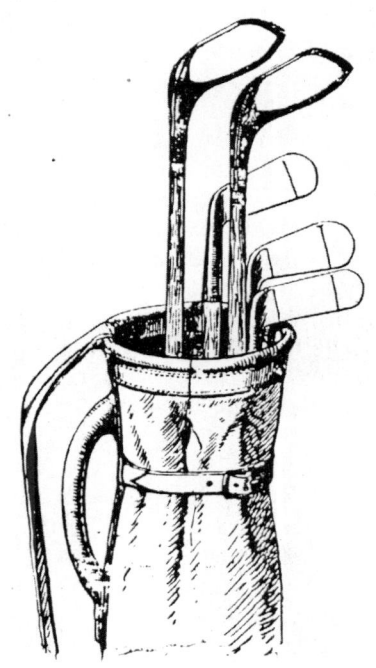

Pete Georgiady's

Abercrombie & Fitch
[New York department store]
Driver--(U) Master model, patent face insert with
7 ivory plugs $150
Brassie--Socket head, stripe top..$50
Spoon--Socket head, face insert..$65
Jigger--H1 model, round back, dot face, monogram CM $45
Mashie--Made by Kroydon $35
Mashie--Stainless, 2 AF CMs, line face $45
Mashie--Model GS3, Burke Monel $60
Mashie Iron--Monel metal, line face $50
Mashie Niblick--Line face, stainless, monogram CM $30
Mid Iron--Model WG5, marked "Burke Monel" $60
Niblick--Model J1L musselback, Monel $65
Niblick--Model NO, Monel $60
Niblick--Model WH9, Burke Monel $60
Putter--Model P1L, Monel blade by Burke $60
Putter--Model WH10, Burke Monel $60
5-Iron--Y model (youth), line face $25

'Aberdeen'
[These clubs are named Aberdeen but each was made by a different company. Cleek marks and model numbers are used to identify the respective maker]
Driver--made by B.G.I., splice head, model number on shaft $225
Driver--(U) Fork splice, made by B.G.I. $400
Mashie--Name in arc, made by MacGregor $25
Mid Iron--Line face, round back, Burke bee & flower CM $35

Abraham & Strauss
[New York department store]
Irons--Lido model, line face, stainless .... $25 each

'Acme'
Cleek--(B) 'The Acme', smooth face, Carrick cross CM $300

Adams, David
[Glasgow]
Driver--Splice head $125

24

Wood Shafted Golf Club Value Guide

Brassie--Small socket head $60
Lofter--Concentric back, line face $60
Mashie--Diamond back, Anderson arrow CM, line face $60
Mashie Iron--Nicoll hand CM, dot face $50
Putter--Blade $60

Jeff Adams "Coordination Putter"
This aluminum putter comes in several variations of head shape. They are all roughly similar but differ in the roundness of the ends and the flatness of the sole.

Produced in the 1920s some models can be found factory fitted with steel shafts though they are not as valuable as their wood shaft counterparts.

Adams, Jeff
* Putter--(A) Coordination model, center shaft, boat shaped head with pointed back $400

'Aim Rite'
[Thomas E. Wilson Co. trade mark appearing on a majority of their clubs, often on the sweet spot of the face. "Aim Rite" clubs listed under Wilson Company, Thomas E.]
Iron clubs--Line face, "Aim Rite" in circle on face $25

Aitken, Alex*
[Gullane s]
Driver--Splice head, transitional shape $250
Driver--Socket head $75
Driver--Short splice head, fiber face insert $200
Brassie--(S) Splice head $500
Brassie--Bulger splice head $750
Wooden Mashie--Pear shaped splice head with dished face . $400
Iron--Smooth face, shaft stamp $100
Putter--(B) Short hosel and blade with very deep face $400

'Alco'
Mashie Niblick--Bronze-type metal oval head, ALCO in star shape CM, line face $75

Alexander & Company, George*
[London department store]
Mashie--Dot face, made by Forgan $30

Alexander, G.
Driver--(B) Hammer head shaped wood with 2 hitting faces $3,000

Allan, John*
[Westward Ho! e and Prestwick s]
Playclub--(L) Brown finish, thick grip, marked "J. Allan" . $4,500
Long Spoon--(L) Dark colored beech head, minor worm damage $3,500
Short Spoon--(L) Lofted face slightly damaged $4,000
Driver--(S) Transitional head, dark color $1,000
Putter--(L) Dark color $2,500
Putter--(S) Thornwood head $2,750

'Alloway'
Putter--(B) Oval head with red guttie face insert $3,500

Allday Company, P.G.*
[Birmingham e]
Putter--Northwood brand, gun metal blade, monogram CM ..$75
Putting Cleek--(A) Northwood brand, model A, mallet head $100
Putter--Northwood brand, Brown-Vardon type in gun metal, steel face $250
Putter--Northwood brand, later splice wood head $125
Putter--Northwood model E, wood head, lead weights $95

Allen Putter Company
Putter--(U) Adjustable, two lofts, swivel center shaft $1,500
Putter--(U) Adjustable, hosel screws to lock angle $750

Allied Golf Company
Driver--Stripe top, socket head $35

Wood Shafted Golf Club Value Guide

Altman, Albert J.
[London]
    Mashie--(B) Smooth face, round back, crimped hosel $225

Altman & Company, B.
[New York department store]
    Driver--Stripe top socket head $75
    Brassie--Stripe top, 'Selected,' ivory insert $100
    Mashie--Made by Everbrite, stainless, dot face $35
    Mashie--Name in script, stainless, dot face $30

Ampco Metal Golf Club Company+
[Milwaukee, WI; Ampco metal is a bronze-like alloy, Dow metal is a harder version of aluminum. All Ampco irons were made from Ampco metal]
*   Driver--Dow metal head, Ampco face insert........................... $175
         Brassie--Dow Metal head, Ampco metal face insert $175
100*   Jigger--Line face $80
         Driving Iron--Line face, name in box $75
         Mid Iron--Lie face--Marked "more yards per stroke" $75
         Mashie--Line face $75
*   Niblick--Marked "more yards per stroke", line face $80
         Putter--Thick blade $100
         Set of 8 irons $750

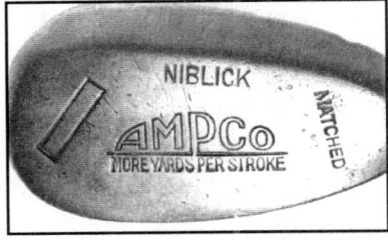

Ampco Metal Golf Club Company
Using their rustless bronze alloy this company produced a line of non-steel irons in the 1920s. Their metal woods were made of Dow metal (which resembled zinc or tin) with a yellow Ampco metal face insert.

An Company, The
    Iron--Juvenile, large bee CM $40

Pete Georgiady's

    Putter--Juvenile blade, line face, large bee CM $50

Anderson, Anderson & Anderson, Ltd.*
[London waterproof manufacturers and retailers also selling golf requisites]
    Driver--Splice head, pear shaped head $350
    Driver--Socket head, escutcheon CM $250
    Driving Iron--Company escutcheon with two globes CM,
    also Anderson arrow CM, smooth face $150
    Mashie--Company escutcheon, line face $150
    Mashie-Rustless, beveled toe, large crown CM $75
    Putter--(B) J. Anderson bronze mallet, steel face,
    escutcheon CM $400
    Putting Cleek--Company escutcheon & Gourlay
    moon/star CMs $200

Anderson & Blyth*
[St. Andrews]
    Driver--Juvenile socket head $75
    Driver--Socket head, white fiber insert $90
    Driver--Invincible model, large socket head, fiber face insert $125
*   Brassie--Socket head, name in arc $80
    Cleek--Stewart pipe CM, line face $50
    Cleek--Short blade, dot face $50
    Iron--Push model, deep face, dot face $100
    Mashie--(B) Weymiss model, bi-level back $90
    Putter--(S) Splice head $600
    Putter--Wood splice head, fiber slip in sole $200
    Putter--Wood splice head, brass face insert $250

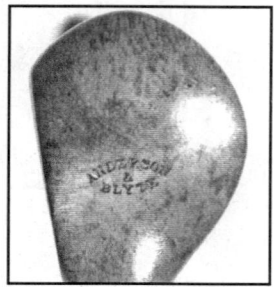

Anderson & Blyth
This firm located in St. Andrews produced some finely crafted hand made clubs. They were only together for a few years and their production output was relatively small.

Anderson & Gourlay*
[St. Andrews]

Wood Shafted Golf Club Value Guide

Approach Mashie--Sovereign series, 3-facet back, A & G CM $75
Driving Iron--Wellington model, line face $70
Mashie--Round back, dot face $65
Numbered Irons--Diamond Iron model, line face, diamond back,
monogram A & G CM $65
Putter--Small iron mallet head, shaped like Ray model,
A & G CM $150

Anderson, D. & W.*
[St. Andrews]

Cleek--Smooth face $250
Iron--Smooth face, name stamped in oval $250
Lofter--Smooth face $300

Anderson & Sons, D.*
[St. Andrews; David Anderson, son of "Old Da'" and younger brother of Jamie, the champion, was assisted in this business by his six sons]

Driver--Spliced-head, Texa ash shaft $350
Driver--(S) Splice head, leather insert $450
Driver--Supreme model, ivorine insert, stripe top
socket head $100
Driver--Semi-circular black fiber insert in face $125
Brassie--Socket head $75
Brassie--Swilcan model, large socket head $95
Cleek--Smooth face, name in oval $100
Cleek--marked "Diamond Cleek", diamond back, line face $65
Driving Iron--Dot face $50
Driving Iron--Zenith model, dash face $50
Driving Iron--Glory model, diamond back, line face $65
Jigger--Glory series, diamond back, dot face $75
Jigger--Monarch series, dot face, beveled heel and toe $75
Lofter--Single fern frond CM, smooth face $225

*100 Mashie--(B) G.F. Smith model (anti-shank),
hollow back, line face $200

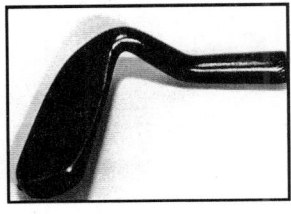

D. Anderson Smith patent 'anti-shank' iron. The Smith mark is in an oval similar to the Anderson mark (right side).

Mashie--Glory series, diamond back $75
Mashie--Smooth face, tiny Millar thistle CM, compact blade $150
Mashie--Smooth face, Condie single CM $250
Mashie Niblick--Premier series, St. Andrew CM,
stainless, line face $50
Niblick--Large size, line face $60
Niblick--Medium size, dot face, diamond back $75
Niblick--Small head, smooth face $300
Putter--Bulge back, dot face $75
Putter--Excelsior model, concentric back, diamond/dot face $100
Putter--Triumph model, offset blade, peaked top edge $150
Putter--100 model, concentric shaped head $100
Putter-Glory series, diamond back $85
Putter--Iron blade ....$ 50

R. Anderson & Sons
This patent crescent shaped iron was one of the first unusual patents (1891). Irons are rare, the center shaft driver is even more scarce.

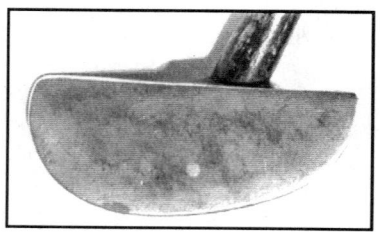

Anderson & Sons, R.*
[Princes Street, Edinburgh]

    Driver--(B) short head, through-bore center shaft $4,250
    Driver--Socket head $125
    Driver--Socket head, leather face insert $150
    Driver--(A) Small head, checkered face $350
    Brassie--(A) Marked "Cleek", small head $500
    Cleek--C.1895, smooth face, greenheart shaft $150
I   Iron--(B) Crescent shaped center shaft head $1,500
    Lofter--(B) Crescent head, center shaft $2,000
    Lofter--Smooth face, large head, Spalding Gold Medal $65
    Mashie--Compact blade, smooth face $80
    Putter--(S) Wooden socket head $250
    Putter--Blade, heavy hosel $100
    Putter--Gun metal blade $150

Anderson, Carl H.

Wood Shafted Golf Club Value Guide

[Lake Geneva, WI, et al]
    Driving Iron--Super Stroke series, monel, line face $45

Anderson, David*
[Bromley & Bickley G.C. e]
    Brassie--Socket head, shaft stamp $60

Anderson, Grant
    Jigger-Acorn Brand, acorn CM, dot face $60

Anderson, James*
[Anstruther s; often referred to as the "original" cleek and iron maker, James began the club head forging business in 1865 and died in 1895. The firm continued into the 1930s under his son Alex. Clubs marked with the name in a 1/2" diameter circle generally date from the 19th century. The name mark in the 5/8" circle and the name mark within two concentric circles are 20th century clubs]

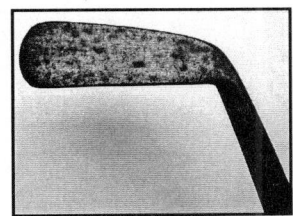

James Anderson (of Anstruther). The typical cleek from the 1880s had a long blade with shallow face, the top and bottom edges being almost parallel. The hosel was usually about 4 1/2" long.

◇◇Smooth face irons (1/2" dia. CM unless noted)
*100   Cleek--C.1875, long thin blade, 4 1/2" hosel
       with deep nicking $500
       Cleek--Made for Goudie & Co., convex back,
       double circle CM $75
       Iron--Smooth face $100
       Iron--Double circle CM $75
       Lofting Iron--C.1890, long blade, slightly dished face,
       thick hosel, dark stained shaft $400
       Lofting Iron--C.1890, large F.H. Ayers markings on shaft,
       slightly concave $300
       Mashie--Double circle CM, short blade $80
       Mashie--C.1890, short head, deep face blade, heavy hosel .. $350
       Mashie Iron--(B) Fairlie model, serial number $200
       Niblick--C.1895, medium size head $150
       Niblick--C.1885, small head $800

Pete Georgiady's

Niblick--(B) G. Lowe's patent (anti-shank), like Fairlie
model, serial number, smooth face, small head $300
Niblick--Small head, smooth face, Sherardized, marked
for Army & Navy Store $400
Putter--(B) Kurtos model, convex face and back $300
Putter--Deep face blade $300
Putter--C.1895, thick blade and hosel $200
Putter--Gun metal blade $225

◇◇Scored face irons showing model number where applicable
- Approaching Cleek--38, musselback, dot face $60
- Cleek--3, dot face $60
- Cleek--4, centraject-type head $65
- Cleek--127, musselback $65
- Cleek--(B) 1919, "Non Slice" model $80
- Driving Iron--85, round sole, line face, arrow CM $65
- Driving Iron--121, dot face, arrow CM $50
- Jigger--88, musselback, dot face, arrow CM $60
- Mashie--Double circle & arrow CMs, line face $50
- Mashie--Royal Crown brand, line face $55
- Mashie--21, diamond back, arrow CM $50
- Mashie--22, regular back, arrow CM $40
- Mashie--24, flange sole $50
- Mashie--(D) 54, arrow CM, ribbed face $125
- Mashie Niblick--Magic model, oval head, line face $60
- Mashie Niblick--115, Maxwell pattern $85
- Mashie Niblick--(D) 136, Hold-Em model,
  oval shaped head, ribbed face $150
- Mashie Niblick--30, thick sole, dot face $60
- Mid Iron--6, line face $50
- Mid Iron--Juvenile, marked B $50
- Niblick--33, concave dash face, arrow CM $150
- Niblick--150, large head, arrow CM, line face $80
- Niblick--Vardon autograph model, medium size head,
  line face $125
- Pitcher--41, round sole $100
- Sammy--2, dot face, notched at hosel $65
- Sammy--5A, round back, dot face $65
- Sammy--6, thick sole $65
- Sammy Iron--133, dot face $65
- Putter--51, steel blade $50

Wood Shafted Golf Club Value Guide

	Putter--68, dot face, peak on top edge	$100
	Putter--91, iron blade, notched at hosel	$100
	Putter--105B, iron blade	$65
	Putter--151, offset blade	$65
	Putter--Magic model, thick sole, eveled toe, arrow CM	$80
	Putter--Blade with horizontal weight ridge on back	$150
**100	Putter--(B) Small gun metal mallet head, steel face insert	$250
	Putter--As above with wood face insert	$350
	Putter--(B) The Coaxer model, iron blade, bent neck, arrow CM	$125
*100	Putting Cleek--(B) Twisted neck, reg. # 277771	$125

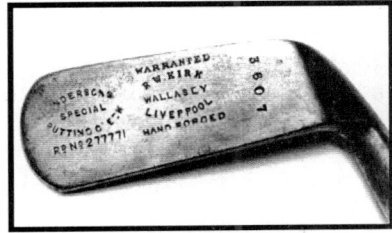

Andersons Registered Putting Cleek with twisted neck.

Joe Anderson mashie with K-in-Circle cleek mark.

Anderson, James ("Jamie")*
[St. Andrews; eldest son of "Old Da'" Anderson. Three time Open Champion, worked for Robert Forgan, several other firms and in his own shop in St. Andrews 1859-1905]

	Playclub--(L) C.1870, beech head, thin shaft, marked "J. Anderson"	$2,500-7,000
	Playclub--(L) In juvenile size	$2,500
	Putter--(L) C.1880	$3,000-4,000
	Putter--(S) C.1895	$1,500-2,000

Anderson, Joe*
[Perth s]

	Driver--Splice transitional head	$300
	Driver--Socket head, circle-K CM	$100
	Mashie--Stainless, O K Brand, dot face	$50
*	Mid Iron--O K Brand, line face	$35
	Mid Iron--Smooth face, OK CM, made for Murrie & Sons	$75
	Putter--(A B) Mallet head, offset with extreme goose neck	$450

Putter--Vardon style, rounded top, shallow face $100
Putter--C.1910, splice wood head $250
Numbered Irons--OK Brand, stainless, line face, fancy
large OK monogram CM $40

Anderson, R.C.B.
[Saratoga Springs, NY]
Driver--Rex model, socket head $75
Spoon--Splice head, deep face, marked for Saratoga & Troy $325
Spoon--Small splice head $300
Mid Iron--Smooth face $75

Anderson, Willie
[Baltusrol, St. Louis, et al, America's first repeat Open Champion (1903-5) who later endorsed clubs made by Worthington Mfg. Co.]
    Driver--Socket head, made by Worthington Mfg. Co. $200
*   Driver--Socket head, steel face insert (5-screw), name in oval $125
    Cleek--Smooth face, marked "W. Anderson, Champion" $150
    Lofter--Concentric back $150
    Niblick--Smooth face, St. Louis $100

Willie Anderson steel faced driver. Willie Anderson was the first American national champion to win two consecutive Opens. He won a third consecutive time and four 'Nationals' in all.

Putter--Iron blade, name in oval $90

Anderson's Rubber Company, Ltd.
Putter--LOTSIRB model in Hawkins Never Rust steel $75

Annan, C.
Driver--(B) Compressed socket head $200

Anson, John
Driver--Splice head, leather face insert $300

'Argyle'
Brassie--Socket head $50

Wood Shafted Golf Club Value Guide

    Iron--Smooth face, u-over-u CM $50
    SET--Juvenile clubs (brassie, mid iron, mashie, putter) $150

Arlington Manufacturing Company+
[Arlington, NJ; a division of the Kempshall Rubber Company. Also see Kempshall]
    Driver--Black Pyralin composition socket head $600
    Putter--Semi-round, center shaft Pyralin head $400

Army & Navy Cooperative Stores, Ltd.*
[London department store making some of their own clubs]

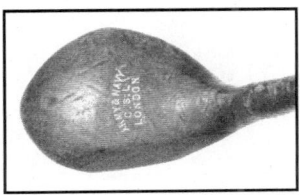

Army & Navy splice head driver. This model has a thin splice neck and shorter head indicative of a club manufactured in about 1905.

*
    Driver--(L) C.1890, late long nose period, beech head $2,000
    Driver--Short splice head $200
    Brassie--(S) Splice head, beech wood $450
    Cleek--Smooth face, name in arc, "C" $150
    Iron--Smooth face, marked in block letters "A & N CSL" ... $250
    Mashie--Smooth face, "A & N CSL" mark $250
    Mashie--Smooth face, marked "Deep Face Mashie" $175
    Mashie--Line face, stainless, name in oval $50
    Lofter--Smooth face, "A & N CSL" $300
    Niblick--Medium size head, smooth face, "A & N CSL" $350
    Niblick--Medium size head, smooth face, heavy thick blade,
    oval name stamp, also marked "Sherardized" $275
    Niblick--Small head, smooth face, Sherardized,
    Anderson small circle CM $400
    Putter--(S) C.1895, wood head, shaft stamp $750
    Putter--Blade, "A & N CSL" $250
    Putter--Hold Fast series, iron blade $200
    Putter--Hold Fast series, gun metal blade,
    small Anderson CM **$225**
    Putter--(B) Anderson gun metal mallet, steel face $250

'Arrow'

[Eagrow Co. brand name]
    Irons--Stainless, line face $30

'Arrowflite'
[Golf Specialty Co. brand name]
    Mashie--(D) Ribbed face, stainless $100
    Mashie--Stainless, line face $45

'Arrowline'
    Mid Iron--Par model, line face $25

Ashford, W. & G.*
[Birmingham e]
    Driver--(B) Skibbie model, combination wood &
    aluminum head $3,500
    Brassie--(S) Transitional beech head, one piece sewn grip,
    foxhead CM $800
    Cleek--Smooth face, Fore Flags CM $200
    Lofter--Smooth face, sewn grip, foxhead CM $250
    Mashie--Smooth face, foxhead CM, sewn grip $250
    Mashie--Smooth face, foxhead CM, cork grip $400
    Putter--(S) Foxhead CM, beech head, sewn grip $900
    Putter--Bent blade model, foxhead CM $300
    Putter--Iron blade, foxhead CM $250

Ashland Manufacturing Company+
[Chicago]
    Mashie Niblick--(D) Model 9-7, ribbed face $100

ATCO
[Alex Taylor brand name; also see Taylor Co., Alex.]
    Mashie--Stainless, line face $25
    Mashie Niblick--Dot face $35
    Putter--Burke model 69 ....$75

Auchterlonie & Crosthwaite*
[St. Andrews]
    Driver--(S) Boxed straight line name stamp $1,800
    Brassie--Short transitional splice head $550
    Approaching Cleek-(B) Registered model, musselback,
    SF, names in circle, registration (sequence) number $250

Wood Shafted Golf Club Value Guide

    Iron--Center shafted, smooth face, 2 fern frond CM $2,000
    Lofter--Smooth face, two fern frond CM $300
    Mashie--Smooth face, oval stamp $150
    Putter--Gun metal blade, boxed straight line stamp $250
    Putter--Gun metal blade, straight name, 2 fern frond CM $300

Auchterlonie, D. & W.*
[St. Andrews; brothers David and Willie started this firm in 1896]
*   Driver--(S) Transitional beech head $500
    Driver--C.1910, splice head, shaft stamp $150
    Driver--Socket head, made for Alex Taylor Co.,
    shaft stamp $60
    Driver--The Champion series, splice transitional
    beech head $200
    Driver--Gold Medal series, socket head $75
    Driver--Auchtie model, stripe top socket head $80

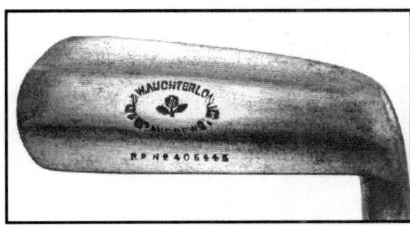 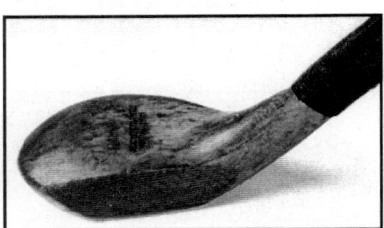

D & W Auchterlonie Registered Putting Cleek.
      D & W Auchterlonie transitional head driver.

    Driver--Dreadnought model, socket head, warship CM $150
    Brassie--(S) C.1900-1910 .... $700
    Brassie--Socket head, made for Wanamakers $75
    Brassie--Socket head, name in oval $60
    Baffing Spoon--(S) C.1896, brown head, shaft stamp $1,200
    Spoon--Socket head $95
*100 Approaching Cleek--(B) Smooth face, musselback,
    sequence number, names in arc, Stewart pipe CM $200
    Cleek--Musselback, line face, made by Stewart, pipe CM ... $100
    Iron--Smooth face, made by Condie, rose CM $80
    Mashie--Boy's (juvenile), rose CM, dot face $60
    Mashie--Dot face, small arrow in circle and
    Condie rose CMs $60

Pete Georgiady's

Mashie Niblick--Foulis style, smooth flat face $100
Niblick--Smooth face, small head, golf club CM $300
Niblick--Smooth face, medium head, arc name stamp $100
Named Irons--D & W Auchterlonie model, Stewart pipe CM,
scored face $50
Numbered Irons--Line face, Stewart pipe CM $45
Putter--(S) C.1900, transitional shaped splice head $600
Putter--C.1915, wood splice head, fiber slip in sole $125
Putter--Line face, pipe CM $50
Putter--(B) The Balance model, wood head $300
* Putting Cleek--(B) Chain link face markings,
horizontal weight bar on back, Condie rose CM $200
[Also found with Stewart pipe CM or Auchterlonie golf club CM]

Putting Cleek-Same as registered model but without chain face
markings, Stewart pipe CM $125
Putting Cleek--Dot face, long blade, pipe CM $60

Auchterlonie, Laurence+

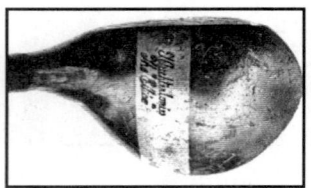

D & W Auchterlonie registered approaching cleek. **Tom Auchterlonie "Ellice" model stripe top driver.**

[Brother of David, Willie & Tom, 1902 US Open champion, Glen View, IL; later several European clubs]

Putter--Professional Model, topspin style blade with
concentric weighting $100

Auchterlonie, Tom*
[St. Andrews]
* Woods--The Ellice series, stripe top ....$75 each
Woods--Itz It Itz In series, double stripe top,
name in script ....$125 each
Woods--Name stamp shaped high at ends, socket head ... $85 each
Driving Iron--Name in circle with small arrow,

Wood Shafted Golf Club Value Guide

      Condie rose CM $60
      Mashie Niblick--(B) Smith model (anti-shank), pipe CM $150
      Mashie Niblick--Line face, stainless, Gibson star CM $50
      Jigger--(B) Itz It Itz In model $85
      Sammy--(B) Itz It Itz In model $100
      Iron clubs--Named, line face, Stewart pipe CM ....$60 each
      Iron clubs--Numbered, scored face, Stewart pipe mark ...$50 each
100 Named Irons--(B) Itz It Itz In series, line face ....$75 each
      Numbered Irons--Stainless, line face, straight line
      name stamp ....$45 each
100 Putter--(B) Holing-Out model, prism shaped head $250
      Putter--(S) C. 1925, wood socket head $250
      Putter--The Ellice series, iron offset blade $60
      Putter--Stainless blade, straight line name stamp $50
      Putter--(B) Itz It Itz In model, blade with small flange $125

Auld, Robert

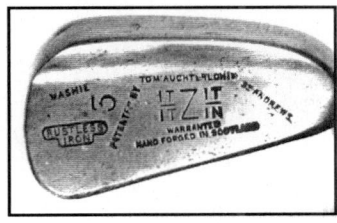 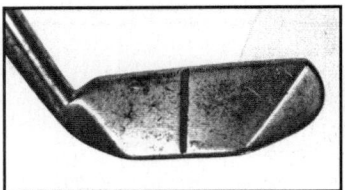

Tom Auchterlonie "Itz It Itz In" series mashie.
      Tom Auchterlonie patent "Holing Out" putter.

[Dunbar s]
      Spoon--Small splice head, light color, leather face insert $150
      Spoon--Socket head $95
      Driving Iron--Smooth face, Stewart pipe CM $60
      Putter--Iron blade, name in oval $50

Aveston, Willie*
[Cromer e]
      Brassie--Transitional splice head $250

Ayers, F.H.*

Pete Georgiady's

[London]
    Driver--(L) Dark color, leather face insert $2,000
    Driver--(S) C.1890, shaft stamp $1,600
    Driver--(B) Dagnall model, socket head $1,000
    Driver--(B) P.A. Vaile model, gooseneck socket head $650
    Driver--The Olympic model, socket head $150
    Iron clubs--Smooth face, marked for Army & Navy Store
    (A & N CSL) or Ayres
        Cleek--Marked "C" $150
        Driving Iron--Marked "D" or "DI" $150
        Iron--Marked "I" $125

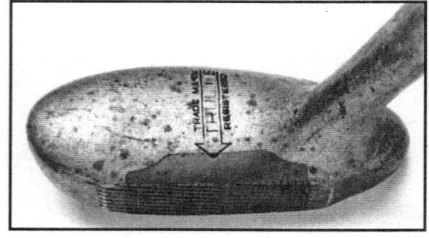 

F.H. Ayres "Tru-Put" Schenectady-type putter.
    F.H. Ayres boy's mashie, made for Army & Navy CSL.

    Mashie-Marked "M" $125
*   Mashie-(Boy's) Marked "BM" $200
    Driving Mashie-Marked "DM" $175
    Lofter-Marked "L" $175
    Niblick-Marked "N", small head...$500
    Putter-Marked "P", steel blade
    Iron--(B) The P.A. Vaile model, swan neck hosel, dot face ..$600
    Iron--A2, Harry Vardon autograph, Maltese cross CM $75
    Jigger--Dot face, small Maltese cross CM $65
    Mashie--Line face, small Maltese cross CM $60
    Mid Iron--The Cert model 2, square extension on sole,
    Maltese cross CM $200
    Mid Iron--Line face, small Maltese cross CM $60
    Niblick--Smith-type (anti-shank) $200
    Niblick--Large head, Maltese cross CM, line face $75
    Putter--Gun metal blade, thick hosel $175
    Putter--(S) C. 1895, beech wood head, short thick shaft $800
    Putter--(A B) The Cert model, square head

Wood Shafted Golf Club Value Guide

    with 4 hitting surfaces $1,200
    Putter--(B) The Cert model, made from wood $2,500
* Putter--(A) CSP model (early version), like Schenectady,
    shaft in exact center of head $325
* Putter--(A) Tru-Put model, Schenectady style,
    fiber face insert $250
    Putter--Oak Brand, made for W.G. Oke, oak tree CM $80
    Putter--The Facet model, bar-back weighting,
    maltese cross CM, name on face $125
    Putter--The Hesketh model, Maltese cross CM, long hosel,
    name in script $125
    Putter--Long, tapered hammer head, like polo mallet $500
    Putter--Model S31, Staynorus stainless, name in script,
    Maltese cross CM $60
    Putter--SX model, long blade, semi-long tear drop
    shaped hosel, beveled top edge $125
    Putter--The Birko model, iron blade $70
    Putter--The DW Grand model, top flange, script name $125
    Putter--Steel blade with pointed toe $100
    Irons--Delta series, round sole, line face,
    Cheshire autograph ....$65 each
    Irons--Deltoid series, round sole, line face,
    Cheshire autograph ....$65 each

Ayrton, W.

F.H. Ayres model CSP putter. The CSP stood for 'centre shaft putter.' This club was similar to a Schenectady but the shaft was more upright and located in the center of the club head, not towards the heel.

    Cleek--(B) Gun metal head with black gutta percha face insert,
    markings on hosel $3,000

Ayton, Laurie
[Chicago, IL]
    Driver--Socket head, ivor insert $80
    Mashie Niblick--Line face, pipe CM $55

B

B.A.M. Company+
[Bridgeport Athletic Manufacturing Co.: the name for B.G.I. after 1905]
    Driver--Socket head, light finish, oval name stamp $150
    Brassie--Socket head, oval stamp $150
    Spoon--Socket head, for BGI $150
    Iron--smooth face, oval stamp $125

B.G.I. Company+
[Bridgeport Gun Implement Co., Bridgeport, CT; 1897-1904]
◇◇Listed by model number (stamped on shaft below grip)
    41--Driver, Simpson model, socket head $150
    43--Brassie, Simpson model, socket head $150
    51--Driver, Chevy Chase model, socket head $125
    51--Driver, Chevy Chase model, splice head $250
    61--Driver, Hibbard model, splice head $225
    71--Driver, Dunn model, splice head $250
    73--Brassie, Dunn model, bulger face, splice head $225
    81--Driver. Kilgour model, splice head $225
    81--Driver, Kilgour model, socket head $125
    90--Driver, standard straight face, splice head $225
    91--Driver, bulger face, splice head $225
    92--Brassie, straight face, splice head $225
    92--Brassie, straight face, socket head $125
    93--Brassie, bulger face, splice head $200
    96--Putter, wood splice head $400
    97--Brassie niblick, New model, splice head $500
    004--Cleek, juvenile $125
    006--Lofting iron, juvenile $150
    009--Iron, juvenile $150
    010--Putting cleek, juvenile $150
    091--Driver, juvenile $250
    093--Brassie, juvenile $250
    101--Driving iron, J.D. Dunn model $100
    102--Putting cleek, gooseneck $125
    103--Driving cleek, Carruthers-type hosel $175
    104--Cleek, regular hosel $100
    105--Mashie, centraject model $100

Wood Shafted Golf Club Value Guide

106--Lofting iron $100
107--Lofting cleek (jigger), concave $150
108--Lofting mashie, Taylor model $125
      *   109--Iron $80

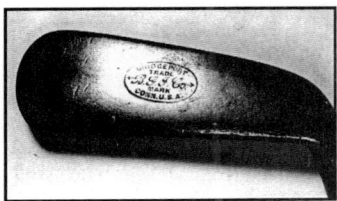

BGI model 109 iron. Clubs from BGI were extremely well made, if only for seven years, and are favorites among collectors. The model number is stamped on the shaft just below the grip.

110--Putting cleek $100
111--Niblick $125
112--Driving Mashie $100
113--Putter, gun metal blade $125
114--Medium mashie $80
115--Mashie, convex back $100
116--Medium mashie, deep face, Taylor model $125
117--Driving mashie $80
118--Approaching mashie, Simpson model $125
119--Putting cleek, twisted neck $125
120--Putting cleek, deep face $150
121--Mashie iron $100
122--Cleek, short blade $100
123--Light mid iron, Simpson model, line face $100
124--Mashie, Taylor model $125
391--Driver, small splice head $225
392--Brassie, Simpson model $200
500--(B) Driver, one piece, straight face $1,500-2,000
501--(B) Driver, one piece, bulger face $1,500-2,000
501--(B) Driver, one piece, lion CM, Kempshall face insert $2,250
503--(B) Brassie, one piece, bulger face $1,500-2,000
502--(B) Brassie, one piece, straight face $1,500-2,000
590--Driver, Tom Morris model, splice head $350
590--Driver, Tom Morris model, socket head $175
591--Brassie, Tom Morris Model, socket head $150
690--Driver, McEwan model, splice head $250
690--Driver, McEwan model, socket head $150
693--Driver, Dundonald model, socket head $175
694--Brassie, Moore model, splice head $200
791--Driver, Brooklawn model, splice head $175

891--Driver, St. Andrews model, splice head $175
893--Niblick Brassie, Kilgour model, splice head $500
893--Niblick Brassie, Kilgour model, socket head $250
991--Brassie, Kilgour model, deep face, splice head $250
Driver--(B) Fork splice head, leather face insert $750
Putter--(A U) Schenectady, marked in double circle
Wright & Ditson outside, BGI inside $300
Putter--(A U) Sprague model, block shaped head, ball-in-socket adjustable hosel **$2,500**

B T N
[see Butchart-Nicholls]

Ball, Tom*
[Raynes Park e, et al; brother of John Ball]
Driver--(S) Beech head, name stamp in script $600

Baltimore Putter Company+
Putter--(A U) Triangular shaped adjustable head rotates for
three different lofts $2,600

'Banner'

Banner brand mashie. Most Banner brand irons displayed the club type and loft in the toe area of the face. The face grooves of the niblick were vertical; all other irons had horizontal grooves.

[Brand line of the Kroydon Company]
Driver--Model 7116, circular steel face insert w/ 2 screws ...$100
Driving Iron--Diagonal line face, 15-degree loft $60
Driving Mashie--20 degree loft, wide line face $50
* Mashie--35 degree, wide line face $45
Mashie Iron--30 degree loft, wide line face $50
Mashie Niblick--45 degree loft, wide line face $45
Mid Iron--25 degree loft, wide line face $45
Niblick--50 degree loft, vertical line face $100
Niblick--Leo Diegel series, chrome, crossed clubs CM $30
Spade Mashie--40 degree loft, wide line face $50

Putter--Pendulum style with center shaft $500

Barker, H.H.
[Garden City, NY]
　　Driver--Socket head, white face insert fastened with 6 dowels $85

Barnes, Heffron
[New York, NY]
　　Putter--Adjustable, angle gauge at hosel $1,500

Barnes, Jim
[Pelham, NY, et al]
　　Mashie--Spalding anvil CM, line face $75
　　Mid Iron--Autograph series, marked Tacoma, dot face $90
　　Niblick--Medium round shaped head, line face $85

Barnes, N.
[Leeds e]
　　Mashie--The Birco series, Ayers cross CM, stainless $40

Batley, James*
[Bushey Hall e, et al]
　　Driver--Socket head $60
　　Mashie Niblick--line face, name in oval $40
　　Putter--Ayers Maltese cross CM, steel blade, pointed toe $100

Bayless Manufacturing Co.
[E. Hartford, CT]
　　Driver--(U) Stripe top socket head, laminated bamboo shaft $200
　　Woods--(U) Set of driver, brassie, spoon, bamboo shaft $750

Baxter, Alex+
[Chicago, et.al.]
　　Cleek--Dot face, PG Mfg. Anvil CM $90

'Beaumont'
　　Putter--(A U) Mallet head, black rubber aiming dot on crown $100

Beckley-Ralston Company, The+
[Chicago]
　　Driver--Excelsior model socket head $90

Brassie--Jock Hutchison model, socket head $75
Chipper--Shotmaker 378 model, banana shaped head,
square grip $50
Putter--No. 9, long head $50
Putter--Marked "J. Black Certified," blade $50
Putter--Solid steel rod for shaft $40

Bell, Frank
[Carnoustie]
        Long Spoon--C 1875, marked "F.Bell" $4,500

Bellwood, Frank
[Garden City, Long Island, NY]
        Driver--Socket head, stripe top $125
        Mid Iron--Stewart pipe CM, dot face $45
        Putter--Copy of wooden Travis model $250

Bembridge, A.
[Coombe Wood, London e]
        Putter--(B) The Coombe model, brass blade, aiming flange ..$125

Bendelow, Tom
[Chicago]
        Mashie Iron--Line face, signature name, Wilson large W CM .$50

Benetfink & Company*
[London retail store]
        Driver--Socket head $75
        Iron--The Concentric series, dot face, diamond back $50
        Mashie--Name in oval, line face $45
        Putter--Offset blade $50

Beveridge, James*+
[St. Andrews, s; later Shinnecock Hills, NY]
        Driver--(S) C.1895, transitional head, deep face $2,400
        Brassie--Transitional splice head $400
        Brassie--Socket head $200
        Long Spoon--(L) C.1880, lancewood shaft $4,000
*   Cleek--Smooth face, marked Southampton, LI $250
        Niblick--(S) Wood club with very lofted face, short head . $3,000

Wood Shafted Golf Club Value Guide

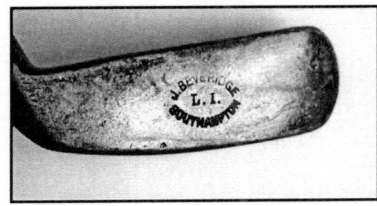 

James Beveridge cleek.

Billings & Spencer "Par-A-Lel" model iron.

Billet, H.N.
[Bridport e, et al]
    Putter--Wood head in cylinder shape $3,500

Billings & Spencer Company+
[Hartford, CT]
    Mashie--Through bore hosel, dot face $50
    Niblick--Marked "Junior Champion" in script $45
*   Named Irons--(U) Par-A-Lel series, circular
    scored face ....$125 each

'Birdie'
    Putter--Thick blade $30

Bisset, Andrew*
[North Berwick s]
    Brassie--Socket head $60
    Iron clubs--Stewart pipe brand, scored face ....$50 each

Black, J.L.
    Driving Iron--Spalding anvil CM, dot face $40

Black, Thomas
100   Putter--(B) Wood mallet, socket head, roller mechanism
    in sole $4,000

Blackheath Golf Company*
[London]
    Jigger--Coronet series, crown CM, dash face $40
    Niblick--Large head, smooth face $150

Pete Georgiady's

Iron clubs--Sun with rays radiating outward on face .... $60 each

Boggs, Arthur
[Cincinnati, OH]
Iron clubs--Iron Man model, stout man CM, dot face $75

Bonner, F.
[Carlisle e]
Mid Iron--The Scot series, kilted Scotsman CM $40

'Bonnie B'
Putter--Heavy blade, line face $35

Boomer, Percy H.
[St. Cloud, Paris, et al]
Jigger--Autograph series, dot face, Gibson star CM $60

Bourne & Bond
[Louisville, KY]
Putter--(A) Ray-type, BB CM in double circle $75

Boyd, Tom
[Staten Island, NY]
Driving Iron--Line face, Stewart pipe CM $50
Putter--Blade, pipe CM $50

Boyden
Iron--(B) Patent fork splice in middle of wood shaft $150

Boye
Putter--(A U) Adjustable where shaft attaches to head $650

Boyle, Charles
[Havana, Cuba]
Driver--Fancy face insert $100
Spoon--Socket head, face insert $100
Niblick--Dot face, palm tree and Gibson star CMs $75
Putter--Square toe, flat sided hosel $150
Putter--(A) Mallet style head $100

Bradbeer, Charles

48

Wood Shafted Golf Club Value Guide

[Hendon e, et al]
    Niblick--Junior Giant model, stainless, Goudie bear CM $800

Bradbeer, Edwin
[Cirencester e, et al]
    Putter--Iron blade, smooth face $60

Bradbeer, James*
[Finchley e, Radlet e, et al]
    Brassie--(B) The "Peggy" model, 20 end grain dowels
    set in face, socket head $300
    Brassie--Socket head $90
    Iron--Top Line model, bird & bee CM, top edge extension . $250
    Putter--Deep face blade, 40 holes drilled through face $800
*   Putter--Drilled face model, holes in face $450
    Putter--Own model, long stainless blade, Gibson star/G CM $100
    Putter--Horseshoe shaped CM, long shallow blade $80
    Numbered Irons--The Jay Bee series, bird & bee CM ....$55 each

Braddell & Sons, Thomas*
[Belfast i]

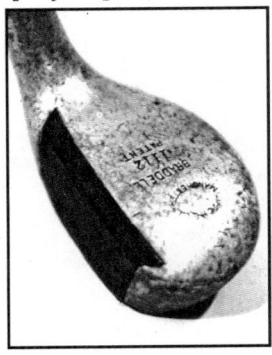
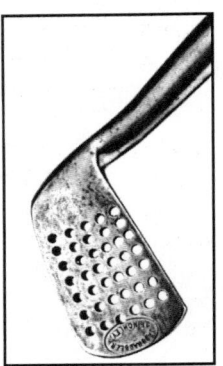

Driver--Splice head, **James Bradbeer's drilled face putter.**

The Braddell driver was made from aluminum and fitted with a leather face and a horn edge slip on its sole.

    leather face, shaft stamp $300
*   Driver--(A B) Leather face, horn insert, serial number
    marked on crown, shamrock shaft stamp $800
    Brassie--(A B) As above $900
    Brassie--Splice head, golden beech, leather face $300
    Cleek--Smooth face, long blade, shamrock CM $300
    Mashie--Smooth face, shamrock CM, shaft stamp $250

Niblick--Medium size head, smooth slightly concave face,
shamrock CM $450
Putter--Heavy iron blade, shamrock CM $250

Brady, Frank
Putter--(U) Deadly Overspin model, gun metal head,
curved face, hollow back $800

Brady, Mike
[Boston, Detroit, et.al]
Driver--Socket head, stripe top, autograph mark $75
Cleek--King series, dot face $60
Mashie--Model 6601, Monel, line face,
made for Winchester $100

'Brae-Burn'
Named Irons--Line face .... $30 each

Braid & Ogilvie
Iron--Smooth face, name in arc $100

Braid, James*
[Five time Open Champion; his shop at Walton Heath, e, made a few clubs but most with his autograph were produced by William Gibson & Co.]
Driver--Splice head, marked Romford $300
Cleek--Stewart pipe CM, dot face $100
Mid Iron--Walton Heath mark in oval $50
Niblick--The "Giant" model, James Braid series,
medium size head, Gibson star CM, line face $90
Putter--Orion model, Gibson star CM, broad sole $150

Braid, W. & G.+
[New York; brothers William and George worked for Forgan before coming to America in 1898. They made clubs in the U.S. for about 10 years then moved back to Scotland]
Driver--Short splice head, line name stamp $175
Brassie--Socket head $100
Niblick--smooth face, thick sole $75

Brand, Charles*
[Carnoustie s]

Wood Shafted Golf Club Value Guide

    Driver--Short splice head $150
    Baffing Spoon--(S) C.1890, lofted face $3,000
    Cleek--C.1890, smooth face, long thin blade, 4 3/4" hosel,
    shaft stamp $600
    Cleek--Smooth face, single Condie fern CM $250
    Iron--Harrower heart CM, diamond face $75
    Mashie--C.1900, smooth face, deep face blade $200
    Mashie--Rampant lion CM, line face $45
    Niblick--C.1895, small head, thistle CM $500
    Niblick--Large head, rampant lion CM, dot face $75
    Putter--Standard blade, lion CM $65

Brand, Fred
[Pittsburgh, PA]
    Driver-Small dark socket head $80

Brand, G.
    Putter--Wood splice head with extreme gooseneck $1,800

Breare, J
    Mid Iron--Line face, stainless steel $35

Breeze, G. Brodie*
[Glasgow]
    Woods--Stripe top socket head, Royal Crown brand .... $75 each
    Mid Iron--Royal Crown Brand, crown CM, dash face $45
    Putter--Excelsior model, Royal Crown Brand,
    crown CM, blade $75
    Putter--Royal Crown Brand, Excelsior series, iron blade $50

Brews, George
[Blackheath e]
    Driver--(S) C.1885, dark stained head, shallow face $2,300
    Brassie--C. 1900, splice head, lancewood shaft $300
    Cleek--Short iron blade, smooth face, Condie rose CM $125
    Cleek--Smooth face, Condie flower CM,
    marked "Blackheath" $150
    Mashie--Stewart pipe CM, smooth face $100
    Putter--(B) Trusty model, wood mallet head with large
    brass backweight $175

Brewster, Francis
[London]
100   Driver--(B) Simplex model, centre shafted cross-head club,
boat shaped head **$2,200**
Spoon--(B) Simplex model, as above $2,000
Niblick--(B)Simplex model, as above $2,500
Niblick--(A B)Simplex model, in aluminum $2,500
Putter--(B)Simplex model, as above $2,000

'Briarcliff'

Brewster "Simplex" patent brassie. Also called (incorrectly) 'crosshead' clubs referring to an earlier variant of the torpedo shape.

Putter--Blade, line face $35

Brine, J.W.
[Boston, MA sports outfitting store]
Iron clubs--Line face, company crest CM, made by Burke $35 each

British Golf Company, Ltd.*
[London]
Cleek--Straight line name stamp, smooth face $75
Mashie--Dot face $50
Putter--Iron blade $60
Putter--(A) Centre shaft, boat shaped duplex head $250
Putter--(A) Two-faced model, rectangular head, no hosel $300
Putter--The British model, center shafted, steel head $250
Putter--Offset blade $75

Brodie & Sons, R.*
[Anstruther s]
Iron--Stainless, triangle/BS&A CM, made for Thornton $50

Wood Shafted Golf Club Value Guide

Jigger--Zenith series, stainless, dot face, triangle CM $50
Mashie--Stainless, line face, triangle/BS&A CM $50
Iron clubs--Regular steel, triangle/BS&A and Tom Morris
CMs, line face, made for Tom Morris shop .... $60-100 each
Iron clubs--Stainless, triangle/BS&A and Tom Morris
CMs, line face, made for Tom Morris shop .... $50-80 each
Spade Niblick-Line face, triangle CM,
made for Morris shop $150
Niblick--Stainless, triangle/BS&A CM,
made for Nicholson Brothers $50
Putter--Stainless, line face, triangle/BS&A CM $75

Brodie Company, W. & D.*
[Anstruther s]
    Mid Iron--Dash face, stainless, initials in 4-lobes CM $60
*   Mashie Niblick--Bobbie model, rustless $75

D & W Brodie & Co.
used a 4-lobed cleek mark encasing the firm's initials.

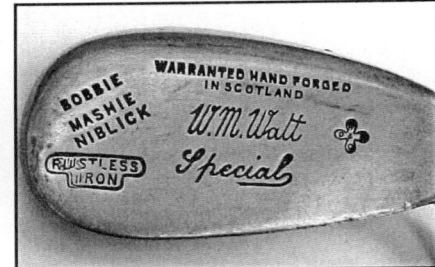

Brougham, Reginald T.*
[London]
    Driver--(A B) Transitional shaped head with wood block
inserted in face, shamrock CM, "Clubs Are Trumps" legend $900
Brassie--(A B) As above but lofted face $1,200

Brown & Smart+
[Chicago]
    Putter--Stewart pipe CM, iron blade $70

Brown, A.W.
    Brassie--Bulldog socket head, fiber insert $125

Brown, Daniel*

Cleek--Smooth face, made by Stewart, pipe CM $70

Brown, David
Driver--Socket head $100
Putter--The Nipper model, made by Alex "Nipper" Campbell $90

Brown, George*
[St. Andrews]
Mid Spoon--(L) Dark head, hickory shaft, marked "G. Brown" $15,000

Brown, Harry
Niblick--Model 17, line face, Winton diamond CM $45

Brown, J.
Putter--(S) C.1885, dark brown head $1,200

Brown, J.R.
[Montrose s; patentee of the Brown Patent Perforated Irons (i.e. "rake" iron); see J. Winton]

Brown, Jim
Iron--Smooth face $60

Brown, Melville
[Malone, Belfast i]
Driver--Bulger scare head $750

Brown, Wallace
Playclub--(L) Beech head, Forgan shaft stamp $3,000

Brown, William
[Dunksey s]
Brassie--Socket head $50

Bryant, George W.
Mashie--Stainless steel, 'Rustless' sun face CM $50

Buchanan's
[London retail store with club making facilities]
Driver--(S) Dark finish splice head $300

Wood Shafted Golf Club Value Guide

    Mashie--(B) Altman's pattern, round back, smooth face $200

'Bula'
    Putter--Danga wood shaft with rib pad grip, iron blade,
    Gibson star CM $75

Bunker, R.A.
    Putter--(A) Mallet head $60

Burgess, Charles
[Woodland, MA; many clubs marked with his nickname "Cha"]
    Iron clubs--Indian head CM, scored face ....$75 each
    Mashie Niblick--Marked Cha Burgess $65
    Putter--Gun metal, round top $175

Burke Golf Company+
[Newark, OH; began manufacturing tennis equipment prior to entering the golf market, C.1910. They produced a large number of clubs including many prestige lines]
◇◇Misc. clubs

	Driver--Splice head, aluminum sole plate $125
	Driver--Socket head, steel face insert with 2 screws $150
	Driver--Socket head, winged B.G. Co. CM $200
100	Driver--(A) End Grain model $400
	Iron clubs--William Burke Leader Model in shield, stainless steel, dot face ....$35 each
	Mashie--(D) Glencoe series, model 1369, ribbed face $75
*	Iron clubs--Long Burke series, line face, shield CM ....$40 each
	Mashie--Wilson model, "Egyptian mashie" $100
	Putter--made for the Edward Tryon Company, Phila., dot face $45
	Putter--(A) End Grain model, heel shafted mallet head $350
**	Putter--(A) End Grain model, Schenectady shaped head $400
	Putter--Model 1363, Glencoe stamp, peaked top of blade $125
	Putter--Brown-Vardon style steel head $200
	Putter--Sandy Mac model, flange sole, lion CM $45
	Rotary model--(D) Mashie, checkered face, Monel $300
	Rotary model--(D) Mashie niblick, checkered face, Monel . $300
*100	Rotary model--(D) Mashie niblick, 'Stars and Stripes' pattern, half checkered, half slot face, Monel $450

Long Burke series mashie.
Burke Rotary iron with 'Stars and Stripes' face.

◇◇Misc. clubs (with model number)
    3--Mid Iron, thistle & scales CMs $40
    4A--Jigger, Commander series $40
    11--Mashie, thistle & scales CMs $40
    26--Mid Iron, thistle $ scales CMs $40
    36--Mashie, made for Rev-O-Noc Co. $60
    BR-1--Mashie, Mike Brady model, dash face $80
    BR-2--Mashie niblick, Mike Brady model, dash face $80
    D5--Cleek, Hammer Forged brand, lion CM $45
    D-1--Mashie niblick, Dave Ogilvie model $80
    GS6--Putter, Monel blade, 7" hosel $175
    MC-1--Cleek, McLean model, dot face $80
    MC-2--Niblick, McLean model $80
    S-2--Mid iron, George Sargent, Monel $80
*   S-3--Mashie, George Sargent, Monel, line face $80
    S-4--(D) Mashie niblick, Geo. Sargent, Monel, ribbed face ...$150
    S-10--Niblick, W.C. Sherwood model, large head $80
    Z-1--Mashie, slotted hosel, dot face $125

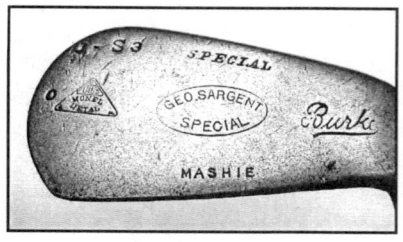

Burke model S-3 mashie in the George Sargent series.

◇◇◇By model series with model number if so designated

◇◇'Bee & Flower' series irons

Wood Shafted Golf Club Value Guide

  Named Irons--Bee & flower CMs ....$40 each

◇◇Burke Autograph series
  Woods (driver, brassie, spoon)--Black fiber insert with screws, stripe top, aluminum sole plate ....$45 each

◇◇Burke Stainless series irons
  Numbered Irons (1-8)--Line face, fleur-de-lis CM ....$35 each
  A-Suffix Numbered Irons (3A, 4A, 7A, 8A)--Slight gooseneck, line face, fleur-de-lis CM ....$40 each
  Putters (9, 10, P1, P2)--Blade ....$40 each

◇◇Burke Standard series
  Driver--Plain face $40
  Brassie--Plain face $40
  Spoon--Plain face $45
  X-1--Cleek, line face $35
  X-2--Driving iron, line face $35
  X-3--Mid iron, dash/line face $30
  X-4--Mid iron, round back, line face $40
  X-4--Mashie iron, plain back $35
  X-5--Jigger, dash/line face $35
  X-6--Mashie, deep face, dash/line face $35
  X-7--Mid iron, diamond back, line face $45
  X-7--Spade mashie, plain back $35
  X-8--Mid iron, offset head $40
  X-8--Mashie niblick, plain back $35
  X-8A--Mashie niblick $35
  X-9--Niblick, plain back $35
  X-10--Putter, blade $40
  X-11--Mashie, line face $30
  X-17--Jigger, line face $45
  X-18--Putter, blade $35
  X-19--Putting cleek, blade $35
  X-23--Niblick, medium head $35
  X-33--Mid iron, concentric back $40
  X-36--Mashie, line face $30
  X-38--Mashie niblick, line face $30
  X-43--Driving iron, line face $35
  X-44--Cleek, round back $40
  X-50--Putter, deep face $40

X-62--Mashie, deep face $40
X-64--Niblick, very deep face $40
X-68--(D) Mashie, ribbed face $75
X-69--Putter, square toe, broad sole $75
X-70--(D) Mashie niblick, ribbed face $75
X-77--Putter, round top, broad sole $75
X-78--Putter, gooseneck blade $50
X-90--Mashie, round back $40

⋄⋄Children's clubs
    Juvenile series clubs $35-50 each
    Driver
    Brassie
*   Iron
    Mashie
    Putter

    Junior series clubs $35-50 each
    Driver
    Iron
    Mashie
    Putter

    Midget series clubs $65-90 each
    Driver
*100 Iron
    Mashie
    Putter

⋄⋄Columbia and Columbia Special Series
    Driver--Plain face $40
    Brassie--Plain face $40
    D1--Mashie niblick, lion & crown CM $40
    D1--(D) Mashie niblick, ribbed face $100
    S4--(D) Mashie niblick, fibbed face $100
    S8--(D) Ribbed face $100
    Driving Iron--Dash face, lion & crown CM $25
    Mashie--Regular head, dash face $25
    Mashie--Deep face, dash face $25
    Mashie--(D) Inverted waffle (deep mesh) face $150
    Mashie Niblick--Dash face $25

Wood Shafted Golf Club Value Guide

Mashie Niblick--(D) Ribbed face $100
Mid Iron--Dash face $25
Niblick--Dash face $25
Putter--Regular blade $25
Putter--Gooseneck blade $30

◇◇Deluxe series
Woods (driver, brassie, spoon)--Black fiber insert,
aluminum backweight .... $60 each

◇◇Golfrite series
Driver--Splice head, aluminum sole plate $125
Driver--Ivor face with 7 red pegs, aluminum backweight $100
Brassie--Ivor face, as above $100
Spoon--Ivor face, as above $90
GR2--Mid Iron, dot & line face $60
GR6--Mashie Niblick, dot & line face $60
Numbered Irons (1-8)--Stainless, line face, scales CM ...$30 each
Set of 8 .... $350
Numbered Irons (1-8)--Iron, line face, scales CM ....$30 each
Set of 8 .... $350

◇◇Grand Prize series
0--Cleek, narrow face, line face $50
1--Spoon, bulldog head, deep face $100
1--Cleek, line face $40
01--Cleek, Monel $50
2--Mashie, narrow face $40
3--Driving iron, long blade, line face, scales CM $45
03--Driving iron, Monel $50
4--Mid iron, round back $40
04--Mid iron, Monel $50
5--Approaching cleek, dot face $60
5--Mid iron, deep face, short blade $40
05--Mid iron, Monel $50
6--Mid iron, round sole, scales CM $45
7--Mid iron, diamond back, dash face $50
8--Mid iron, offset blade, line face, scales CM $40
9--Mashie niblick, semi-gooseneck, dash face $45
09--Mashie niblick, Monel $55
10--Driver, splice head $125
10--Mashie, offset head $40

Pete Georgiady's

010--Mashie, Monel $50
11--Spoon, large head $90
11--Mashie, medium blade, line face $40
011--Mashie, Monel $50
12--Brassie, splice head $125
12--Mashie, round sole, short blade $45
12--Putting cleek, blade $45
13--Jigger, musselback, scales CM $55
013--Jigger, Monel $65
14--Spoon, small bulldog shaped head, fancy face insert $95
14--Mashie, deep face, flange sole $55
014--Mashie, Monel $60
15--Mashie, half musselback, dot face $75
15--Mashie, long blade, flange sole $50
16--Driving iron, round sole, line face $45
17--Jigger, narrow face, line/dash face $50
017--Jigger, Monel $60
18--Putter, blade, line/dash face, scales CM $40
018--Putter, Monel $60
19--Putting cleek, blade, scales CM $45
20--Putter, gooseneck, scales CM $45
020--Putter, Monel $55
21--Putter, round sole, straight neck $40
22--Driver, small head, deep face $60
22--Mid iron, J.H. Taylor model, line face $60
23--Niblick, medium size head, dash face, scales CM $45
023--Niblick, Monel $55
24--Driver, Balista combination face insert $150
24--Niblick, short blade, line face $45
25--Niblick, thistle & scales CMs, flange sole, line face $60
25--Brassie, Balista combination face insert $150
25--Mashie niblick, deep face, line face $40
025--Mashie niblick, Monel $55
26--Mashie niblick, line face $40
26--Mid iron, short blade $40
026--Mid iron, Monel $50
26--Putter, flange sole $50
27--Mid iron, musselback $50
027--Mid iron, Monel $60
28--Niblick, dreadnought style large head, scales CM $50
028--Niblick, Monel $60
29--Putting cleek, musselback $60
029--Putting cleek, Monel $70

Wood Shafted Golf Club Value Guide

30--Driver, bulls-eye face insert $90
30--Putter, musselback, semi-gooseneck $50
030--Putter, Monel $60
31--Driving mashie, scales CM $45
32--Brassie, bulls-eye face insert $90
32--Driving mashie, round sole, short blade $50
33--Mid iron, concentric back, dash face $45
033--Mid iron, Monel $55
34--Driver, thick Ivor face insert $80
34--Mid iron, medium length blade, line face $40
35--Brassie, thick Ivor face insert $80
35--Mashie iron, heavy blade, dash face $45
36--Mashie, deep face $40
36--Putter, slight gooseneck $50
036--Mashie, Monel $50
37--Approaching cleek, scales CM $60
037--Approaching cleek, Monel $70
38--Pitcher, line face, scales CM $55
038--Pitcher, Monel $65
40--Driver, socket head, plain face $40
40--Mashie niblick, line face, scales CM $40
41--Mashie iron, short blade $50
42--Brassie, plain face $45
42--Putter, blade with point on top, scales CM $60
43-Spoon, plain face $50
43--Driving iron, long blade, deep face $40
043--Driving iron, Monel $50
45--Mid iron, concentric back, deep face $50
045--Mid iron, Monel $50
45--Wood cleek, bulls-eye face insert $200
45--Wood cleek, fiber face insert $150
46--Mashie, concentric back, scales CM $45
046--Mashie, Monel $55
51--Putter, straight neck, very deep face $55
52--Putter, flange sole, gooseneck $55
052--Putter, Monel $65
53--Mid iron, long blade, deep face, flange sole $60
053--Mid iron, Monel $70
54--Driver, Victory model $100
55--Niblick, offset head, line face $45
056--Niblick, Monel $55

56--Brassie, Victory model $100
56--Cleek, celtic shaped offset head, deep face $45
056--Cleek, Monel $55
57--Cleek, diamond back, line face, scales CM $50
59--Cleek, musselback, line face $50
62--Mashie, medium length blade, line face $40
062--Mashie, Monel $50
63--Putter, long narrow blade, slight gooseneck $50
64--Niblick, very deep face $60
66--Mashie, musselback, scales CM $55
066--Mashie, Monel $65
67--Spoon, Victory model $125
68--(D) Mashie, Shur Stop model, ribbed face $100
69--Putter, broad flange sole, square toe $75
069--Putter, Monel $85
70--Driver--plain face $45
70--(D) Mashie niblick, Shur Stop model, ribbed face $100
070--(D) Mashie niblick, Monel $110
72--Brassie, plain face $45
73--Spoon, plain face $50
73--(D) Mashie niblick, Shur Stop model,
ribbed face, offset head $100

 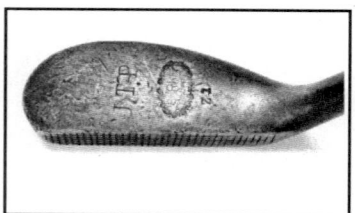

Burke model 74 mashie niblick.
Burke model Z1 long headed aluminum putter.

*100   74--(D) Mashie niblick, Shur Stop model, slotted face $100
074--(D) Mashie niblick, Monel, slotted face $120
74--Driver, fiber face insert $55
75--(D) Cleek, ribbed face $100
76--Brassie, fiber face insert $55
76--(D) Niblick, ribbed face $125

Wood Shafted Golf Club Value Guide

77--Putter, round top, broad sole $75
77--Spoon, fiber face insert $80
78--Putter, extreme gooseneck, scales CM $60
80--Driver, semi-bulldog head $75
82--Brassie, semi-bulldog head $75
84--Niblick, concave face, scales CM $85
085--Driving iron, bulger face, Monel $100
086--Mid iron, bulger face, Monel $100
087--Mashie, bulger face, Monel $100
088--Mashie niblick, bulger face, Monel $100
089--Putter, bulger face, Monel $125
90--Driver, long narrow head $100
90--Mashie, round back, line face $50
91--Mashie, diamond back $60
91--Putter, flange sole $75
92--Brassie, long narrow head $100
92--Putter, blade, slight gooseneck $50
140--Driver, bulls-eye face insert $90
142--Brassie, bulls-eye insert $90
144--Driver, pear shaped head, semi-bulger face $125
146--Brassie, pear shaped head, semi-bulger face $125
320--Driver, dreadnought head $90
322--Brassie, dreadnought head $90
511--Brassie, J.H. Taylor model $100
522--Spoon, J.H. Taylor model, round sole $125
600--Driver, large head $80
602--Brassie, large head $80
800--Driver, bulls-eye face insert $90
802--Brassie, bulls-eye face insert $90
844--Driver, plain bluger face $45
846--Brassie, plain bulger face $45
849--Spoon, plain bulger face $50
849--Spoon, small head $75
857--Spoon, fiber face insert $80
857--Spoon, plain face $50
875--Spoon, fiber face insert, round sole $80
G-1--Putter, gun metal blade, scales CM $65
G-2--Putter, gun metal, straight neck, wide sole $75
G-3--Putter, gun metal blade, musselback, scales CM $75
G-4--Putter, gun metal blade, flange sole $75
S-1--Putter, George Sargent model, round back, steel $75

Pete Georgiady's

    S-1--Putter, George Sargent, Monel $85
    Schenectady Putter--(A) $125
*   Z1--(A S) Putter $125

◇◇Grand Prize series numbered irons
    Numbered Irons (1-8)--Dot face, regular blade .... $35 each
    A-Suffix Numbered Irons (3A, 4A, 7A, 8A)--Dot face,
    slight gooseneck ....$40 each
    Putters (9, 10)--Blade ....$40 each
    Individual Irons (21-26)--Flange sole, line face ....$40 each
    Individual Irons (42-45)--Musselback, line face ....$40 each
    Individual Irons (71-72)--Diamond back, line face ....$40 each

◇◇Hutchison Autograph Series
    74--Driver, fiber face $100
    76--Brassie, fiber face $100
    77--Spoon, fiber face $125
    6640--(D) Niblick, slotted face $100
    6641--(D) Mashie Niblick, slotted face $100
    H-1--Mid iron, Monel, flange sole, line face $75
    H-2--Mid iron, Monel, plain sole, line face $60
    H-3--Medium iron, Monel $75
    H-4--Mashie iron, Monel $75
    H-5--Mashie, line face, Monel $60

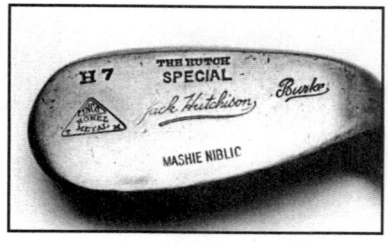 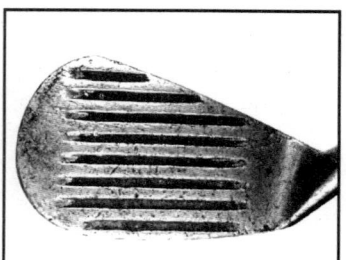

Burke Jock Hutchison model H7 mashie niblick.
    Burke Jock Hutchison model H6 spade mashie
    showing deeply slotted face. grooves

I   H-6--(D) Spade mashie, Monel, slot face $150
*   H-7--(D) Mashie niblick, Monel, offset head, slot face $150
    H-8--(D) Niblick, Monel, slotted face $200
    H-9--Putter, Monel blade $75

Wood Shafted Golf Club Value Guide

◇◇Lady Burke series

Lady Burke model 25 mashie niblick.

1--Cleek	$30
2--Spoon	$50
2--Driving iron, line face	$35
3--Mid Iron, line face	$35
4--Mashie iron, line face	$35
6--Jigger, line face	$40
7--Mashie, line face	$35
9--Spade mashie, line face	$35
10--Mashie niblick, line face	$35
11--Niblick, line face	$35
13--Putter, blade	$35
17--Jigger	$40
18--Putter	$40
23--Niblick	$35
* 25--Mashie niblick, thistle & scales CMs, dash face	$45
26--Mid iron	$30
40--Driver, Ivor face	$75
40--Driver, plain face	$40
42--Brassie, Ivor face	$75
42--Brassie, plain face	$40
42--Mid Iron, line face	$35
43--Spoon, plain face	$45
44--Mid Iron, line face	$35
45--Wood cleek, fancy face	$200
45--Wood cleek, fiber face	$125
68--Mashie	$30
69--Putter, square toe, broad sole	$75
70--Mashie niblick	$30
90--Mashie, round back	$50
91--Putter, broad flange sole	$90
92--Putter, gooseneck blade	$40
G-2--Putter, gun metal	$65
430--Driver	$50

432--Brassie $50
800--Driver, fiber face $90
800--Driver, fancy face $90
802--Brassie, fiber face $90
802--Brassie, fancy face $90
844--Driver, plain face $40
846--Brassie, plain face $40
849--Spoon, plain face $45

◇◇Parplay series woods
P40--Driver, black fiber insert with screws $45
P70--Driver, as above $45
P42--Brassie, black fiber insert, brass sole plate $45
P72--Brassie, as above $45
P43--Spoon, black fiber insert, brass sole plate $50
P73--Spoon, as above $50

◇◇Pickwick clubs
[Also see Winchester Arms Co. for additional Pickwick models]
Named/Numbered Irons--Chrome, line face,
small shamrock CM .... $30 each

◇◇Plus Four series
Woods (driver, brassie, spoon)--Red fiber face
insert with screws, aluminum sole plate .... $45 each

◇◇Prestwick clubs
Woods--Socket head, plain face .... $40 each
Woods--Socket head, plain face, model number .... $60 each
Named Irons--Name in oval, scales CM, line face .... $35 each
Mashie--(D) Ribbed face $100
Putter--Like the Brown-Vardon, round hosel $100

◇◇Ranger series
Woods (driver, Brassie, spoon)--Aluminum face insert
and sole plate .... $45 each

◇◇Sportsman series woods
S30--Driver, plain face, stripe top $40
S32--Brassie, as above $40
S33--Spoon, as above $45

S40--Driver, as above $40
S42--Brassie, as above $40
S43--Spoon, as above $45
S70--Driver, long head $40
S72--Brassie, as above $40
S73--Spoon, as above $45
S320--Driver, large head $40
S322--Brassie, as above $40
S323--Spoon, as above $45

◇◇Ted Ray Autograph Series
852--Driver, bulger face $125
854--Brassie, bulger face $125
R-1--Mashie, Monel, dash face $75
R-2--Cleek, Monel, dash face $75
R-3--Mongrel iron, Monel $100
R-5--Mongrel mashie, Monel $100
R-6--Mid iron, Monel, line/dash face $75
R-7--Mashie, Monel $75
R-8--Pitcher, Monel $90
R-9--Jigger, Monel $90

◇◇Harry Vardon Autograph Series
[Some Burke Vardon series irons also appear with model numbers beginning with A instead of V. Those marked A are the first series and carry the same relative values as the later V series.]
830--Driver, splice head $250
832--Brassie, splice head $250
840--Driver, Ivor face $150
842--Brassie, Ivor face $150
842--Brassie, plain face $125
844--Driver, bulger face $125
846--Brassie, bulger face, fiber face $125
846--Brassie, plain $125
857--Spoon, fiber face $175
857--Spoon, no insert $175
V-1--Cleek, line face $100
V-2--Driving iron $100
V-2--Driving iron, Monel $125
*   V-3--Mongrel iron $200
V-3--Mongrel iron, Monel $225

Burke model A-3 from the Vardon series in Monel Metal. In the Vardon series sometimes the model number begins with an A instead of a letter V.

       V-4--Mid iron $100
       V-4--Mid iron, Monel $125
       V-5--Mid iron $100
       V-6--Mongrel mashie $200
       V-6--Mongrel mashie, Monel $225
       V-7--Jigger $125
       V-7--Jigger, musselback, Monel $150
       V-8--Approach mashie $150
       V-8--Approach mashie, Vardon, Monel $175
       V-9--Mashie, Vardon autograph $100
       V-9--Mashie, Vardon, Monel $125
       V-10--Mashie niblick, Vardon autograph $100
       V-10--Mashie niblick, Vardon, Monel $125
       V-11--Mashie niblick, Vardon autograph $100
       V-12--Niblick, Vardon autograph $100
       V-12--Niblick, Vardon, Monel $125
       V-13-Putter, Vardon autograph $90

◇◇Walter Hagen series irons
       Mashie Iron--Monel, Hagen autograph, line face $100
       Mashie Niblick--Monel, autograph, dot face $100

◇◇Zenith series
       Woods (driver, Brassie, spoon)--Stripe top,
       plain face, aluminum backweight .... $40 each

Burr-Key Bilt+
[R.H. Buhrke Co., Chicago]
       Driver--Majestic series, socket head $40
       Driver--(U) Ritewood series, multi-part face insert $125
       Brassie--Regal series, ivorine face insert, 5 black dowels $80
       Brassie--Regal series, red face insert $75
       Driving Iron--Classic series, brass disc in face $75

Wood Shafted Golf Club Value Guide

Mashie--(D) Baxpin model, ribbed face $100
Iron clubs--Mohawk series, dot face .... $30 each
Iron clubs--Princess Pat series, line face .... $35 each
Iron clubs--Burr-Key Built series, dot face .... $30 each
Iron clubs--Majestic series, line face .... $30 each
*   Iron clubs--Stylist series, dot face, stainless .... $30 each
Iron clubs--RHB Monogram series, stainless $40each
Iron clubs--Medalist series, stainless, line face .... $35 each
Iron clubs--Andy Robertson series .... $40 each
Spade Mashie Niblick--Andy Robertson series $45
Spade Mashie Niblick--Classic series, brass disc in face $85
Putter--Finalist, blade $30
Putter--Majestic, blade $30
Putter--Mohawk series, regular blade $30
Putter--Rambler series, thick blade $30
Putter--Speedway series, chrome, blade $30
Putter--Stylist series, blade, chromed head $30
Named Irons--Classic Series, brass disc in face .... $60 each

Burr Key Lady Stylist mid-mashie. Burr Key clubs are typical of mass produced sets from the 1920s—serviceable but uninteresting for many collectors.

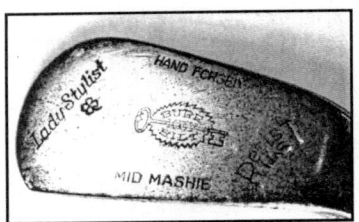

Bussey, George G.*
[London sports outfitter; patented a two-piece iron head with blade braised to a hosel for improved quality]

        Driver--Transitional splice head $500
        Brassie--Splice transitional beech head, one piece sewn grip $500
100*   Cleek--(B) Short smooth face blade, marked
        "Patent Steel Socket", one piece sewn grip $350
        Iron--(B) Patent steel hosel, "Patent Perfection Handle"

Most **George Bussey patent irons** featured separate steel blades and hosels brazed together. The putter had a steel socket joined to a bronze blade.

Pete Georgiady's

    marked on sewn grip $325
    Iron--(B) Marked as above, smooth face, sewn 1-piece grip...$300
    Lofting Iron--(B) Long blade, smooth face,
    sewn one piece grip $350
    Mashie--(B) Smooth face compact blade, wide toe $300
*   Putter--(B) Gun metal blade, steel hosel, sewn 1-piece grip ...$400
    Putter--(B) Iron blade, marked "Thistle", sewn 1-piece grip...$350
    Putter--(B) Thistle series, steel socket model $250

Busson, J.H.
[Formby e]
    Driver--Autograph model, socket head $50
    Brassie--Autograph model, stripe top $50
    Putter--XLALL model, iron blade, square socket $200

Butchart, C.S.*+
[Worked at several locations in Britain and Ireland; moved to America in about 1918 where he served as professional to the Westchester Country Club, NY and was a principal in the Butchart-Nicholls Company]
    Driver--C.1920 Butchart Bilt series, late splice head with
    aluminum insert $250
    Driver--Genuine Butchart model, split bamboo/hickory
    laminated shaft $200
    Driver--Butchart Bilt model, stripe top, fiber insert $75
*   Niblick--Ayers CM, Autograph series own model $70
    Iron clubs--Autograph series, Stewart pipe CM, line face $60 each

C.S. Butchart adopted the tradename "Butchart Bilt" after moving from London to New York. This model was imported from F.H. Ayres.

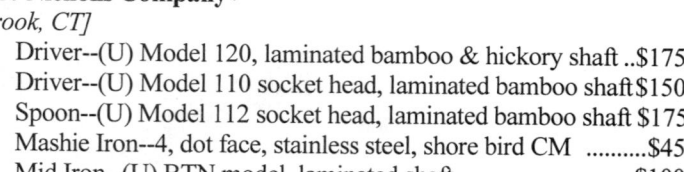

Butchart-Nicholls Company+
[Glenbrook, CT]
    Driver--(U) Model 120, laminated bamboo & hickory shaft ..$175
    Driver--(U) Model 110 socket head, laminated bamboo shaft$150
    Spoon--(U) Model 112 socket head, laminated bamboo shaft $175
    Mashie Iron--4, dot face, stainless steel, shore bird CM $45
100   Mid Iron--(U) BTN model, laminated shaft $100

Wood Shafted Golf Club Value Guide

Niblick--11, laminated bamboo & hickory shaft $100
Niblick--(U) Model 11, bamboo shaft $75
Putter--(U) 12, laminated bamboo & hickory shaft $125
Putter--(U) BTN model, laminated shaft $150
Numbered Irons--(U) Bamboo shaft .... $65 each
Set--(U)Bamboo shaft, irons 1-11, putter 12 .... $1,000

Butchart-Nicholls laminated shaft was made from alternating hickory and bamboo strips.

C

Cafferty, Peter*
[Edinburgh]
    Putter--Top Spin model, stainless, negative loft $200

Caird, Adam
[Tynedale e]
    Driving Iron--Diamond back, name in circle,
    diamond/dot face $60

'Caledonia'
[MacGregor store brand]
    Driving Iron--Name stamp in arc, dot face $30

Callan Brothers*
[London]
    Iron clubs-Leaf brand, 3-leaf CM, stainless .... $60 each
    Putter--Leaf brand, 3-leaf CM, stainless $75

Callaway, Christopher
[Haslar & Gosport e; later Europe and U.S.]
    Named Irons--Pipe brand, name in oval .... $50 each
    Putter--(S) Splice head $400

Campbell, Alex+

[Boston, MA, Cincinnati & Dayton, OH]
  Driver--Socket head, stripe top $100
  Iron--Smooth face, Stewart pipe CM $75
  Mashie--Stainless, line face $50
  Named Irons--Alex Campbell irons, Stewart pipe CM,
  scored face ....$60 each
  Jigger--The Nipper model $80
  Putter--The Nipper model $85

Campbell, Jamie
  Mid Iron--Smooth face $100

Campbell, Matt
[Boston]
  Mid Iron--Lined face, Burke scales CM $60

Willie Campbell socket head driver. Campbell was the first big-name Scottish pro to work in America. He died in 1900.

Campbell, Willie*+
[Bridge o' Weir s & Boston, MA]
* Driver--Socket head, name in diamond $175
  Driver--Splice head, shaft stamp $250
  Brassie--Socket head, Boston address $150
  Iron clubs--Marked "I.J.S.G. Co." in double oval ....$100 each
  Mashie--Smooth face, name in diamond $75
  Mid Iron--Marked "Wm. Campbell, Boston" in
  semi-circle stamp, smooth face $125
  Putter--Gun metal blade, oval name stamp $100
  Putter--Gun metal blade, name in arc, "Franklin Park" $250

Campbell, W.W. (William W.)
[Colorado Springs, CO]
  Woods--Socket head ....$85 each
  Mashie--Smooth face, Spalding 2 roses CM $50
  Jigger--Rampant lion CM $50

Wood Shafted Golf Club Value Guide

Cann & Taylor*+
[Founded, Winchester e, most clubs produced at Richmond, Surrey e and two US sites; a partnership of Open Champion J.H. Taylor and club designer George Cann]
◇◇Early clubs
    Driver--(S) Splice head, marked "Cann & Taylor" in block letters $300
    Driver--Small splice head in oak wood $400
    Brassie--(S) Short, bulldog shaped head with long splice $175
    Spoon--Short splice head $225
    Iron--Smooth face, marked for Winchester (England) $250
    Lofter--Smooth face, marked Winchester and Wimbledon .. $200
    Mashie--Smooth face, marked Richmond and Pittsburgh $200
    Mashie--(B) Smooth face, marked "Winchester & Richmond and Deal Beach, USA" $275
    Putter--Gun metal blade, marked "Winchester & Richmond and Deal Beach, USA" $150
    Putter--Gun metal blade, stamped for Asbury Park $200

Cann & Taylor mashie iron.
J.H. Taylor's use of the mashie in the 1895 Open popularized that club.

Carew niblick with medium sized head.

◇◇Clubs with J.H. Taylor Autograph CM
    Driver--Autograph CM on head with Williams & Cie.
    oval import mark $125
    Driver--Stripe top socket head, shaft stamp $90
    Driver--Confidus model $100
    Brassie--Stripe top socket head, shaft stamp for
    Williams & Cie., Paris $100
    Spoon--(B) Cynosure series, stripe top socket head $125
    Spoon--Confidus model $125
    Cleek--Smooth face $80
    Lofter--Smooth face, long blade $100

Mashie--Smooth face $80
Mashie--Smooth face, heavy blade $100
Mashie--Line face, autograph CM & registration number $50
Mashie--(B) Mule's Patent spring face $500
Mashie--Fliweel model, flywheel CM, dot face $50
Mashie--Quickstop model, oval head, dash/dot face $75
Mashie Iron--Line face, short blade with deep face $90
*100 Mashie Iron--Smooth face, short blade with deep face $100
Mashie Niblick--Dot face, autograph CM with
registration number $50
Mid Iron--Mascot model, greyhound CM. line face $70
Iron clubs--Cynosure series, line face .... $50 each
Mid Iron--Smooth face $80
Niblick--Smooth face, small heavy head $350
Putter--Bent blade style, marked "Taylor's Putter" $150
Putter--Fliweel series, gem style $100
Putter--Model V-15 blade, Vardon autograph, Fliweel CM $125
Putter--(B) Billiard Cushion model, top edge of face raised .$300
Putter--(A B) Mallet head, negative loft,
Taylor autograph w/ registration number $250

Cannon, William Kempton
[Cambridge e]
Mashie--Flange sole, line face, cannon CM $75
Lofter--(B) Pointed toe, line face $150

Carew
* Iron clubs-Name in oval with arrowheads $75

Carrick, F. & A.*
[Musselburgh s; iron tool manufacturers, used a small cross cleek mark, C. 1860-1904]
Cleek--Circa 1875, long face, 4 ½-5" hosel, straight
line name stamp, cross cleek mark $650
Cleek--(B) 'The Acme', smooth face, Carrick cross CM $350
Cleek--Circa 1890, long face, 4 1/2" hosel, name stamp in arc,
cross cleek mark $400
Cleek--Circa 1900, shorter face, 4" hosel $300
Iron--Circa 1875, 4 3/4" hosel, straight line name stamp $750
Iron--Circa 1885, 4 1/2" hosel, no name stamp, cross CM $350
* Lofter--Circa 1880, long blade, not concave, 4 1/2" hosel,

Wood Shafted Golf Club Value Guide

straight line name stamp $400
Mashie--C.1880-85, straight name stamp $400
Mashie--Circa 1885-90, name stamp in arc,
medium length blade with deep face $300
Mashie--c.1890, short blade, wide toe,
marked for J.H. Hutchison $500
Niblick--Circa 1875, small almost circular head,
thick heavy hosel, marked only "Carrick" $1,500-2,500
Niblick--Circa 1890, smooth face, round head marked
with Carrick cross CM $1,200-1,500

Carrick iron. This club probably was made prior to 1880. It has a hosel slightly over 4 1/2" in length and the cross cleek mark was struck near the heel of the club.

Carruthers, John
[London]
    Putter--(A B) Mallet head with hooked face $1,200

Carruthers, Thomas*
[Edinburgh; inventor of the short hosel, through-bore iron club]
100   Cleek--(B) Smooth face, short blade, short hosel
        drilled through, Carruthers name in oval stamp $300
        Iron--Smooth face, hosel *not* drilled $200
        Mashie--(B) Smooth face, regular length hosel
        drilled through $250
*   Niblick--(B) Smooth face, regular length hosel
        drilled through $250
        Putter--(B) Smooth convex face, short hosel drilled through $300

Carter, George*
[Guildford e]
    Driver--Socket head, straight line name stamp $75
    Mashie--Signature marking, line face $75

Cassidy, J.L.*
[Aldburgh e, et al]
    Driver--Starbeck model, socket head $95
    Putter--(A B) The Vee model, mallet head, V-shaped
    aiming bar on top $125

Catlin, A.
[Barnet e, et al]
    Driver--Socket head $60

Carruthers niblick with patented drilled hosel.
    Cawsey mashie fitted with Cawseygrip grip.

Cawsey, Harry*
[Skegness e, et al]
    Driver--(B) Angsol model, beveled sole socket head $250
    Brassie--(B) Picmup model, socket head, round sole $150
    Brassie--(B) Spli-Sok model, combination
    splice/socket joint $350
    Spoon--(B) Angsol model, H-shaped sole plate $250
*   Mashie--Cawseygrip model $125
    Spade Mashie--Line face, Stewart pipe CM $60
    Niblick--Cawseygrip model, 2 hands CM $100
    Putter--Tramline model, wood mallet head, brass sole $125
    Putter--Cawseygrip model, 2 hands CM, square handle $175

Chambers, F.
    Driver--C.1905, splice head $150
    Driver--Socket head $50

Chambers, J.
    Putter--(S) Beech head with pointed toe, shaft stamp $400

Wood Shafted Golf Club Value Guide

'Champion'
    Putter--Cross in shield CM $45

Chattell Company, C.C.+
[Chicago]
    Iron--Juvenile, CCC CM $50
    Mashie--Stainless (nickel) steel, musselback, dash face $75
    Mashie Niblick--stainless, CCC CM $50
    Mashie Niblick--Foulis model, smooth concave face,
    CCC CM $250
    Spade Mashie--CCC CM, dot face $40
    Putter--Blade, CCC CM $60

Chestney, Harry*
[London]
    Spoon--small socket head $70

Chicago Golf Company
[Chicago]
    Iron clubs-Line face, large shamrock CM .... $35 each

Chicago Golf Shop+
[Chicago, IL]
    Approach Cleek--Model 19, Celtic series musselback,
    Forgan crown CM $75

Churchill, James
[Quincy, MA]
    Mashie--(U) Rectangular cut out in sole, dot face $300

'Clan'
[in bell CM, see F.A.O. Schwarz]

'Clan'
[find more Clan clubs in the Spalding listings]
    Cleek--Smooth face $250
    Cleek--Smooth face, juvenile, stamped shaft $200

Clan Golf Company*
[London]

Driver--(S) Transitional shaped head, original black
paint finish, large thistle CM $850
Brassie--Light colored head, large thistle CM $600
* Cleek--Smooth face, thistle CM $300
Iron--Smooth face, long blade with deep face, large thistle CM $400
Mashie--Smooth face, compact blade, large thistle CM $300
Putter--"Made by Spence & Gourlay for Frank Bryan,
Clan London", club pip CM $60

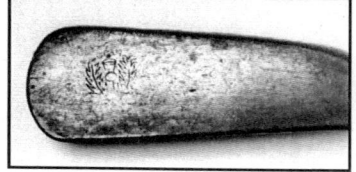 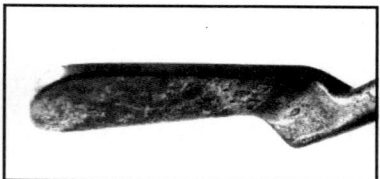

Clan Golf Company cleek with its large sized thistle cleek mark.

J. & D. Clark bent blade putter looking down on the top edge.

Clark, A.
Mashie--Smooth face, Millar small thistle CM $150
Clark, D.W.
[Lansdowne, PA]
Putter--Shield CM $50
Putter--Name in small oval $60

Clark, J. & D.*
[Musselburgh s]
Driver--Transitional shaped short splice head, bulger face $450
Driver--Splice head, marked for Tryon, Philadelphia $250
Brassie--(B) Compressed splice short head $350
Cleek--Smooth face, short round back blade,
name in small oval $150
Cleek--Smooth face, Carrick cross CM $250
Lofter--Smooth slightly concave face, ash shaft $350
Mashie--Smooth face, compact blade $200
Mashie--C. 1900, dot face $100
Niblick--Small head, long hosel, smooth face $800
Putter--(S) Dark stained wood head $900
* Putter--Bent blade style $275
Putter--Blade, name in oval $80
Wooden Niblick--Splice head, bulger face, brass sole plate ..$450

Clark, Peter
Mashie Niblick--Diamond face $60

Clark, Tom
[Kansas City, MO]
Mashie--Flange sole, name in script, unusual diamond cartouche design on face $200

'Climax Fife'
Putter--Crown CM, made by Wm. Gibson $40

Clucas, J.
[Bridlington e, et al]
Putter--Iron blade $40

Clydesdale Rubber Company*
[Glasgow]
Lofter--Smooth face, straight line name stamp $100
Mashie--Smooth face, Nicoll small hand CM $200

Cobb, R.T.
Brassie--(L) C.1890, long wide head $600

Coburn, George*
[West Bromwich e, et al]
Brassie--Socket head $60
Niblick--Line face, medium size head $40

Cochrane & Company, J.P.*
[Edinburgh; headed by James Pringle Cochrane who had formerly worked for the S.G.C.M. Co. Originally a major factor for golf balls they became a large iron club manufacturer as well, using two CMs, a knight in armor and a bowline knot]
Driver--(U) The Everlasting Model, combination wood in steel casing $1,250
Driver--Walter Hagen autograph model, large socket head .. $150
Driver--Socket head, marked "J.P. Cochrane & Co." $80
Brassie--Walter Hagen autograph model, socket head $125
Brassie-Joe Kirkwood autograph series, face insert $125
Cleek--Juvenile (marked "B"), smooth face, knight CM $95

Pete Georgiady's

*	Mashie Niblick--(B) XL Model, thin sole, thick top edge.......$250
	Mashie--"Challenger Rustless Metal" on face $80
	Mashie Niblick--Extra large oval head (like giant niblick), knot mark, line face $2,000
	Mid Iron--Deep face, knight CM, made for T & G McKenzie $60
	Niblick--Small head, smooth face, marked J.P. Cochrane $400
100	Niblick--Mammoth model, huge face, knot CM $1,200-2,000
	Niblick--Mammoth model, "Junior" giant niblick $800
	Pitcher--(D) Dedli model, grooved face, knight CM $150
	Putter--(B) The Mac model, thick, short blade, knot CM $100
	Putter--The Nigger model, long thin blade and hosel $350
	Putter--The Nigger model, deep face iron blade $350
*	Putter--UOT model, cut out section at toe $600
	Putter--Blade, Clyde Alloy stainless $60
	Putter--(U) Travers model, rectangular wood head, centre shaft $600
	Putter--Walter Hagen series model 28, knot CM, stainless blade $90
	Putter--Model Z, flat side on hosel, broad flange sole, knight CM $90
	Putting Cleek--JPC model, JPC monogram CM $75
	Putter--Holem model, musselback, knight CM $85
	Putter--Model 28, Walter Hagen autograph, knot CM, stainless blade $100
	Putter--(A) Mallet head, knight CM $125
	Putter--Q model, bent neck, Challenger rustless iron $75
	Numbered irons--Walter Hagen autograph model, rustless, knot CM $75each
	Numbered irons-Repeter series ....$60 each

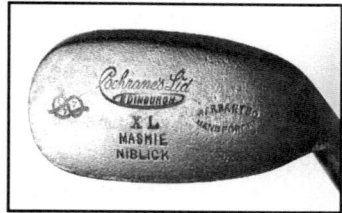 

Cochrane Model XL mashie niblick.

Cochrane Model UOT putter.

Cogswell & Harribone
[London & Feltham e]
*100   Driver--Dint patent with C&H CM on silver sole plate $400
        Putter--Gun metal gem-style, large C&H CM
        and Halley swords CM $150

Dint driver with silver face plate. Clubs made for Cogswell & Harribone carry the C H mark.

Collins, William+
[Ryton-on-Tyne e and Staten Island, NY]
        Spoon--Socket head, marked for Tenafly, NJ shop $125
        Iron--Smooth face, marked Fox Hills $150
        Mashie--Smooth face $75
        Niblick--"The Willie Collins" in script, by Spalding $75

Collis, Harry
[Homewood, IL]
        Lofter-Concave face, long thin blade, rounded sole $100

Columbia Special
[see Burke]

'Comet Brand'
[see Craigie, J. & W.]

Compston, Archie
[Manchester e, et al]
        Driver--Socket head, stripe top $45
        Numbered Irons--Own model, made by A. Patrick .... $45 each
        Numbered Irons--Champion autograph series by
        Thos. E. Wilson .... $60 each

Condie, Robert*
[St. Andrews]
        Cleek--Smooth face, rose CM $85

Pete Georgiady's

  Cleek--Smooth face, short 2 1/2" hosel, rose CM $140
  Iron--Black gutta percha insert in face of blade
  (imitating Nicoll patent), C.1900 .... $2,500
*   Mashie--Smooth face, name in oval, rose CM, Slazenger
  name in oval $100
  Mashie--Smooth face, Condie single fern CM $225
  Mashie--Dot face, rose CM $60
  Mashie--Boy's size, dot face, early rose CM $60
  Mid Iron--Dot face, Tom Morris model, rose mark $85
  Lofter--Smooth face, long blade, small rose CM $125
  Niblick--Smooth face, small head, rose CM $300
  Niblick--Medium head, smooth face, rose CM $100
  Niblick--Large head, dash face, rose CM $65
  Putter--Gun metal blade, rose CM $65
  Putter--Excelsior model, iron blade, rose C $65

  Named Irons-Smooth face, rose CM .... $50-75 each
  Named Irons-Line or dot face, rose CM .... $45-60 each

Robert Condie deep faced mashie made for Slazengers bearing an early version of his rose cleek mark.

Connellan & Campbell+
[Boston, MA]
  Driving Iron--Smooth face, Stewart pipe CM $100

Connellan Brothers
[Boston, MA]
  Mid Iron--Smooth face, St. Andrew Golf Co. stag head CM ..$80
  Iron--Smooth face, marked Connellan Selected in oval
  with scrollwork design $60

Connelly, H.E.
  Putter--Vimbo model, wood socket head, brass sole $250

Conroy, Thomas J.+
[New York]

Wood Shafted Golf Club Value Guide

    Driver--Splice head, brown color $150
    Cleek--Smooth face, name in crest $75
    Mashie Niblick--Smooth face, name in arc $100

Corey & Savage+
[Schenectady, NY]
    Putter--(A) Center shaft, RL boat shaped head $300

'Corona'
    Niblick--Line face $25

Cosby, E.
    Woods--Socket head, braided whipping at socket and grip ends,
    made by Wm. Gibson, hand holding arrows CM .... $200 each
    Mashie Niblick--(D) The Dead'un, rows of holes
    drilled through face $650
*   Named Irons--Braided whipping, hand/arrows CM ......$125 each

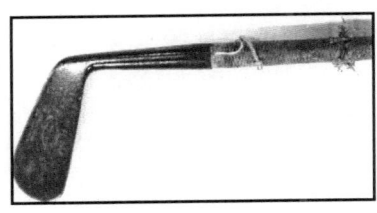 

Cosby patent iron showing the braided whipping above the hosel (with some slight fraying and unraveling)

                     Comet Brand putter made by J. & W. Craigie.

Cowan Golf Company*
[Sunderland e]
    Brassie--(A S) Mills-style fairway club, cross hatch face $250
    Putter--(A) Model F, Rodwell-type, arrow aiming line $175

Cowan & Clasper Ltd.
[Sunderland e]
    Putter--(A) Model 322, mallet head $150

Cox & Sons
[Southampton e]
    Mashie Niblick--Dot face, Gourlay moon/star CM $45

'Craftsman'
  Putter-Brass blade, long square hosel $75

Craigie, J. & W.*
[Montrose s; originally timber merchants, the Craigie brothers produced quality wood and iron clubs around the turn of the century]
  Driver--Splice head, black color, straight line name $400
  Brassie--Socket head, straight line name stamp $175
  Brassie--Comet Brand, small head, comet CM in oval mark $150
  Wood Cleek--Socket head, face insert $225
  Mashie--Line face, rifle mark $80
  Mid Iron--Smooth face, rifle CM, shaft stamp $100
  Lofter--Smooth face, long blade, rifle CM $225
  Lofter--Smooth face, short blade, rifle CM $100
  Niblick--Smooth face, small head, rifle CM $400
  Niblick--Line face, large head, rifle CM, oval name stamp ...$100
* Putter--Comet Brand, iron blade, comet CM, line face $75

Crawford McGregor & Canby Company+
[Dayton, OH; see MacGregor]

Crawford-Bartlett Company
[Chicago]
  Mashie--Child's club for game of Lawn Golf,
  W in diamond CM $50

Crighton, J. & R.*
[Carnoustie s]
  Cleek--Dot face, heart CM $75
  Iron--Line face, heart CM $75
  Mashie--Dreadnought model, dot face $75
  Mashie Niblick--Oval shaped head, line face, heart CM $80
  Niblick--Large head, dot face $75
  Putter--Heart CM, iron blade $80
  Putter--Steel mallet head, heart CM $250

Croke, Jack
[Oak Park, IL]
  Driver--Socket head, name in script $75
  Niblick--Dot face, heavy head, S&G club pip CM $60

Wood Shafted Golf Club Value Guide

Crook, Henry
[Leigh-on-Sea e]
    Iron--Line face, blacksmith's forge CM $60

Crosthwaite, Andrew W.*
[St. Andrews]
*   Putter---(S) Marked "Crosthwaite" $850

Andrew Crosthwaite wood head putter. This club was probably made after the firm of Auchterlonie and Crosthwaite was disbanded in 1896.

Crosthwaite & Lorimer*
[St. Andrews]
    Brassie--(S) Transitional shaped head $450
    Iron---Smooth face, heavy blade $200

Crowley, James
[Glasgow]
    Playclub--Beech head $1,500
    Iron clubs--Nicoll Indicator series,
    Crowley name in oval .... $50 each
    Putter---Gun metal head, three legged Manx figure CM $100

Crowley, R.
    Playclub--(S) Beech head, bulger shape $1,200

'Crusader'
    Putter--9, shield CM $40

Cumming, George+
[Toronto, ONT]
    Driver--Large socket head $100
    Mashie--Dot face blade $65
    Mashie Niblick--(D) Corrugated face, Spalding roses CM .. $125
    Spade Mashie--Dash face, Forgan flagstick CM $75

Cunningham, William*
[Edinburgh]
    Driver--Dreadnought-style large socket head $85
    Brassie--Stripe top, socket head $60
    Brassie--Gullen model, socket head $75
    Iron clubs--Stewart pipe brand .... $60 each

Cupples Golf Company+
[St. Louis, MO]
*   Iron clubs--Rhino series, rhinoceros CM, dot face .... $45 each
*   Iron clubs--Pro series, target CM .... $35 each

Cupples Golf "Rhino" series mashie.

Cupples Golf "Pro" series mashie.

Currie, J.D.
    Driver--Socket head, juvenile $50

Currie, T.
    Brassie--Short splice head $175

Currie, William
    Driver--(S) Beech head $350
*   Driver--(B) Bronze head with red gutta percha or rubber
    covering all the face $5,000

Curtis, H.L.*
[Bournemouth e]
    Driver--Socket head $75
*   Driving Mashie--Autograph model $75
    Mashie--Line face, oval name stamp $45
    Mashie--X35, dot ball face, autograph CM $75

Sammy--Autograph CM, round back, dot face $75
Niblick--(B) Smith model (anti-shank), smooth face $175
Putter--Wood centre shaft head, brass sole $300

Cuthbert, G.
[Carnoustie]
Iron clubs--"Caddie" Brand .... $40 each

Cuthbert, J.
[Stanmore e, et al]
Driving Iron--Dot face $35
Putting Cleek--Three crowns CM, made by Premier Golf Co. $85

'Cutlas'
Putter--(A) Mallet head $75

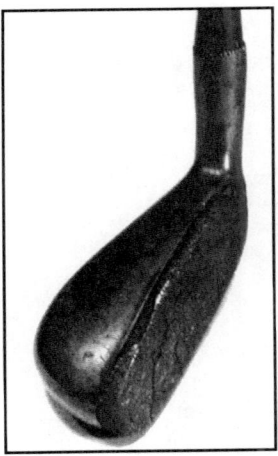

H.L. Curtis driving mashie with name stamped as an autograph.

William Currie patent bronze driver.

D

D.S. & Company+
[Dame. Stoddard & Co., Boston, MA]
Mid Iron--Trimount series, smooth face, knurled hosel $80
Mashie--Smooth face, D.S & Co. $60

Putter--Iron blade, dot face $50
Putter--Gun metal blade $125

D.S. & K.+
[Dame, Stoddard & Kendall, Boston, MA]
Driver--Socket head.. $55

Dagnall, George*
[Sevenoaks e, et al]
Driver--(B) Socket head, The Dagnall $250
Mashie--(D) "Handy Andy Kutspin Highball Iron",
large dot/dash face $600
Mashie Niblick--(D) Handy Andy Kutspin model,
brick face with deep circle punches $400
Putter--Bobby model, low profile dot face, sloped back $125

Dailey, Allan
Driver--Stripe top socket head $50

Dalgleish, J.
[Kansas City, MO]
Driver--Splice head $150
Putter--Blade, Spalding anvil CM $55
Putter--Missouri Topspin model, top flange $250
Putter--Old Elm Special model, offset blade $60

Dalrymple, Sir Walter H.*
[Famous amateur golfer and club patentee; clubs made by R. Forgan, J.H. Hutchison and other makers]
* Duplex Club--(A B) Cylindrical aluminum hammer
shaped head with two hitting surfaces, shaft stamp $2,000
Duplex Club--(B) Brass cylindrical hammer head, one surface
used for chipping and one for putting, marked
by J.H. Hutchison $4,800

Dalrymple patent duplex club. The two-faced hammer head shaped club designed by Dalrymple came in several versions. This on is aluminum and made by Robert Forgan.

Wood Shafted Golf Club Value Guide

'Daniel'
    Putter--(A B) Rectangular head with adjustable
    weights in toe $2,500

Dargo, J.H.*
[Edinburgh]
    Driver--Socket head $50
    Mashie--Line face, oval stamp, Gibson star CM $40
    Mid Iron--Line face, oval stamp, shaft stamp $35

Davega+
[New York City sporting goods house]
    Driver--Metropolitan series, socket head $35
    Brassie--Wicklow series, stripe top $40
    Driving Iron--Gairlock series X2, line face $30
    Iron--Gairlock series, X-88, Burke bee/flower CM $35
    Mashie--(D) Baxpin model 2A, ribbed face $85
    Putter--Tommy Armour model $50
    Putter, Wicklow series, blade, line face $35
    Putter--Gairlock series, blade $35
    Irons--Cameo series .... $30 each
    Irons--Gairlock series .... $30 each
    Irons--Imperial series, stainless, line face, heart CM .... $30 each
    Irons--La Salle Club series, star & crescent CM .... $30 each
    Irons--Lassie, dash face .... $30 each
    Irons--Metropolitan series, dot face, chromed .... $30 each
*   Irons--Wicklow series, star CM, chrome .... $30 each
    Numbered Irons--Tommy Armour model .... $40 each

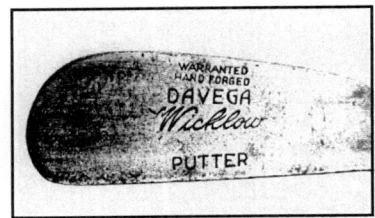

Putter forged by William Wilson for Willie Davis.

                           Davega Wicklow model putter.

Davey, Ashley*
[Margate e, et al]
    Cleek--Smooth face, Stewart serpent CM $100
    Mashie--Line face, Stewart pipe CM $50
    Mashie--Excelsior series, A.H. Scott lion CM, dot face $60
    Niblick--Gun metal head with large extension at top,
    smooth face, two surface face (concave) $2,250
    Putter--Gun metal blade, oval name stamp $80

Davidson, C.*
[Musselburgh s]
    Deep Face Mashie--Line face, three crowns CM $60

Davidson, Robert*
[Montrose s]
    Playclub--(L) Long head, whippy shaft $6,000-9,000
    Baffing Spoon--(L) Lofted face, name stamped in script ... $6,500
    Driving Putter--(L) Straight face, thick neck,
    dark stained head $8,000

Davidson, W.*
[Musselburgh s]
    Driver--Splice head, name in block letters $250

Davis, Willie F.+
[William H. Vanderbilt brought this young Scotsman to the U.S. to serve as the first professional to the Newport, RI Golf Club, later at Shinnecock Hills. During the 1880s Davis worked in Canada]
    Playclub--(L) Marked 'W. Davis', C.1890 Montreal $8,000
    Brassie--(S) Beech head, marked 'Thornton' $750
    Brassie--Splice head $300
    Cleek--Smooth face, name stamp from Newport $200
*   Putter--Iron blade, Willie Wilson 'St. Andrew' CM $200

Day, Arthur
[Ganton e, et al]
    Mashie Niblick--Eeze series, line face $50

Dayton Art Metal Co.
[Dayton, OH]
    Putter--Birdie model, flying bird CM $50

Wood Shafted Golf Club Value Guide

Dayton's
[Minneapolis, MN department store]
    Putter--Interlachen series, flange sole,
    Burke lion & crown CMs $75

De La Torre, A.
    Mashie--Line face, made by Stewart, pipe CM $45

'De Luxe'
    Putter--Maxwell pattern, kangaroo & kiwi CMs,
    made in Australia $50

Dean, H.E.
    Mashie--Stewart pipe CM $45

Dean, R.M.
    Cleek--Smooth face, juvenile, shaft stamp,
    dark stained shaft $125

'Dedli'
    Putter--(U) Blade with large cylindrical weight chamber
    on top edge, Marsh patent $2,500

'Demon, The'
[name also used by Slazenger]
    Iron--Made by Fred Blaisdell, smooth face small 6-point
    asterisk CM $100

Denholm, Andrew*
[Brighton e]
    Driver--Transitional splice head $350
    Driver--Splice head, thick scare, leather face insert $200
    Driver--Socket head $50

Des Jardins, A.
[Montreal, QUE]
    Driver--Laval model, stripe top $60

Dewar, Hugh
[Troon s]

Mashie Niblick--A9, triangle CM, line face $50

Dewsbury & Son, Jos.
Numbered Irons--Dewralex series, rustless dot face ...... $40 each

Diamond Manufacturing Company+
[St. Louis, MO]
Mashie--M-31, name in double diamond, dash/dot face $60

'Diamond State Brand'
Mashie--(D) Marked for Wilfred Reid, corrugated face $100

Dickinson, M.
Brassie--Splice head, hickory shaft $300

Dickson, J. & A.*
[Edinburgh]
Brassie--Short splice head $225
Spoon--Short splice head $250
Cleek--Smooth face, short blade, Braid Rd. address $100
Iron--(B) Simplex model, two-tine hosel,
like short Seely Patent $1,500
Jigger--Dot punch face $50
Mashie--Convex face, calfskin grip $400
Mashie--Deep face, X face, Gibson star CM $75
Niblick--C.1895, small head, smooth face $400
Putter--Gun metal blade $150
Putter--Iron blade, bent hosel, small Gibson star CM $150

Dint Patent Golf Company, Ltd.
[Malvern Link e]
100   Woods (driver, brassie, spoon)--"The Dint", socket head,
German silver sole & face plates $400

Doerr
[Made by Laclede Brass Works, St. Louis, MO; also see Laclede]
Putter--(U) Doerr Topem model, stainless, top flange $150
Putter--(U) Doerr Topem model, phosphor bronze,
negative loft, bottom flange, deeply scored line face $300

Doleman, Frank*

Wood Shafted Golf Club Value Guide

[Edinburgh]
    Driver--Splice transitional head, dark stain on head & shaft $450
    Brassie--(S) Transitional splice head $650
    Iron--Smooth face, straight line name stamp $125
    Mashie--Smooth face, Gibson star CM $100
    Putter--(S) C.1895, beech head, heavily leaded $650

Donald & Son, J.
[Weston-Super-Mare e]
    Mashie--Dot face, swan CM $60

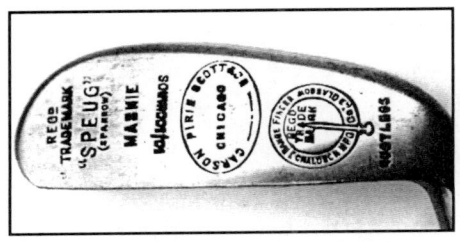

Donaldson "Speug" model mashie.

Donaldson Rangefinder series spoon with Rangefinder symbol on the sole plate;

Donaldson Manufacturing Company, Ltd., J.*
[Glasgow]
    Driver--(B) Rangefinder-Rapier series, Duralwood
    socket head $100
    Driver--Rangefinder-Rapier series, socket head $75
*   Woods (dr br sp)--(B) Rangefinder series, double stripe top,
    splice head .... $125 each
    Iron--Birdie model, bird CM, stainless, line face $60
    Iron--Skelpie model, pointed toe, line face $70
*   Iron--Speug model, round sole, dot face $80
    Iron clubs--Rangefinder series, line face, circular CM ....$50 each
    Mid Iron--Rapier series, dot face $45
    Niblick--Power 80 model, Rangefinder series, large head
    sand iron $200
**   Putter--Bunny model, stainless mallet head, brass face plug,
    bunny CM $175

Putter--Rangefinder series, blade, dot face $60

Donaldson, J.A.
[Glenview, Chicago]
Mongrel Mashie--Stewart pipe CM, line face $80

Donaldson, J.T.
[Glasgow]
Putter--Shallow face, round back $75
Numbered Irons--Dot face $30

Dow, Robert*
[Montrose s]
Driver--C.1900 Transitional splice head $500
Driver--Short splice head $300

Draper-Maynard Company+
[Plymouth, NH sporting goods firm]
Driver--Socket head, Ideal model..$75
Brassie--The Lucky Dog Kind series, dog CM $75
Mashie--(D) Lucky Dog series, corrugated face $125
*   Mashie--Lucky Dog series, dot face, stainless, dog CM $40
Niblick--Bulls Eye model, dot

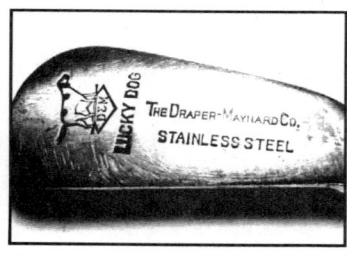

Draper-Maynard mashie. The company made a general line of sporting goods and thus used a sporting dog as their symbol..

face, dog in circle on face $85
Spade mashie--Doggie series, dog CM, dot face $40
Named Irons--Ideal series, stainless, dot face ....$35 each
Numbered Irons--Kingswood series, dog CM, dot face, chrome ....$40 each

Dubow, J.A.
Putter--Silver Cup model, offset blade $30

Wood Shafted Golf Club Value Guide

'Duncan Twin'
    Putter--(B) Adjustable head combination putter/chipper ... $1,400

Duncan, George*
[Hanger Hill, Ealing e, et al]
    Driver--Dreadnought type socket head $100
    Brassie--Ivorine insert, socket head $85
    Brassie--(U) Duncan model by Spalding, one piece sole
    plate backweight $100
    Cleek--Curious model $150
    Named Irons--Akros model, George Duncan autograph,
    Gibson star CM .... $75 each

Duncan, William
    Brassie--Greenock model, socket head $60

Dunlop, A
    Putter--Shoor Flite series, gem-type $75

Dunn Brothers*
[Mitcham, London; brothers John D. and Gourlay Dunn]
    Driver--(B) Unbreakable compressed splice head $450
    Mashie Iron--Smooth face, plume of feathers CM $300

Dunn, John Duncan
[Nephew of Willie Dunn, Jr.; headed B.G.I. and British Golf Company]
    Brassie--Splice head, fiber insert $275
    Brassie--Splice head, olde English lettering, small crown CM,
    fiber insert $200
    Lofter--Marked "British Made", made by British Golf Co. $85
    Mashie Niblick--Stainless, Morehead ship's wheel CM,
    dash face $50
    Mid Iron--Ionic series, 2 crowns CM $50
    Niblick--Smooth face, maltese cross in circle CM,
    "British Made" $100

Dunn, Seymour+
[Nephew of Willie Dunn, Jr. for whom he worked; later to Lake Placid, NY]
  *   Brassie--Model 72C, splice head, crown CM $175
    Iron clubs--"Vi et Arte" model, crown CM .... $80 each
    Pitcher-"Viet et Arte" model 102 .... $100

Mashie Niblick--Smith model anti-shank, crown CM with
legend "Vi et Arte" $200

Dunn, Thomas*
[Son of old Willie Dunn; worked at Wimbledon, North Berwick, Bournemouth and London]

Playclub--(L) Circa 1880, black stained head $2,500-5,000
Brassie--(S) C.1890, beech head, shaft stamp $1,450
Brassie--Transitional head $550
Mid Spoon--(L) Late long nose $2,700
Short Spoon--(L) Circa 1880, leather face insert $3,200
Spoon--Transitional head, calfskin grip $1,200
Baffing Spoon--(L) Circa 1880, beech head $5,500
Iron--Smooth face, straight name stamp $350
Lofter--Smooth concave face, long blade $600

Dunn, William (Sr.)*
[Blackheath e & Musselburgh s]
*   Long Spoon--(L) Very long head, stained dark,
    ash shaft $6,000-8,000
    Mid Spoon--Medium stain, fruitwood head $6,000-8,000
    Putter--Hook face, long thin head $5,000-8,000

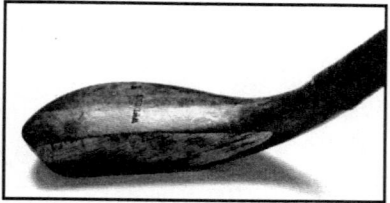

William Dunn long nose long spoon from the late featherball or early gutta percha era.

Dunn, William (Jr.)*+
[Ardsley Casino, NY and NYC; made clubs with his brother Tom in England until 1894 when he emigrated to America. Had his own business but also managed the B.G.I. and MacGregor golf works in the late 1890s]

100   Driver--(B) One piece, shaft stamp
      "Dunn & Son, Bournemouth" $2,400
      Driver--Short splice head, NY markings, dark color $550
      Driver--(U) Indestructable (sic) model, combination
      aluminum and wood head $1,500
      Driver--Splice head, "Unbreakable" $150
      Driver--Model 20 splice head, MacGregor shaft $250

Wood Shafted Golf Club Value Guide

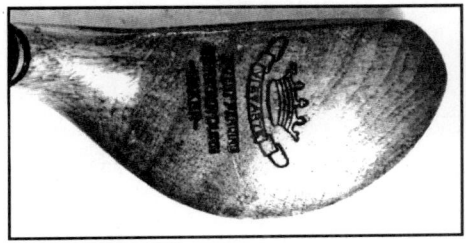

Seymour Dunn brassie with crown mark.

Willie Dunn splice head brassie made about 1900.

Driver--Splice head, child's size $300
Brassie--Splice head with bulger face $400
* Brassie--Short splice head in persimmon $300
Brassie--Splice head, marked "Dunn Selected" $250
Brassie--Splice head marked "Dunn Selected" $275
Brassie--(U) Convex sole model, socket head, leather face . $300
Chipper--(A U) Oval hammer shaped head with two hitting surfaces, center shaft $1,500
Cleek--Head forged by Williams with "W" mark on hosel, MacGregor shaft stamp $300
Iron--Smooth face, "Dunn Selected" in script $175
Iron--Smooth face, "Dunn Selected" in block letters $150
Iron--Smooth face, short blade, Dunn-MacGregor 'bowtie' CM $275
Iron--Smooth face, marked New York in arc, MacGregor shaft, I on hosel $200
Mashie--Smooth face, "Dunn Selected" in script $175
Lofter--Smooth face, name in block letters $175
Niblick--Smooth face, small head, marked "Ardsley", small eagle CM $800
Putter--(U) 'Rotary model' two flange gunmetal head $850
Putter--Park-style bent neck blade, "Dunn Selected" in script $200
Putter--Gun metal blade, Condie rose CM, marked Ardsley, NY $200
Putter--(A S U) Topspin-type, negative loft face $400

'Durexo'

Driver--Socket head, made by Alex Patrick $75

Duthie, Alex
[Several locations in Canada]
Heavy Iron--Dot face, Gibson star CM $70
Light Iron--Dot face $60
Medium Iron--Dot face $60

Dwight Directional driver.

Dwight Directional niblick.

Both woods and irons are very rare.

Dwight, J.W.+
Dwight Directional Clubs
[Des Moines, IA]
*   Driver--(U) Directional model, conic shaped head with
              brass backweight $2,000-4,000
100*   Mashie--(U) Directional model, boat shaped head,
              centre shaft, dot face $1,800-3,000
*   Niblick--(U) Directional model, well-lofted boat shaped head,
              centre shaft, dot face $2,500-3,500
              Putter--Dwight Directional series, center shaft,
              dot face $2,000-3,000

E

Eagen, Peter
[Princeton, NJ]
Brassie--Name in script, socket head $60

'Eager Special'
        Putter--Offset blade $40

Eagrow Company+
[Milwaukee, WI]
        Named Irons--Arrow model, stainless, line face ....$35 each

'Edco'
[Ernest Derrick Company, London]
*   Niblick--Dash face, triangle CM $45
        Putter--Gun metal blade, triangle CM $65

EDCO niblick sold by the retail store of A.W. Gamage & Co. in London

Edgar, J
[Settle e, et al]
        Putter--100 model, gem style, flower CM $100

'Edgemont'
[MacGregor economy series; see MacGregor]

'Edinboro'
[made by B.G.I.]
        Driver--Splice head $150
        Cleek--Smooth face $125
        Mashie--Smooth face $95
        Putter--Gun metal blade $150

'Elm Ridge'
        Mid Iron--Chrome, line face $20

Edinburgh Club
        Mashie--Smooth face $60

Elvery's
[London, Dublin, Cork i retailer]
    Putter--Star Maxwell model, Maxwell pattern,
    Gibson star CM $75
    Putter--Vardon style, shallow face, curved top $150

'Emperor' Brand
    Putter--Wood socket head, swan neck bent hosel,
    marked for Slazenger on toe $650
    Putter--As above, unmarked $450

'Esto Perpetua'
    Putter--Gun metal blade $60

'Eureka'
    Driver--Made by Frank Johnson, socket head $125

'Everbrite'+
[Baltimore, MD; made by Curtis Bay Copper & Iron Works]
    Mashie--High nickel content stainless, dot face $60
    Mashie Niblick--Dot face $60
    Putter--(A) Schenectady-type, Everbrite mark on sole $25

F

Fair, The
[Chicago department store]
    Driver--Socket head, Waverly Horton autograph $85

'Fairfield'
[B.G.I. economy brand line of clubs, made from selected "seconds"]

◇◇Listed by model number (stamped on shaft below grip)
    004--Cleek, smooth face, juvenile $100
    006--Lofting iron, smooth face, juvenile $100
    009--Iron, smooth face, juvenile $100
    010--Putting cleek, juvenile $100

Wood Shafted Golf Club Value Guide

012--Driving mashie, smooth face, juvenile ... $100
091--Driver, splice head, juvenile ... $200
093--Brassie, splice head, juvenile ... $200
201--Driving Iron ... $75
202--Gooseneck putting cleek ... $125
203--Driving cleek ... $75
204--Cleek ... $65
205--Centraject mashie ... $100
206--Lofting iron ... $75
207--Concave lofting cleek (jigger) ... $150
208--Lofting mashie ... $100
209--Iron ... $65
210--Putting cleek ... $100
211--Niblick, thick sole ... $125
212--Driving mashie ... $100
214--Medium mashie ... $75
215--Mashie, convex back ... $100
216--Medium mashie, deep face ... $100
217--Driving mashie, long blade ... $100
218--Approaching mashie ... $100
219--Putting cleek, twist neck ... $100
220--Putting cleek, deep face ... $125
221--Mashie iron ... $100
222--Cleek, short blade ... $100
290--Driver, straight face, splice head ... $250
223--Light mid iron ... $100
224--Mashie, J.H. Taylor pattern ... $125
291--Driver, bulger face, splice head ... $250
292--Brassie, straight face, splice head ... $225
293--Brassie, bulger face, splice head ... $225

'Fairview'
[House brand for The Fair department store, Chicago, IL, later by Lowe & Campbell]

       Iron clubs--Smooth face (Fair Store) ... $75 each
       Iron clubs--Scored face, Aim Rite clubs by Wilson
       for Lowe & Campbell ... $30 each

Faith Manufacturing Company+
[Chicago]
*   Named/Numbered Irons--Big Ball series, chromed head,

line face, ball CM .... $25 each
Numbered Irons--Superflight series, chromed head,
dot face .... $25 each

The Faith Manufacturing Company, Chicago, produced several lines of clubs at the end of the hickory shaft era.

Far & Sure Golf Company*
[Edinburgh]
    Driver--(S) Short narrow splice head $750
    Brassie--(S) Transitional splice head $600
    Iron--Smooth face, straight line name stamp $250
    Putter--(S) Transitional wood splice head $900

Feltham & Company*
[London]
    Brassie--Splice head, bulger shape $250
    Mashie--Smooth face $80
    Niblick--Smooth face, small head $400

Fenn, A.H.+
[Poland Spring, ME, et al]
    Driver--Short splice head $200
    Driver--Socket head $80
    Mashie--Line face, Spalding Gold Medal series $75

Fergie, William*
[Edinburgh]
    Driver--Short splice head $200
    Brassie--(S) Transitional splice head $450
    Lofter--Smooth face, oval stamp $200
    Putter--(S) Splice head $600
    Putter--Wood socket head, fiber face $250

Ferguson, J. (Jacky)
[Musselburgh s; brother of Robert]
    Driver--Short splice head $175

Ferguson, Robert*
[Musselburgh s, Open Champion]
    Putter--(S) Dark head $2,500-3,500

Fernie & Ross
[St. Andrews]
    Cleek--Ross's Own Model, Carruthers hosel, dot face $95
    Niblick--Eden series, hand holding wreath CM, line face $75

Fernie, George
[Troon s, et al]
    Spoon--(S) Brass sole plate, transitional head $750

Fernie, Harry
[Gosforth e]
    Driver--Name in script, socket head $80

Fernie, John
[Barnet e, et al]
    Numbered Irons--Par series, stainless, dot face ....$30 each

Fernie, Tom R.
[Royal Lytham e]
    Driver--Socket head $100
    Baffy--(B) "Wooden mashie", socket head $300
*   Cleek--RTJ model, Fernie autograph, Stewart pipe CM $125
    Iron clubs--Stewart pipe model, autograph ....$80 each
    Iron clubs--Stewart pipe model, name in oval stamp ....$70 each
*   Iron clubs--Line face, sword and crest CMs ....$75 each

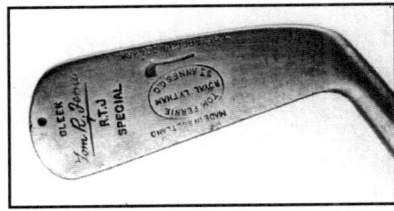 

Tom Fernie cleek in the Stewart 'R.T.J.' model.

Tom Fernie putter in the Perfectus/Claymore series with sword CM.

Fernie, Willie*
[Troon s, et al]
      Driver--Transitional shape splice head, leather insert $300
      Driver--Splice head, oval stamp $200
      Brassie--Short splice head $150
      Cleek--Smooth face, pipe CM $100
      Putter--Steel blade, oval stamp $100
      Putter--Bent hosel with steel blade ahead of shaft $400

'Field'
[Marshall Field Company, Chicago]
      Mashie--Juvenile, name in shield $30
      Mid Iron--Junior model, straight line name stamp $25

Fife Golf Company
[Kinghorn, Fife s; produced by William Gibson]
      Iron clubs--Castle CM, line face .... $40 each
      Putter--Gun metal blade, castle CM $75

Finnigan's*
[Liverpool department store]
      Brassie--Socket head, oval shaft $150

Fitzjohn Brothers+
[New York]
      Mashie--Smooth face, name in double oval $75

Fitzjohn, Ed
[Oneita NY, Albany, NY et.al.]
      Mid-iron--(U) Leitch patent (Spalding) with raised ridge on
      center of back, dash face $150
      Putter--Adjustable, shaft bolted to center back of blade $2,500
      Putter--(U) Center shaft attached to back of blade, shaped like an
      inverted question mark $3,500

Fitzjohn, Val
      Driver--Short splice head $200

Fletcher, W.
[Luton e, et al]
      Driver--Gravitum model, socket head $80

Wood Shafted Golf Club Value Guide

> Brassie--Hornby model, ivorine face insert $90
> Putter--Iron blade, dot face $40

Flood, Val
[New York]
> Driver--Splice head, name in circle, eagle head CM $350
> Brassie--Splice head, full sole plate $150
> Brassie--Socket head, name in signature $100
> Jigger--Dot face $90
> Mashie--Spalding rose CMs, dot face $50

Forgan, Andrew*
[Glasgow s; younger brother of Robert Forgan]
> Playclub--(L) Dark head $2,500
> Driver--Splice head, tree CM $350
> Driver--(S) Splice head, tree CM $600
> Brassie--Splice head, tree CM $350
> Lofter--Smooth face, long blade, long hosel $300
> * Mashie--Smooth face, compact blade, tree CM $150
> Niblick--Smooth face small head, made by James Anderson $600
> Putter--Gun metal blade, tree CM $200
> Putter--(S) Light color splice head $650

Andrew Forgan mashie. The Andrew Forgan cleek mark of the pear tree was only the second golf trademark registered in Great Britain.

Forgan & Son, Robert*
[St. Andrews; Robert Forgan grew from Hugh Philp's assistant to be principal of the largest and best known club making firm in the world. Appointed club maker to H.R.H. The Prince of Wales in 1863, early Forgan clubs are marked with the prince's symbol of a plume of three feathers. When the prince became King Edward VII in 1901, Forgan began using the crown mark.

Because of the firm's large output during the long nose and semi-long nose periods, the Forgan name is most often found on old wooden clubs. For that reason ranges of prices are given to accommodate differences in style, age and condition]

Pete Georgiady's

◇◇Early clubs with Prince of Wales plume mark
    Playclub--(L) C.1880, long head, plume over warrant CM $7,000
*   Playclub--(L) C.1870-1880, long head $3,500-5,500
    Spoon--(L) As above $3,500-5,500
    Baffy--(L) As above $4,000-6,500
    Putter--(L) As above $2,500-5,500
    Cleek--Smooth face, 4 1/2" hosel $250-500
    Iron--As above $250-500
    Lofter--As above $250-500
    Niblick--As above, small head $300-500

◇◇1890s clubs with Prince of Wales plume mark

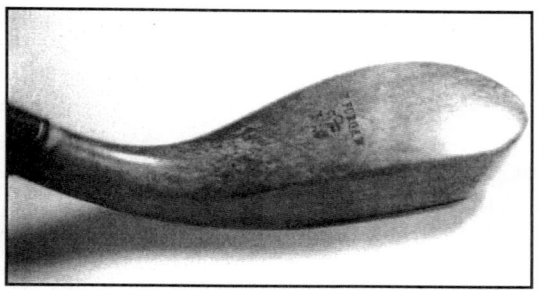

Robert Forgan long nose play club, from about 1875-1880 with plume mark. It was a large club-making firm and more Forgan-made long headed clubs exist today than those of any other maker.

100   Playclub--(L) 1880-1900 vintage $1,000-2,500
**   Playclub-(L) Child's club circa 1890, no bone or lead $900
    Spoon--(L) As above $1,000-2,500
    Baffy--(L) As above $1,000-3,000
    Putter--(L) As above $800-2,500
    Cleek--Smooth face, 4" hosel $150-300
    Iron--As above $150-300
    Mashie--As above $150-300
    Niblick--As above, small head $200-500
    Niblick--As above, medium head $150-300
    Putter--As above, steel blade $100-300
    Putter--As above, gun metal blade $100-300
    Driver--(B) Fork splice joint $350
*   Driver--(S) C.1890-1900, shorter transitional
    shaped head $300-800
    Driver--(S) Red fiber face insert $500-800
    Brassie--(S) As above $500-800

Wood Shafted Golf Club Value Guide

Fairway club-(A B) Cylindrical head with striking surface on each end (Dalrymple patent) $2,000
Lofter--(B) Fairlie model (anti-shank), smooth face, plume CM $400
Lofter--Smooth face, compact blade $150-300
* Lofter--Smooth face, long blade $150-300
Mashie--As above $100-200
Putter--(S) As above $200-800

◇◇◇20th century clubs

Driver--Swilken model A, large socket head, face insert $60

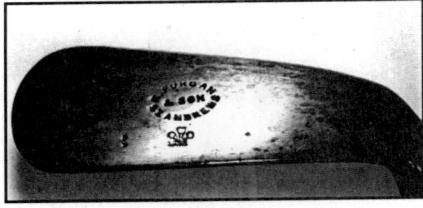
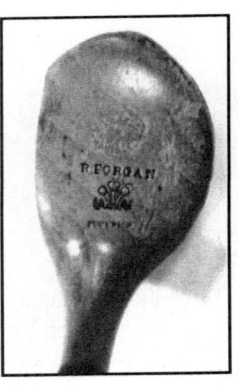

Forgan lofting iron with plume mark, circa 1890.

Forgan splice head Superior model driver.

Driver--(B) Forganite model, socket head $150
Driver--Dreadnought model, oversize socket head $100
Driver--Socket head, Andrew Kirkaldy autograph $100
** Driver--Maxmi model, 4-screw ivor face insert, rounded sole $125
Brassie--(B) Angle Shaft model, oval shaft $175
Brassie--(B) Forganite model, socket head $150
Brassie--Dreadnought Junior model, socket head $100
Spoon--Bulldog model, ivor insert $125
Putter--(A B Maxmi model, sounded sole $150
Putter--(A) Maxmo model, mallet head $80
100   Putter--(B) Maxmo model, wood mallet, 2 metal sole plates $175
Putter--The Tolley model, wood socket head $200
Putter--The Tolley model, socket head in Forganite $250
Putter--(B) The Whee model, combination wood & metal shaft $600

Pete Georgiady's

Putter--Ebony wood socket head $300
Putter--Gem style, rounded back, dot face $75
Putter--Iron blade, dot face, oval name stamp $50
Putter--(A) Kent model, mallet head $75
Putter--Marked "Putter Iron," dot face, shallow face blade,
Forgan company markings on toe of face $75
* Putter-Wood socket head, bulger shape, metal sole plate $200
Putter--Model B9, boy's size, iron blade, dot face $40
Putting Cleek--Long blade & hosel, line face $75

◇◇Celtic series

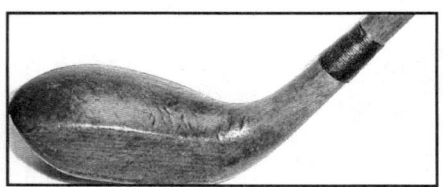 

Forgan Company wood headed putter, heel-shafted in a socket. Sole plate shows Forgan markings circa 1915-25.

Approach Cleek--Model 19, Celtic series musselback,
crown CM $60
Iron clubs--Celtic model, name in script, line face ....$50 each

◇◇Crown CM

Driver--Crown CM, socket head $60-125
Driver--Juvenile size, smaller head, 21" shaft
(no lead backweight) $125
Brassie--Crown CM, socket head $60-125
Cleek--Dot face, crown CM $50
Driving Iron--Dot face, crown CM $50
Driving Iron--A. Kirkaldy model, crown CM dot face $90
Iron--Line face, crown CM $40
Mashie--Simple crown CM, pipe CM, dot face $65
Mashie-(B) Fairlie model anti-shank, dot face, crown CM $175
Mashie Niblick--Also carries Nicoll hand CM, Zenith series ..$50
Niblick--Small head, crown CM $200
Niblick--Marked B (boy's), dot face, crown CM $65
Putter--Gun metal blade, crown CM $90

Wood Shafted Golf Club Value Guide

Putter--Steel blade, crown CM $50
Putter--Steel blade, bent hosel like Park model $90

Forgan "Stopded" model mashie has a strongly grooved, but not corrugated face for back spin.

◇◇ Flagstick CM (Spence series)
    Chipper--Stroke-Saver model, P.A. Vaile swan neck, round sole $300
    Cleek--Juvenile, marked B, flagstick CM $50
    Mashie--Line face, flagstick CM $50
*   Mashie--Stopded model $60
    Mashie Niblick--Line face, oval head, flagstick CM $60
    Spade Mashie--Dot face, flagstick CM $65
    Putter--Offset blade, flagstick CM $65

◇◇ Forgan name in script
    Mashie Niblick--Oval head, name in script $50
    Niblick--Name in script, dash face $50
    Mashie--Scotia series, marked "Taylor's Pattern", smooth face $90
    Mid Iron--Clan series, line face $30

◇◇ Matched sets
    Crown series
    Woods (driver, Brassie, spoon)-- Socket head .... $60 each
    Numbered Irons (1-7)--Stainless, line face .... $30 each

    Eeze Series
    Numbered Irons (1-6)--Line face .... $35 each

    Gold Medal series
    Woods (driver, Brassie, spoon)--Stripe top, socket head $60 each
    Numbered Irons (1-9)--Line face .... $30 each

Meteor series
Woods (driver, Brassie, spoon)--Socket head, white
aiming dot .... $65 each

Scotia series
Woods (driver, Brassie, spoon)--Stripe top .... $75 each
Numbered Irons--Regular or stainless .... $35 each

Forrest, Charles*
[North Berwick s, East Berkshire e]
    Mashie--Albion brand, abstract thistle CM, line face $50
    Lofter--Forest Clubs brand, smooth face, 'FF' CM $100

Forrest, J.
[Sheffield e]
    Brassie--Splice head, ivorine insert $125

Forrester, George*
[Elie s; Forrester was acknowledged by his contemporaries as one of the most innovative club designers of his time. He patented many types of wood and iron clubs though his most important contribution was his concentric back iron]

100   Driver--(B) Socket head, round name stamp with
        patent number, shaft stamp $250
        Driver--(B) As above, head made of black composite fiber ..$650
        Brassie--(S) Bulger shaped splice head $500
        Brassie--Short splice head $300
        Brassie--(B) Socket head, round name stamp with patent
        number, shaft stamp $250
        Spoon--(L) C.1885, dark finish $4,000
        Cleek--(B) Bulbous toe, smooth face $600
        Cleek--Smooth face $125
*   Cleek--(B) 1919, "Non Slice" model, Anderson arrow CM $80
        Iron--(B) Round back, bulger face $350
        Lofter--Smooth face, Forrester and Anderson round CMs $150
        Mashie--(B) Two humps on back (Double Balance model),
        smooth face $800
100   Mashie--(B) Concentric back, round name stamp with
        patent number $200
        Niblick--Smooth face, small head $300
        Putter--Little Gem model, small gem style blade $75

Putter--(B) Top Edge model, top edge bent toward face $600
* Putter--(A) Boat shaped Schenectady-type $250

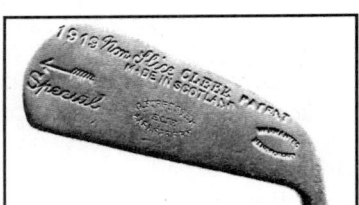

Forrester cleek, "Non Slice" model 1919, made by Anderson.

Forrester aluminum boat-head putter.

Forrester, James
[Elie; son of George, James ran the branch location in London before arriving as successor to the family business in Elie]
Brassie--Stripe top socket head $75

Forth Rubber Company, Ltd.*
[Edinburgh, Glasgow, Dundee s]
Driver--(S) Splice transitional head, bulger face $400
Driver--Bulger short splice head $300
Cleek--Smooth face, name in rectangle $75
Iron--Small Nicoll hand CM, smooth face $150
Iron--Small circular name CM, smooth face $125
Mashie--Smooth face, Forth Rail Bridge CM $300
Niblick--Smooth face, medium head, name in box $125
Putter--(S) Transitional splice head, name in block letters ... $400

Fortnum & Mason*
[London specialty store]
Driver--Socket head, stripe top, name in script $45
Spoon--Very small socket head, name in block letters,
fiber face insert $60
Mashie--Fort Mason brand, stainless, dot face $40
Niblick--Fort Mason brand, giant head, stainless,
dot face $1,800

Foster Brothers*
[Ashbourne e]
    Driver--Socket head, ridged sole plate $90
    Driving Iron--Dot face, skeleton CM $85
    Jigger--Line face, skeleton CM $100
    Putter--(A B)The Bogee model, square hosel, rectangular head with broad sole $200

Fraser, Chick
    Driving Iron--Line face, Nicoll hand CM $40

Foulis, David+
    Lofter--Stewart pipe CM, smooth face $75
    Mashie Niblic--(D) Spalding Foulis model 3, hammer, 2 Thistle CMs, patent date, ribbed face $450
    Putting Cleek--Spalding Dysart series, steel blade, name in oval $75

Foulis, James+
[Chicago; U.S. Open Champion 1896, inventor of the flat sole, concave face mashie niblick, which many other makers imitated]
    Brassie--(S) Splice head, leather face insert $500
    Cleek--Smooth face $100
    Cleek--Octagon back, smooth face $400
*100 Mashie Niblick--(U) Flat sole, concave face, star mark $250
    Mashie Niblick--As above marked "Pat. Applied For" $400
    Niblick--Small head, slightly concave face $500
    Putter--Iron blade $200

James Foulis, Jr. patent mashie niblick. The original design had a concave face.

Foulis, Robert+
[Chicago and St. Louis]
    Lofting Iron--Smooth face, Stewart pipe CM $100

Fovargue, A.
    Mid Iron--Concentric back, name in horseshoe $60

Wood Shafted Golf Club Value Guide

Fryer, James
[Edinburgh]
  Driver--Made by Forrester, splice head $125

Fulford, Harry*
[Bradford e]
  Sammy--Dot face $100
  Iron clubs--Stewart pipe brand, scored face .... $60 each

G

Gadd, Charles*
[Roehampton e]
  Putter--(A) Autograph model, mallet head, beveled top $125

Gair, Alexander*
[Edinburgh]
  Cleek--Midget Marvel model, 2-sided approach club $250

Galloway, Thomas*
[Pittenweem s]
*   Iron clubs--Edinburgh Gold Medal stamp, dot face .... $75 each

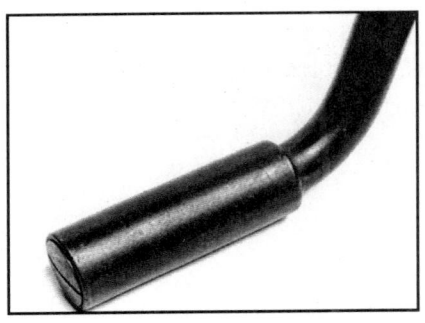 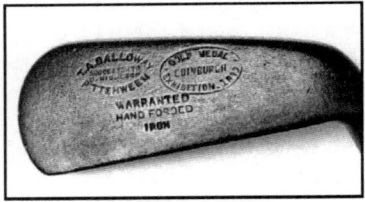

Galloway iron.
Payne Gallwey roller putter.

Gallwey, Sir R. Payne
*100   Putter--(B) Gallwey roller model $1,500-2,000

Gamage Company, A.W.*
[London retail store]
        Driver--The Gamage series, socket head $75
        Driver--The Gamage series, short splice head $150
        Driver--(S) Transitional splice beech head $350
        Brassie--(S) Transitional splice head $350
        Iron clubs-Name in oval, Spalding hammer CM ....$40 each
        Iron clubs--Kromwell model, dot face ....$40 each
        Mid Iron--Juvenile, marked B, by Anderson/Anstruther $50
        Niblick--The Gamage series, smooth face, small head $350
        Putter--(B) Duncan Twin model, adjustable
        head combination putter/chipper $1,400
        Putter--Bent neck, heart & arrow + lion CMs, marked "Park Putter" $90

Gardner, Stewart
[Garden City, NY et al]
        Driver--Socket head, stripe top, red fiber insert $100
        Iron clubs--Stewart pipe mark, line face ....$60 each

Gassiat, Jean*
[Biarritz, France and Baden-Baden, Germany]
*   Putter--Large square wood socket head, name in script $700
        Putter--Large square wood head marked with reg. number ..$800
        Putter--LCL model, name in oval $700

Gassiat model wood head putter, nicknamed the "Grand Piano" because of its size ad shape. It could be used by right or left handed players.

Gaudin, P.J.*
        Driver--Socket head, stripe top $60

'Gee-Bee'
        Mashie--Child's toy club, roughly cast head $20

Gibson, Charles*
[Royal North Devon Golf Club, Westward Ho! e]

Wood Shafted Golf Club Value Guide

Driver--(S) Bulger style splice head, leather face insert $1,500
Driver--(S) Bulger splice head, wood face insert $1,200
Brassie--Beech splice head, leather face insert $800
Spoon--The Nippy model, well lofted face, fiber insert $300
Iron--Diamond back, juvenile, dash face, stallion CM $95
Mashie Iron--Short blade, deep face, stallion CM $75
Niblick--Flange sole, dash face, stallion CM $60
Niblick--(B) Smith style anti-shank, stallion CM $200
Putter--(S)Wood splice head $450
Putter--Wood mallet, socket head $250
Putter-Gassiatt-type, large wood head $700
* Putter-Winner model, rampant horse CM $75
1-Iron--Excellar series, phoenix CM, Line face $65

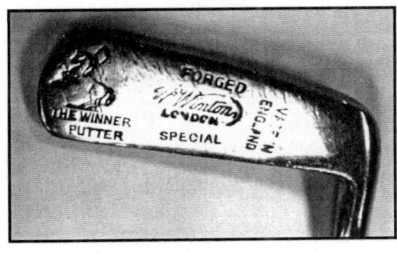

Charles Gibson Winner model blade putter.

Gibson, Jr., C.H.*
[Oxford, later Westward Ho!; son of Charles Gibson]
 Driver--Socket head $60
 Niblick--Spalding hammer CM, line face $60

Gibson, R.J.
[Calcutta, India; son of Charles Gibson]
 Mid Iron--Triplex model, Paragon series, shield with
  3 Xs CM $75
 1-Iron--Excellar series, phoenix CM $65

Gibson & Company, William*
[Kinghorn, Fife s. In the early part of the 20th century, William Gibson was the largest manufacturer of golf clubs in the world.]
 Driver--"Gibson's of Kinghorn" in script, stripe top,
  socket head $75
 Driver--Mignon series, bulger socket head, star CM $100
 Driver--Socket head, star CM $65

Brassie--Stripe top, socket head, star CM ...$65
Brassie--Bulldog shape ...$125
Spoon--Short socket head, star CM ...$100
Baffy Spoon--Small socket head, fiber insert ...$125
Cleek--Smooth face, marked "Long Face Cleek", star CM ...$100
Cleek--Smooth face, Carruthers hosel ...$90
Cleek--Leather face (copied after Nicoll) ...$1,800
Cleek--Pixie series, offset head, dot face ...$90
Full Iron--Star CM, line face ...$45
Iron--(B) Murray model, iron head with splice joint ...$2,000
Iron--Carruthers hosel ...$100
Jigger--Shallow blade, dot face ...$60
Jigger--Stainless, star CM ...$45
Jigger--Jerko model, dot face ...$75
Light Iron--Star CM, dot face ...$75
Mashie--Smooth face, marked for Robert Simpson,
small star CM ...$100
Mashie--Starona series, star on face ...$45
Mashie--Stella series, model 22, diagonal bi-level back,
line face ...$65
Mashie--King-Horn model, star in circle CM, dash face ...$35
Mashie--Star Maxwell model, stainless, Maxwell pattern,
dot face ...$60
Mashie--Vardon autograph model, musselback, dash face ...$100
Mashie--(B) Smith model (anti-shank), concave back,
star CM ...$175
Mashie--(B) Fairlie model (anti-shank) ...$150
Mashie--(D) Jerko model, corrugated face ...$125
Mashie--Baxpin model, diamond/dot face ...$60
* Mashie Niblick--Akros model, George Duncan autograph,
star CM ...$60

William Gibson & Co. George Duncan 'Akros' series mashie niblick. This particular club was exported to the Williams Company in France

Mashie Niblick--(D) Jerko model, corrugated face ...$125

Wood Shafted Golf Club Value Guide

      Mashie Niblick--Baxpin model, Maxwell pattern, stainless ... $75
      Mashie Niblick--The Skart model, line face $60
*   Mashie Niblick--(D) The Dead'un model, holes drilled
      through face, star CM $650
      Mashie Niblick--Dandy model, diamond back, dot face $85
      Medium Iron--Star CM, line face $75
      Medium Iron--(B) Smith model (anti-shank), smooth face .. $200
      Mid Iron--The Horn model, hunting horn CM $45
      Mid Iron--Stella model, stainless, line face $35
      Mid Iron--Starona series, stainless, Maxwell pattern $60
      Mid Iron--Marked Osborn's Rustless, tiny hand & heart CM $60
*100 Niblick--Skoogee model, concave face $450
      Niblick--Superior model, stainless, dash face, star CM $40
      Niblick--(D) Winchester series, ribbed face, star CM $200
      Niblick--The "Giant" model, James Braid series,
      medium size head, star CM, line face $85
      Niblick--Big Ben model, giant head $1,800
      Pitcher--The Pitcher, round sole, dot face $85
      Pitcher--Model 92, shallow face, very thick sole $75
      Pitcher--(D) Jerko model, ribbed face $150
      Sammy--Pixie series, line face $100
      Numbered Irons--Superior series, stainless, deep
      star CM ....$35 each
      Putter--Star Maxwell series, Maxwell pattern,
      extra thick flange $75
      Putter--Dominie model, rounded back $125
      Putter--(B) The Princeps model, top edge weighted $300

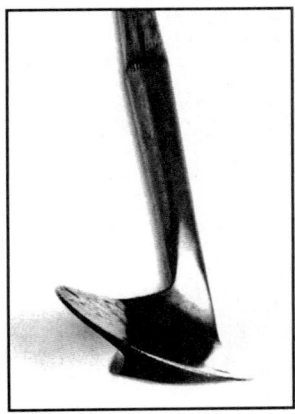

Gibson Skoogee model sand wedge.

William Gibson Dead'un model made for Edwin Cosby.

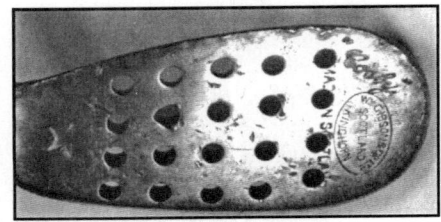

Pete Georgiady's

	Putter--(B) Skinner model, protruding face	$300
	Putter--Gem style, dot face	$75
	Putter--Jonko model, flat sole with large hump at sweet spot	$2,500
100	Putter--(B) Brown Vardon model, iron head	$200
	Putter--(B) Brown-Vardon style, Monel, star CM	$200
	Putter--(B) Brown Vardon model, gun metal head	$275
	Putter--Cara Mia model, stripe top wood mallet, socket head	$175
	Putter-The Skart model, shallow face, round back, same in script	$100
	Putter--Triple star model, stainless, offset blade	$50
	Putter--Marked "bent neck putter"	$60
100	Putter--Orion model, broad flange sole, name in script	$80
	Putter--Kilgour Match model, blade	$90
	Putter--(A S) Model AA, long head	$150
	Putter--(A) Model BB, medium length head	$100
	Putter--(A) Schenectady style	$175
	Putter--All Square model, square hosel, offset blade	$175
	Putter--Bradbeer's Own, long stainless blade, star CM	$100
	Putter--Accurate model, iron blade, bent neck	$65
	Putter--Iron blade, gooseneck	$65
	Putter--(B) Civic model, flange sole, holes drilled through face, star CM	$400-600
	Putter--Eskit model, offset hosel, pointed toe, square grip	$125
	Putter--Gleneagles model, low profile blade, grooved sole, square shaft, medium hosel	$125
	Putter--Varsity model, heel and toe weighting	$200
	Putter--Cosby series, hand holding arrows & star CMs, gooseneck hosel	$125
	Putter--F.G. Tait model, blade shape, star CM	$80
	Putting Cleek-Tait model, star CM inside double circle	$80
	Putting Cleek--Genii series	$95
	Putting Iron--Iron blade, dot face, star CM	$70

◇◇**Hugh Logan's Genii Model irons**

Three generations of Genii irons exist, marked:
"Patent Pending" (oldest),
"Patent No. 22170" (most common), and
"Patent No. 308040" on a stainless head (most recent)

Wood Shafted Golf Club Value Guide

*100   Cleek--(B) Genii model, smooth face, notched at hosel,
"patent pending", star CM $150
also available in
Mashie
Mashie Cleek
Mashie Niblick
Medium Iron
Mashie Iron
Putting Cleek
Mashie--(B) Genii model, line face, patent number,
star CM $60
   Other Genii club types with patent number similarly valued

Mashie--(B) Genii model, line face, patent number, stainless,
star CM $45
   Other Genii club types in stainless similarly valued

Gibson Hugh Logan series Genii model medium iron.

Gibson Arnaud Massy autograph series putter.

◇◇James Braid Autograph series
    Cleek--James Braid model, musselback, dot face $75
      also produced as (at similar value)
    Driving Cleek (later Driving Iron)
    Medium Iron
    Light Iron
    Heavy Iron
    Niblick
    Putter
    Mashie

◇◇Arnaud Massy Autograph irons
    Medium Iron--Arnaud Massy autograph model, star CM $75

The Massy series also included these clubs (at similar value)
Cleek
Iron
Mashie Niblick
Iron (round back)
Mashie (long face)
Jigger
Niblick
Mashie (deep face)
* Putter

◇◇Selected Autograph series clubs representing various players made by William Gibson and bearing his star CM
Named Irons--George Duncan autograph, Akros series . $60 each
Named Irons--Percy Boomer autograph series,
shallow line face, star CM .... $60 each
Named Irons--A. Kirkaldy autograph series, line face .... $75 each
Named Irons--F. Cheshire autograph series, dot face ..... $90 each

◇◇Selected miscellaneous clubs
Mashie Niblick--(D) George Duncan autograph series 126,
slotted face $125
Named Irons--George Duncan autograph series, dot face $90
Push Iron--R.H. de Montmorencie autograph series,
dot face $100
Spade Mashie--George Sargent autograph series,
line face, star CM $75

Gimbel's
[New York City department store]
Iron clubs--Gimbel name between 2 Spalding thistle CMs $40

Glasgow Golf Company*
[Charles L. Millar, proprietor]
Driver--Socket head, thistle CM $100
Iron clubs-Rustless, company name in 2 triangles .... $45 each
Putter--Blade, thistle CM, dot face $50

'Glencoe'
[Burke store brand]
Mashie--(D) Model 1369, corrugated face $75

Wood Shafted Golf Club Value Guide

Glover Specialty Company+
[Bridgeport, CT]
    Brassie--Read Balanced model, socket head $75
    Driver--Read-Barnes model, metal face insert $125
    Putter--Read model, square wood head, heel shafted $400

'Gold Standard'
    Driver--(U) Stripe top socket head, bamboo shaft,
    sewn grip $150

'Golden Eagle'
[A brand from the Eagrow Company, Milwaukee, WI]
    Mashie Niblick--Ampco metal blade, line face $50

Goldsmith Company+
[Cincinnati, OH]
    Driver--Socket head, name in block letters $55
    Mashie--Hyde Park series, line face, Maltese cross CM $35
    Mid Iron--Model G, diamond back, line face $40
    Mid Iron--Line face $35
    Putter--Bronze alloy blade, Maltese cross CM $45
    Putter--Lady Claremont series, two Maltese cross CMs $45
    Putter-Bronze alloy, circular waffle-style face $75

Golf Company, The+
[Kansas City, MO]
    Putter--The Highlander model, 2-sided, line faces $40

Golf Company, The*
[St. Andrews]
    Putter--(S) Beech head, dark stain $1,000

Golf Goods Manufacturing Company+
[Binghamton, NY; around 1900 this firm was headed by Willie Tucker who produced some of his Defiance clubs here]
    Driver--Socket head, stamped "G.G.M.Co." $250
    Driver--Model 104, splice head $500
    Cleek--Smooth face $175
    Iron--Smooth face $150
    Mashie--Smooth face, thick blade $200

    Lofter--Smooth face, long blade $200
    Niblick--Small head $800
    Putting Cleek--Thick iron blade $250

Golf Shop, The
[Chicago]
    Mid Iron--Name in script, dot face $30
    Jigger--Anderson arrow CM, musselback, dot face $50
    Mashie--(D) Hold em model, Anderson arrow CM,
    corrugated face $150
    Mashie--444 model, deep face, small shamrock CM $35
    Putter--Gun metal dominie-type head $225

Golf Specialty Company
[Baltimore, MD]
    Mashie--(D) Arroflite model, ribbed face $100

Golfers' Supply Company*
[Glasgow]
    Mid Iron--Smooth face, marked 'Scotsman' $100
    Putter--Iron blade, marked 'Scotsman' $125

Goodrich Sales Company+
[Chicago]
    Iron--(U) Adjustable "All-One" club $2,000

Goudie & Company*
[Glasgow and Edinburgh]
    Driver--(S) Transitional beech splice head $400
    Cleek--Made for Goudie & Co., convex back,
    Anderson double circle CM $75
    Putter--(B) "Taylor's Patented Hosel", smooth face $125
    Putter--Gun metal blade $100

Gouick, T.
[Dundee s]
    Putter--Center shafted, pendulum style $600

Gourlay, Bert
[Glasgow]
    Driver--Socket head $50

Wood Shafted Golf Club Value Guide

Gourlay, James*
[Carnoustie s; maker of iron club heads]
  Cleek--Name in horseshoe CM, smooth face $75
* Iron--Smooth face, crescent moon & star CM $100
  Mashie--Concentric back, diamond face, anchor CM $60
  Mashie Cleek--Moon & star cleek mark, name in horseshoe .. $75
  Mashie Niblick--Oval head, diamond/dot face $60
  Mid Iron--Moon/star CM, diamond back $60
  Niblick--Large head, dot face, back beveled to toe and heel $100
  Sammy--Round back, round sole, moon & star CM $60
  Putter--P.A. Vaile model, swan neck,
  made for F.H. Ayers Co. $400
  Putter--Bent neck, crescent moon & star CM $75
  Putter--Beveled Edge model, radiused top edge $125
  Putter--Sovereign model, floral design on face,
  rounded back $100
  Putter--Offset blade, musselback,
  crescent moon & star CM $75
  Putter-Deep face blade, crescent moon & star CM $150

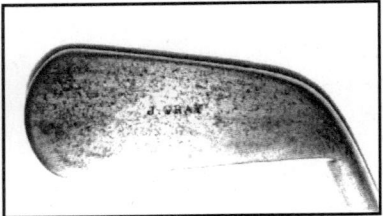

James Gourlay iron with moon & star CM.
    John Gray general iron from about 1875.

Gourlay, Walter
[St. Andrews]
  Putter--Dot face, blade $45

Gourley, Thomas
  Mashie--Spalding Gold Medal, marked for Marine & Field ... $75
  Putter--Offset iron blade, marked for Baltusrol $80

Govan, James
    Putter--Made by Spalding, 2 roses CM,
      marked Pine Valley $100
    Putter--A-1 model, blade behind hosel, gun metal,
      line face $300

'Grampian Range'
[A series made by J.H. Turner; see Turner]
    Iron clubs--(B) Mountain CM, line face,
      weight holes in upper edge of blade ....$150 each

'Grand Leader'
    Putter--Gun metal blade $75

Grant, Frank
    Driver--Model 33, deep face, socket head $50

Grant Company, W.T.
[New York]
    Jigger--Chromed, curved swastika & large fleur de lis CMs ..$35
    Iron clubs--Piccadilly series $25

Gravitator Golf Ball Company*
[London]
    Putter--(B) The Multiface model, 4 removable
      face inserts $4,000

Gray, A.*
[Carnoustie s; C.1860-68]
    Cleek--Long hosel, name stamp in script $3,000
    Iron--Name in large block letters, very heavy hosel $6,000
    Niblick--Deep faced, short blade $7,000

Gray, Ernest*
[Littlehampton e, et al]
    Driver--Splice head, light finish $150
    Driver--Socket head $70

Gray & Sons, H.J.
[Cambridge e]

Cleek--Long blade, smooth face $125
Mashie--Smooth face, compact blade $100
Niblick-Mammoth style, extra large head,
Cochrane knot CM $1,200-1,500
Putter--Steel blade, name in circular CM $100

Gray, John*
[Worked in Prestwick about 1850-1890 as one of the pioneer iron club makers and was one of the first to regularly stamp his name on iron clubs. First name was stamped Jn. or J.]

100*	Cleek--Long hosel, smooth face	$1,250-2,000
*	Iron--Long hosel, deep face	$1,250-2,000
	Lofter--Long hosel, long and slightly concave face	$1,250-2,500
	Niblick--Long thick hosel, small thick head	$2,000-3,000

Great Lakes Golf Company+
[Milwaukee, WI]

	Driver--Stripe top socket head	$45
	Driver--Glen-Eagle series, socket head	$40
*	Iron clubs--Great Lakes name in stylized script, swastika CM	$45 each
	Mid Iron--Baltic series, swastika CM, dot face	$45
	Niblick--Stainless, GL in circle on face	$30
	Niblick--Kiltie series, dot face	$25
	Putter--Model 10F, blade	$25
	Putter--New Yorker series, chrome blade	$30
*	Numbered Irons--Lakeshore brand, Tommy Armour series, diamond CM	$50 each
	Numbered Irons--Al Watrous Straight Eight autograph series, line face	$50 each
	Numbered Irons--Bobby Cruikshank autograph series, GL face mark	$50 each
	Iron Set--Bobby Cruickshank autograph series, 8 irons and putter	$650

Green, W.G.
[Rumson, NJ]

Iron clubs-Line face, four-square CM
(Swastika variant) ....$75 each

Pete Georgiady's

Grosse Ile Putter Company+
[Grosse Ile, Detroit, MI]
    Putter--Stainless, flange sole $60

Grove & Company, George
[London]
    Mid Iron--The Hawk series, stainless, flying bird CM $50

Guise, F.
    Putter--Shiva, small musselback, oval shaft,
    Winton diamond CM $125

'Gyroscope'
    Mashie--(D) Diagonal grooves, circular CM $200

Great Lakes model 44 mashie iron with Sawstika CM.
    Great Lakes putter from the Tommy Armour series.

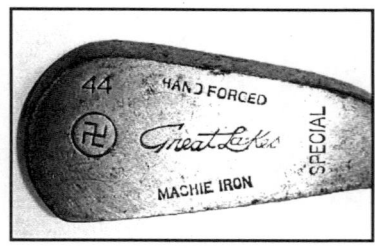
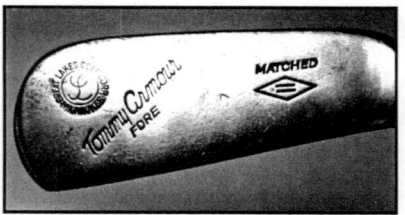

H

Hackbarth, Otto+
[Primarily worked in Cincinnati, OH]
    Driver--Socket head $80
    Spoon--Very small splice head $400
    Spoon--(U) Small socket head, 'Pat. Pending' $125
    Mid iron--Stewart pipe brand, line face $50
    Mashie--Made by Wilson, Hackbarth shaft stamp $50
    Niblick--Smith model anti-shank model $200
*100 Putter--(A U) "Coathanger shape," two-tined hosel,
    brass weight strip in sole $300-500

Wood Shafted Golf Club Value Guide

The Otto Hackbarth patent putter.

Important Note:
The weighted blade of the Hackbarth putter placed heavy stress on the hosel tines, often cracking or breaking them. A repaired club is worth appropriately less that the above range. Also, replica copies are known to exist.

Hagen, Walter+
[After 1926, all Hagen brand clubs were made by L.A. Young Company. Earlier clubs, like the Cochrane series, are noted otherwise. Most Hagen clubs had a small 'H' on the club face at the sweet spot]

◇◇Clubs and putters not belonging to other model sets
    33-Iron--Ranger utility club $100
    44-Iron--Tom Boy series, Ranger model utility club $100
    66-Iron--Ranger utility club $100
*100   Sand Iron--(U) Smooth concave face,
    large flange on sole $350-600
    Sand Iron--The Iron Man model, large flange, flat
    lined face $150-200
*100   Putter--Sterling silver head, hallmarked, *usually with presentation inscription ,*
    made by Lambert Brothers, NY $1,000-1,500
    Putter--(A) The Haig model, mallet head, regular grip $150
    Putter--(A) The Haig model, mallet head,
    paddle handle grip $200
    Putter--Lucky Len model, wood mallet head, paddle grip $250
    Putter--Wood mallet Gassiat-type, Hagen name in script $400

◇◇Autograph series (see Walter Hagen Autograph series below)

◇◇Belleair series
    Numbered Irons--Line face, 'H' on club face ....$35 each

◇◇Braeburn series
    Woods (dr, br, sp)--Braeburn series, lady's weight ....$50 each

◇◇Champion series
    Woods (dr, br, sp)--Plain face .... $50 each

◇◇Cochranes of Edinburgh (not L.A. Young; made in Scotland)
    Numbered irons--Autograph model, rustless,
    bowline knot CM .... $75 each

◇◇Crown series
    Irons (1-8, putter)--Compact blades, chrome .... $40 each

◇◇Diplomat series
    Woods--Socket head, stripe top .... $45 each
    Numbered Irons--Stainless, dot face .... $25 each

◇◇Getaway series
    Woods (driver, Brassie, spoon)--Socket head .... $40 each
    Wood Set (3 clubs)--Getaway series $300
    Named Irons (8)--Non-stainless, line face .... $30 each

◇◇Heatherdowns series (not L.A. Young)
    Woods--Socket head, stripe top .... $40 each
    Numbered Irons--Line face .... $30 each

◇◇International series
    Numbered Irons--Stainless .... $40 each

◇◇St. James series (not L.A. Young)
    Numbered Irons--Stainless .... $30 each

◇◇Staybrite series
    Numbered Irons--Stainless .... $30 each

◇◇Tom Boy series
    Numbered Irons--Stainless .... $30 each

◇◇Triangle series
    Woods (3)--7 plug face insert .... $60 each
    Woods (3)--Plain face .... $45 each
    Named/Numbered Irons (8 irons & Putter)--Compact
    head, "Duro-Chrome", line face .... $30 each

Wood Shafted Golf Club Value Guide

◇◇Ultra series
    Woods (dr, br, sp)--Ultra series, bull's eye insert,
    metal backweight ....$65 each
    Numbered Irons--Stainless ....$30 each

◇◇"WH" series
    Woods (3)--Socket head, plain face ....$45 each
    Woods (3)--Brass face ....$75 each
    Woods--Splice head, brass face ....$200 each
    Numbered Irons (9)--Line face ....$30 each

◇◇Walter Hagen autograph series
    Woods--Socket head, brass face insert ....$75 each
    Woods--Bulls-eye insert, brass backweight ....$75 each
    Numbered Irons 1-8--"DeLuxe" Registered, stainless ....$30 each
*   Matched Set of Nine (8 irons & putter)--"Deluxe"
    Registered 201, line face $850
    Named/Numbered Irons 1-8--Graduated Registered,
    non-stainless ....$35 each
    Matched Set of Nine (8 irons & putter)--Graduated
    Registered $750
    Numbered Irons--"Autograph" series, line face,
    stainless ....$30 each
    Matched Set of Nine (8 irons & putter)--"Autograph"
    series $650

The "Hagen W.S". set of driver, brassie and spoon was the last Hagen Brand set to be offered with wood shafts. It was discontinued after the 1935 season.

    Hagen W.S. model woods, plain face ....$60 each
    Set of 3 .... $300

By 1930, L.A. Young/Walter Hagen **Walter Hagen patent sand wedge.** Perhaps one of the ten most sought clubs by collectors it has a rich historical background, notoriety and visual appeal.

Pete Georgiady's

golf offered almost no wood shafted drivers though most irons were still available with wood shafts. The below list of iron club models with wood shafts had matching woods that were only offered with steel shafts.

Hagen Irons in the late 1920s and 1930s came in several set groupings. The

Iron Sets:	America Lady	Imperial Crown
Full 10-club set $800	Center Poise	International Tom Boy
9-club set $700	Continental	Moderne
8-club set $650	Crown T.T.	Play Boy
6-club set $500	Crown	Tom Boy
5-club set $350	Hagen Junior	Triangle
	Haig model	Trophy
	Honey Boy	Walter Hagen Autograph

full set included irons 1-9 plus a putter (the putter was #9, the pitching niblick was #8 and the full niblick was #10). Several shorter sets were also sold with sets varying in size almost yearly. The 9-club set was as above minus the 1-iron. The medium set came with numbers 2,4,5,7,8,9 and the small set had numbers 2,5,7,9. Most were sold with various types of metal shafts and were only made with hickory by special order. Hickory shafts were discontinued after 1936 though extra shafts were sold for repairs for several more years.

Hall, Willie

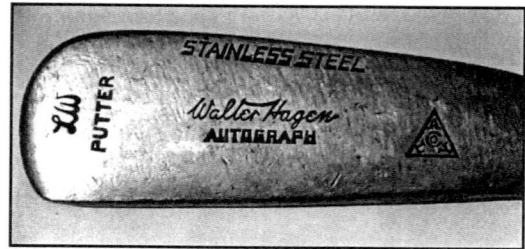

Walter Hagen autograph model putter. The script "LW" represented 'Ladies Weight.'

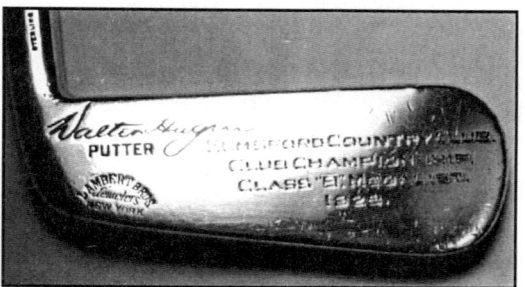

The Walter Hagen sterling silver presentation putter. Frequently, the back of the blade has been engraved with wording for the recipient.

130

Wood Shafted Golf Club Value Guide

    Putter--(A) The Verden model, mallet head $200

Halley & Company, J.B.*
[London]
    Brassie--Autograph series, stripe top, fiber insert $100
    Cleek--Maxwell pattern $50
    Iron--Junior model, crossed swords CM, dot face $40
    Mashie--Stainless, line face, crossed swords CM $40
    Mid Iron--Dot face, H in circle CM $40
    Mid Iron--Model 12, shell CM, line face $45
    Mashie Niblick--Model 28, Maxwell pattern, shell CM $75
    Niblick--Model 37, dreadnought, pyramid CM $75
    Putter--Model 38, blade, crossed swords CM $50
    Putter--Model 40, gun metal head, shallow face,
    pyramid CM $75
    Putter--Two sided, shell CM on sole $65
    Putter--Gun metal, small mallet head, shell CM $125
    Putter--Pyramid model, juvenile size, gun metal blade,
    pyramid CM $40
    Putter--(A) Mallet head, marked J B H $100
    Putter--Ideal model 42, prism shaped back $100
*   Putter--Holton Own Model, like MacGregor semi-putter,
    shell CM $150
    Putter--(B) Long Tom model, shell CM $75

    Juvenile Set--Driver, iron, mashie, putter, iron clubs in
    rustless alloy with shell CM and Ocobo brand canvas bag $300

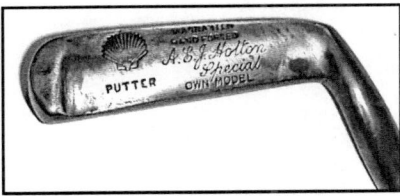

J.B. Halley Company putter. This is an exact copy of the MacGregor semi-putter probably licensed to Halley for sale in Great Britain.

Ham, Arthur
[Skegness e, et al]
    Mashie--Pipe CM, line face $45
    Niblick--Hamsole model, shallow cuts in sole $2,000
    Sammy--Dot/dash face, Gourlay moon/star CM $75

Hamley's
[London toy & game store]
    Irons--Juvenile, smooth face, name in block letters $40

'Handkraft'
    Mashie--Model A-2, chrome head, dot face $25

Harders, Con
    Driver-Stripe top, socket head $50
    Mashie--Chrome head, line face $25
    Mid Iron--Flange sole, line face $40
    Mashie--Name in banner, line face $35

Hardman, Edward
    Brassie--Socket head $50

Hardman & Wright+
[Belleville, NJ]
    Driver--(U) Hardright brand, 'Condensite' composition head, metal neck $250

'Hardright'+
[See Hardman & Wright, above]

Hardy Brothers
[Alnwick e]
    Numbered Irons--Hardy's in script, line face, bamboo shaft .... $80 each
    Numbered Irons--Palakona in script, line face, bamboo shaft .... $80 each

Harland, John
    Brassie--Short socket head $100

Harris, T.
    Mashie--Spalding anvil CM, line face $40

Harrod's
[London department store]
    Named Irons--Dot face, name in circular belt .... $60 each

Harrison, John
Niblick--Smooth face, medium head $80

Harrower, Thomas
[Carnoustie s]
Iron--Dot face, heart CM $60
Iron clubs--Marked 'Harrower' with heart CM $75
Putter--(B) Small steel mallet shaped like Brown-Vardon
with square toe, heart CM $175

Hartford, E.V.
Putter--(U) Gun metal center shafted head, aiming device on
top edge $6,500

Haskins & Pulford
[Hoylake e]
Putter--Gun metal blade $100

Haskins & Sons*
[Hoylake e]
Iron--Smooth face, name in arc $80
Niblick--Stainless, dot face $40

Havers, Arthur
[Coomb Hill, London, et al]
Driver--Stripe top, socket head, name in script $50
Iron clubs--Pipe brand, line or dot face $50

'Hawco'+
[Harold A. Wilson Co., Toronto, ONT]
Driver--Large socket head $50
Iron--Made by Willie Park, smooth face $200
Iron clubs--HAWCO brand, line or dot face $45
Putter--Offset blade, name in oval $50

Haywood, Charles*
[Redditch e]
Iron Clubs--Stainless, line face, CH with spur CM $80

Hearn, J.H.
[Mitcham e, et al]

Mashie Niblick--Sun Spot brand, stainless, sun CM $40

Heather Brand
Mashie--Maxwell pattern, stainless, sprig of heather CM $40

Hemming & Son, Thomas*
[Redditch e]
Iron clubs--Smooth face, lion over long crown CM $95
Mashie--Smith-type anti-shank, smooth face oval head
lion over long crown CM $200
Mashie Niblick--Number 7, oval blade, line face,
thick sole, lion over long crown CM $150

Hemmings Golf Company*
[Redditch e]
Putter--Offset blade, lion over crown CM $150

Hendry & Bishop*

Hendry & Bishop Perwit putter.
Hendry & Bishop 'Auld Reekie' model iron.

[Edinburgh]
Cleek--Mitre brand, mitre CM, dot face $40
Driving Iron--Cardinal series, dot face, mitre CM $40
Iron--(B) Slog-Em model, threaded nut to tighten hosel $600
Jigger--The Master series, line face $75
Lofter-Hiteezi model, thick top edge, thin blade, mitre CM ..$175
Mashie--Mitre Brand, bishop's mitre CM, line face $40
Mashie Niblick--Cardinal model, oval head, line face,
mitre CM $50
Mashie Niblick--Pitch-em model, line face, mitre CM $75
Mid Iron--The Bert model, oval head $50
Niblick--Cardinal model, large head, line face, mitre CM $75

Wood Shafted Golf Club Value Guide

    Niblick--The Master series, round back, line face, mitre CM $65
    Niblick--Cardinal model, marked "Dreadnought",
    extra large head $150
    Niblick--Cardinal model, giant head, dot face,
    mitre CM $1,400-1,800
    Niblick--Cardinal series, Junior Giant model $1,200
    Niblick--The Scottie model, dot face $60
    Niblick--Archie Compston model, smooth concave face $400
    Pitching Mashie--Diamond face, mitre CM $60
    Sand Iron--Smooth concave face, very thick sole $350
*   2-Iron--Auld Reekie model, Cardinal series, dot face,
    mitre CM $65
    Named Irons--Master series, line face $65
    Numbered Irons--Cardinal series, line face, mitre CM ...$40 each
    Numbered Irons-Playmore series, mitre CM ....$50 each

    Putter-The Bedford, flange sole $75
    Putter--Offset blade, mitre CM $50
*100 Putter--(B) Per Whit model, round blade,
    hollow back $400-650
    Putter--Sniper model, long thin hosel and blade $250
    Putter--Eagle Special, iron blade $60
    Putter--Challenge model, shield with cross CM $50
    Putting Cleek--Diamond back, acorn and mitre CMs $75
    Putting Cleek--Long faced, dot face, mitre CM $60

'Henley'
    Driver--Short splice head $150

'Henry's'
    Iron-(B)Centro Machine model, center shaft,
    kidney shaped head $3,000

Henry, Hugh*
[Rye e]
    Brassie--Socket head $60

Hepburn, James*
[Surbiton e, later Long Island, NY]
    Driver--Socket head.. $60
    Driving Mashie--Stewart pipe CM, line face $60

Herd, Alexander ("Sandy")*
[St. Andrews; Open Champion 1902]
  Driver--Short splice head, leather face insert $150
  Brassie--(S) Bulger splice head $400
  Niblick--Ayers maltese cross CM, dot face $90
  Push Iron--A. Herd model, Stewart pipe CM,
  line or dot face $100
  Named Irons--A. Herd autograph model, Stewart pipe CM,
  line or dot face ....$75 each
  Putter--Trusty model, iron blade, Nicoll hand CM $50
  Putter--(S) C.1895, splice head $600
  Putter--(S) C.1910, fiber slip $200

Herd, David*
[Littlestone e; younger brother of Alex Herd]
  Niblick--Smooth face, small head, Condie rose CM $200

Herd, Fred
[Chicago et al]
  Driver--Small splice head $200
  Iron--Dot face, Condie rose CM $75

Herd, James*
[St. Andrews]
  Driver--St. Andrews model, socket head $90

Herd & Herd+
[Chicago, IL]
  Driver--Champion brand, splice head $150
  Driver--Socket head $75
  Baffy--Long narrow socket head $150
  Mashie Iron--Pipe CM, line face $75
  Iron clubs--Stewart pipe brand, line or dot face ....$60 each
  Putter--Flange sole, name in oval $60

Herd & Yeoman+
[Chicago, IL]
* Driver--Champion series, socket head $100
  Brassie--Socket head $70
  Spoon--Socket head, Y shaped sole plate $85

Cleek--(U) Smooth face, through bore hosel $100
Mashie--Smooth face, P.G. Mfg. Co. anvil CM $75
Named Irons--Herd & Yeoman model, Stewart pipe CM,
scored face .... $60 each

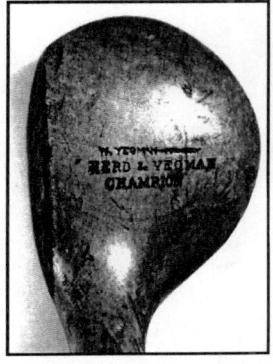

Walter Hewitt Park model putter.

Herd & Yeoman Champion model driver. At some point Herd left the firm; this club is also marked "W. Yeoman — Proprietor."

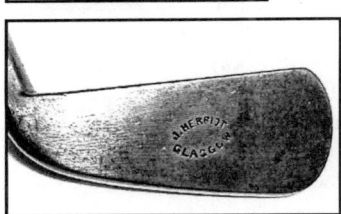

J. Herriot lofting iron. Heavy blade with long hosel made in the late 1880s or early 1890s.

Heron, George
[Peterhead s]
    Driver--Socket head $75
    Mashie Iron--Short blade, cross face $60

Herriot, J.
[Glasgow]
*   Lofter-Smooth face, long hosel, long blade $150

Hewitt, Walter
[Carnoustie s]
    Iron clubs-Arrow through heart CM, dot face .... $75 each
    Putter--Bent neck, heart & arrow CM $80
*   Putter--Bent neck, heart & arrow + lion CMs,
    marked "Park Putter" $90

Hiatt & Company*
[Birmingham e]
    Cleek--Smooth face, 'mild steel' CM $200
    Lofter--Smooth face, long blade, 'Mild steel' CM $200
    Mashie--Smooth face, short blade, circular 'mild steel' CM ..$150

Hillerich & Bradsby Company+
[Louisville, KY; a company better known for its Louisville Slugger baseball bats]
    Woods--(U) "Kork" grip model, socket head .... $125 each

100   Irons--(U) Any model fitted with "Kork" grip .... $75 each

    Approach Iron--Model 5A1, musselback, dash/dot face $50
    Approach Putter--N9, slightly lofted like jigger $100
    Cleek--Model 1 DC, diamond back, arm & hammer CM $40
    Driving Iron--Par X-L series, model 101, musselback,
    dot/dash face $50
    Mashie--(D) Par X-L series, model 80, ribbed face $100
    Mashie--(D) Backspin model 8BSM, ribbed face $100
    Mashie--Hand Forged model, star face marks $200
    Mashie--Juvenile, script H B in circle CM $30
    Mid Iron--Model 80MI, dash face $40
    Mid Iron--Par X-L series, line face $35
    Mid Iron--(U) Par X-L series, patent "kork" grip $75
    Mid Iron--Juvenile, script HB CM $30
    Mashie Niblick--Model S C 1, slotted hosel,
    arm & hammer CM $85
    Mashie Niblick--(D) Model 1 M, grooved face $125
    Mashie Niblick--(D) Backspin model 1BSMN, ribbed face .$100
    Mashie Niblick--(D) Backspin model 3BSMN, ribbed face .$100
    Pitcher--Backspin model 1BSMN, stagdot face $50
    Putter--(A) Par X-L series, mallet head $75
    Putter--(A) Center shaft mallet head $125
    Putter--N 10, shallow face blade $50
    Putter--(A) Par X-L series, Schenectady style, cork grip $200

◇◇The Kernel model
    Woods--The Kernel model, socket head $50
    Iron clubs--The Kernel model, line face .... $30 each
    Putting Cleek--The Kernel model, iron blade $50

◇◇Stewart Maiden model
    Numbered Irons--Stainless, marked "designed by
    Stewart Maiden" ....$40 each
    Putter--# 10, stainless blade, marked "designed by
    Stewart Maiden" $60
    Numbered Irons--Stainless, marked "designed by Stewart Maiden,"
    fitted with B-Bow flat side shaft ....$80 each
    Putter--# 10, stainless marked "designed by Stewart
    Maiden, fitted with B-Bow flat side shaft $100

◇◇Sets
*   Numbered Irons--Grand Slam series,
    hand holding cards CM ....$35 each
    Numbered Irons--N-W series, line face ....$35 each
    Named Irons--Hinsdale Matched Set series ....$30 each
    Numbered Irons--Hinsdale Matched series, chrome ....$30 each
    Woods--Invincible series, socket head ....$40 each
*   Numbered Irons--Invincible series, chrome duo-flange head,
    shield CM ....$30 each
    Woods--Lo-Skore series, golfer profile CM ....$40 each
    Numbered Irons--Lo-Skore series, golfer profile CM .....$25 each
    Numbered Irons--Lady Lo-Skore series ....$25 each

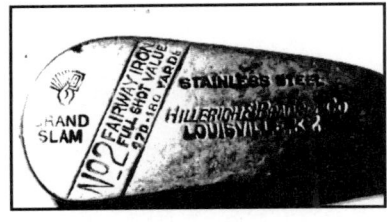 

Hillerich & Bradsby Grand Slam model 2-iron.
              Hillerich & Bradsby Invincible model 2-iron.

Hills, Percy*
[Gosport e, et al]
    Niblick--Large head, line face $60

Hoare, Willie+

Iron--Smooth face, name in oval stamp $85
Mashie--Two acorns CM, line face $60
Mashie Niblick--Dot face $50
Niblick--Round head, smooth face $300

Hobens, Jack
[Englewood, NJ]
Driver--Short splice head $150
Iron clubs--Smooth face, Stewart pipe CM .... $80 each
Iron clubs--Smooth face, Spalding Golf Medal series ..... $70 each
Iron clubs-Scored face, by Spalding .... $50 each

Hobley, A.J.
[Cheltenham e]
Iron clubs--Line face, bench-wheel CM $75

Holmac, Inc.+
[New York City]
Mid Iron--Model 57, swastika CM $45
100   Putter--(U) Rudder putter, T-shaped brass $3,250

Honeyman, Philip+
[Lenox, MA, et al]
Iron--Smooth face, line name stamp $125

Hood, Tom*
[Edinburgh, C.1880-1909]
Driver--(S) Name stamped in script, dark finish $1,800
Playclub--(L) Script stamp, dark finish $5,000
Long Spoon--(L) Script stamp, dark finish $4,500

Hood, Tom*
[Dublin i, C.1900-1920]
Mashie--Line face, Gibson star CM $60
Niblick--Line face, medium head, Stewart pipe CM $65
Putter--Combination wood head with metal
sole/gooseneck hosel $3,000

Hooker, E.A.
Brassie--Socket head $50

Wood Shafted Golf Club Value Guide

'Horn, The'
[William Gibson proprietary brand]
    Iron clubss--Line face, hunting horn CM .... $50 each

Horsman, J.
[New York]
*   Iron clubs--Line face with Burke thistle and
    Horsman horseman CMs .... $50 each

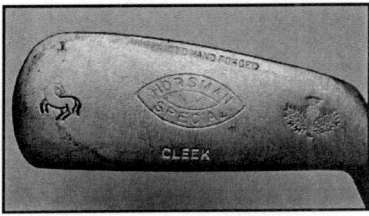 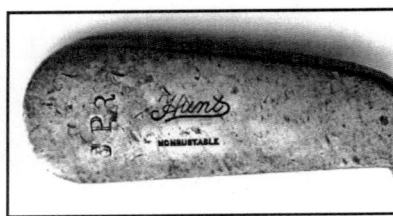

Horsman cleek with Horsman and Burke cleek marks.

                                                 Hunt rustless driving iron.

Horton, Chester
[Chicago]
    Brassie--Model S650, socket head $60
    Spoon--Stripe top socket head $60
    Iron clubs--Reaction Speed series, small eagle CM,
    line face .... $50 each
    Iron Clubs--MacGregor model, name in oval .... $45 each
    Putter--Birkwood 508, Hi Compression series, long hosel $150

Horton, Waverly+
[Chicago]
100   Driver--Wonder Club model, aluminum & wood
       combination $300
       Driver--Socket head, Horton autograph,
       marked for The Fair $85
       Mid Iron--Model 9, Burke hand CM $45
       Niblick--Made by Spence & Gourlay, shaft stamped
       "Waverly Horton" $60
       Putter--(A) Pay Me model, Schenectady style head $200

Howell, V.

Putter--(A B) The Victory, mallet $150

'Hoylake'
Jigger--Name in oval, dot face $40
Mashie Niblick--Slightly concave smooth face $80

Hub, The
[Chicago; also see Lytton]
Iron clubs--MacGregor models, scored face ....$35 each
Putter--Iron blade $40
Putting Cleek--Juvenile $50

'Hunt'+
[Shafts stamped "A.C. & P. Co. Mfgr. Westboro Mass."]
Driver--'Bead' splice head $300
Cleek--Smooth face, yellow colored non-rustable metal head $150
* Driving Iron--Model 504, smooth face, wide toe, yellow colored nonrustable metal $150
Driving Mashie--Smooth face, nonrustable metal $150
Lofter--Smooth face, nonrustable metal $150
Niblick--Small head, concave face, nonrustable metal $600
Putter--Blade, nonrustable metal $200

Hunter, C. & J.
[Prestwick s]
Putter--Iron blade, dot face $60

Hunter, Charles*
[Prestwick s]
Driver--(S) Bulger splice head $400
Playclub--(L) C. 1880, long thin head $6,500
Brassie--(S) C.1890, longish splice head, dark stain $800
Brassie--Socket head $100
Spoon--(L) C.1890, long dark head $1,600
Putter--(L) Long head $3,500

Hunter, Dave
Spoon--(U) Bap model, large head, bulger face $125

Hunter, Harry

Wood Shafted Golf Club Value Guide

[Deal e]
- Driver--(S) Beech head $800-1,000
- Brassie--Splice head, leather insert $175
- Putter--Bent neck blade, Winton diamond CM $75
- Putter-Hunter's model, gooseneck hosel, Winton diamond CM $100

Hunter, Maurice
[Calgary, Canada]
* Iron clubs--Scored face, horsehead CM ....$50 each

Hunter, Ramsey*
[Sandwich e]
- Driver--(S) Splice head, leather face insert $500-1,000
- Driver--C.1910 short splice head $150
- Putter-(B) Offset blade, #4810 .... $250
- Putter--Gooseneck blade, oval name stamp $100

Hunter, Willie
[Richmond, Surrey e; Los Angeles, CA]
- Driver--Short splice head $150
- Iron clubs-Spalding Kro-Flite, stamped with Hunter name ....$35 each

"Huntly"
[England]
*100 Putter--(A) Mallet head, thumb groove in grip end of shaft, made without leather wrap $100-200

Huntly aluminum putter. The Huntley is unique because it came standard with no leather grip, just a thumb groove in the wood handle.
Maurice Hunter niblick (top right).

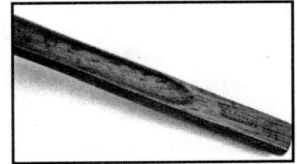

Hurry, D.H.
    Mashie--Smooth face, junior size $100

Hurry, H.
    Brassie--Broad splice head $150

Hutchings, W.
[Derbyshire e]
    Brassie--Socket head $60

Hutchison, J.H.*
[North Berwick s]
    Driver--(S) Light colored head, leather face insert $2,500
    Driver--Compact splice head $400
    Brassie--(S) C.1895, dark finish $2,000
    Brassie--Socket head $250
    Long spoon--(S) C.1895, narrow head $1,800
    Iron--Smooth face, Carrick CM $500
    Lofter--Smooth face, long blade, name in oval $250
    Mashie--(B) Two level smooth face, Condie rose CM $1,200
    Putter--(S) Light color $600
    Putter--Gun metal blade $175
    Putter--Offset blade, Pipe CM $100

Hutchison, John (Jock)
[Pittsburgh, PA and Chicago, IL; other Hutchison line clubs were sold by Burke and Winchester]
    Brassie--Socket head, marked Pittsburgh $125
    Named Irons--Autograph series irons, Stewart pipe CM,
    scored face .... $65 each
    Iron clubs--Burke models, marked for Pittsburgh .... $55 each

I

I.J.S.G. Company+
[see Iver Johnson Sporting Goods Co.]

'Illini'

Putter--Chrome head, long gooseneck hosel, Illinois map CM $90

Imperial Golf Company*
[Sunderland e]
- Brassie--(A S) Model 1 .... $200
- Mid Iron--(A S) Checkered face $200
- Putter--(A S) Model 1 .... $250
- Putter--(A) RM model $100
- Putter--(A) The Verden, mallet shape, domed crown $200
- Putter--(A) Dormie model, short mallet head $100
- Putter--(A) X model, mallet, ridged crown $100
- Putter--(A) Rex model mallet $100
- Putter--(A) Square toe mallet, wood face insert $300

Indestro Company+
[Chicago]
- Driver--Socket head, decal on shaft $25

Inglis, J.R.
[Elmsford, NY]
- Putter--(A) Ray-type head, cross clubs CM $85

'Ionic'
- Driver--Name in script, socket head $30

Irving & Clark
[Sporting goods retailer, Pittsboro, MA]
- Niblick--Medium head, smooth face, heard mark with legend "In the Heart of the Berkshires" $150

Isherwood, A.J.
[Warrington e]
- Driver--Socket head $50

Isles, A.S.
- Putter-(A) Mallet head with hole in center for picking up ball $850-1,000
  [There are at least three variations of this design with differently shaped rubber gaskets for gripping the ball]

Iver Johnson Sporting Goods Company+

[Boston, MA sports outfitter]
*   Iron clubs--Smooth face, marked "Willie Campbell, I.J.S.G. Co." in double oval $100

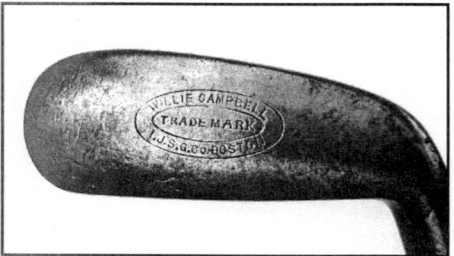

Iver Johnson Sporting Goods Company Willie Campbell model driving iron. These clubs were made late in Campbell's career. He died in 1900.

J

J.B. & Company
[Jack Burns, St. Andrews]
    Iron clubs--The Falcon series, line face, falcon on hand CM .... $60 each

Jackson, John*
[Perth s]
    Playclub--(L) Ash shaft, long thin head $7,500-25,000
    Short Spoon--(L) Ash shaft $10,000-30,000
    Putter-(L) Brown stained head $7,500-20,000

Jacobs, Charles J.*
[Isle of Wight e]
    Driver--(B) Composition splice head $550
    Baffy Spoon--Socket head, fiber face insert $150

Jarvis & White
[Chicago]
    Iron clubs--Line face, Burke fleur-de-lis CM $35

Jeffrey, Ben
[Worthing e]
    Mid Iron--Maltese cross CM, stainless, line face $45

Johns, Charles*
[Purley e, et al]
    Brassie--The Manor model, socket head $60
    Cleek--Round sole, dot face $35

Johnson Company, The A.L.
[Boston, MA]
    Driver--Socket head $50
    Iron--Dot face $35
    Mongrel Iron--Stewart pipe CM, line face $80
    Niblick--Pipe CM, large head, smooth face $175

Johnson, Frank*
[London]
    Driver--(B) Eureka model, full metal face $200
    Iron--Smith model (anti-shank), Cygnet series 306, dot face $150
    Iron clubs--Scored face with key CM $55
*   Mashie--6, smooth face, key CM $80
    Mashie--Premier series, notch hosel $75
**   Putter--Eureka model, metal face $400
    Putter--Frank model, name in script, half barrel shaped head $125

Johnson, W. Claude
    Driver--(B) Round head, removable weights $2,250

Frank Johnson mashie.

    Johnstone Brothers putter made for the Tom Morris shop.

Johnston, Charles
[Cranford, NJ]
    Driver--Socket head, oval name stamp $45
    Mashie--Model 12, Burke hand CM, diamond face $35

Johnston, T.
    Playclub--(B L) Black composite head, oval name stamp . $8,000
    Putter--(B L) as above $9,000

Johnstone Brothers*
[Tayport s]
*   Iron clubs--Line face, hammer in hand CM $100

Johnstone, R.
    Driver--Splice head $150

Johnstone, R
[Seattle]
    Putter--Spalding BV model, two roses CM $250

Jolly, Jack
[Newark, NJ et al]
    Mashie Niblick--Foulis style with musselback $150

Jones, Ernest
[Chislehurst e, et al]

Driver--**Ernest Jones 3-iron** from Women's National Links with special CM shown in inset.

Socket head $100
*   Iron clubs--Line face with large CM for
       National Women's Golf Links .... $75 each

Jones. H.I.
[Chicago]
    Mashie--Line face $25

Jones, Jr., Robert T.
[The Amateur and Open champion; he never endorsed clubs until after his retirement. Stewart's R.T.J. irons were unauthorized replicas, Spalding's were

Wood Shafted Golf Club Value Guide

Jones's own post-retirement design]
    Numbered Irons--R.T.J. series, made by Stewart ..... $80-120 each
    Numbered Irons--RTJ/FO series, made by Stewart $90-140 each
*   Named Irons--Robert T Jones, Jr. autograph series irons,
    made by Stewart .... $300-600 each
    #1 through 9-Iron--Stainless, Robert T. Jones, Jr. signature
    by Spalding, dot face, registration number .... $100-300 each
    Matched Set--6 or 9 Spalding clubs in sequence
    with matching registration numbers .... $200-400 each
    Putter--Calamity Jane model, 3 bands of whipping on
    (wood) shaft, Spalding Kro-Flite CM $150-250

Tom Stewart mashie with Robert T. Jones, Jr. autograph. These clubs were produced in the 1930s after Jones retired from competition.

[The following are steel shafted clubs, usually found with a plastic coated shaft with simulated wood grain or plain yellow plastic coating. These are included because Robert T. Jones, Jr. clubs of all types are becoming more collectible daily]

    Woods--Spalding Jones autograph model .... $5-35 each
    Iron clubs--Kro-Flite models with Robert T Jones, Jr. signature,
    weighted sole .... $5-25 each
    Putter--Kro-Flite Calamity Jane with steel shaft $50-100

Jones, Rowland*
[Wimbledon e]
    Driver--Socket head $80
    Iron clubs--Stewart pipe brand, scored face ....$50 each
    Niblick--Medium head, smooth face, pipe CM $175
    Putting Cleek--Anderson reg'd. #277771 .... $200

Jones, T.W.
[Llandudno w]
    Driving Iron--Line face, anvil CM $40

K

Kay, James
[Seaton Carew e]
    Driver--Socket head $75

Keffer, Karl+
[Ottawa, ONT]
    Putter--(A) Mallet head $100

Kempshall Manufacturing Company*+
[Arlington, NJ & London; an automobile tire manufacturer that entered the golf business making balls and pyralin golf clubs]
    Driver--(U) Socket head, made from black pyralin $700
    Driver--(U) Wood socket head with pyralin marked/dated
    face insert $400
    Duplex Club--(U) Two face fairway club with Brassie and
    spoon lofts, black pyralin $1,200
    Putter--(U) Schenectady style head, black pyralin $500
**100   Putter--(U) Dunn model, black pyralin
    square head, center shaft, brass face $400
    Putter--(U) As above but in white pyralin $600

Kenny, Daniel
    Spoon--Socket head, fiber face insert $60

Kidd, Willie
[Minneapolis MN, et al]
    Spade Mashie--Reg number, line face, WK in circle
    on sweetspot $65
    Mashie Niblick--Running stag CM, name in script $50
    Named Irons-- Wm. Kidd model, Stewart pipe CM,
    scored face ....$60 each
    Putter--'Bassackward' model, hosel bent backward $450

Kilty Kersten Company+
[Milwaukee, WI]
    Woods--Name in oval ....$40 each

Named Irons--Kilty Kersten series, K in triangle CM .....$25 each
Named/Numbered Irons--Lady Lucky Strike series,
K in triangle CM ....$25 each
Numbered Irons--Name in oval, K in triangle CM ....$25 each
Putter--Kilty Kersten series $35

King Hardware Company
[Atlanta, GA]
Iron clubs--King Bee model, bee CM, made by Burke ...$45 each

King-Horn
[William Gibson proprietary brand]
Iron clubs--Line face, star in circle CM ....$35 each

Kinnear, J.B.
Mashie--Deep face, line face, pipe CM $45

Kinnell, J. & D.
[Prestwick s]
Iron clubs--Prestwick brand, smooth face,
two-sided K CM ....$85 each

Kinnell, David*
[Leven and Prestwick s]
Spoon--Splice head $200

Kinnell, James*
[Prestwick, s; Norwich and Purley e]
Brassie--Socket head, deep face $75
Putter--Own model, bar shaped blade, Stewart pipe CM $150

Kirk, R.*
[St. Andrews]
Putter--Fruitwood head, greenheart shaft $12,000

Kirk, R.W.
[Wallasey e]
Driver--Splice head, ash shaft $350
Driver--Splice head, short thick head $150
Iron--Smooth face, rose CM $100
Putting Cleek--(B) Steel blade with twisted neck,

Anderson's reg. 277771, serial number at heel $200

Kirkaldy, Andrew*
[St. Andrews; clubs made by Martin & Kirkaldy]
    Driver--Dreadnought model, large head, Kirkaldy autograph $175
    Mashie--Autograph model, made by Wm. Gibson, line face ...$85
    Putter--Splice wood head, fiber slip $250

Kirkwood, Joe
[San Francisco, CA]
    Iron clubs--Line face, Gibson star CM $50

'Kismet'
[Made by Phosphor Bronze Smelting Co., Baltimore, MD]

The **Kismet putter** was used by Max Marston to with the 1926 U.S. Amateur Championship.

    Putter--Long rectangular metal head, shafted at heel $200

Klees, Charles J.+
[Chicago, IL]
    Brassie--Socket head, name in script $40
    Driving Iron--MacGregor Tomahawk series, dot face $60
    Putting Cleek--Line face, Stewart pipe CM $65

Klein, Willie
    Mashie Niblick--Zenith model 82, hand CM, dot face $60

Klin Brothers+
[Valparaiso, IN]
    Driver--Stripe top socket head, bulger face $50
    Driver--Socket head, name in script $50
    Driver--Drive-Rite model, brass backweight, ivory insert $65
    Brassie--Klin Club series, socket head $50
    Mashie--Model 32, dash face, flower CM, marked "Klin's" ...$45

Wood Shafted Golf Club Value Guide

    Lofter--K-70 model, Klin Brothers flower CM $45
    Numbered Irons--Spalding roses CM, stainless,
    dot face ....$40 each
    Putter--Thick blade, offset head $50

Klin-McGill Golf Manufacturing Company+
[Valparaiso, IN]

    Driver--Socket head, Kiltie model $90
*   Iron Clubs-McGill metal, dash face, diamond-K CM ......$75 each
    Mashie--(D) McGill metal head, rustless bronze alloy,
    corrugated & brick pattern face $400
    Mashie--Bakspin model K-5, stagdot face $65
    Mashie Niblick--(D) Klin Klub series, deep slot face w/ comb
    grooves at sole, McGill metal $600

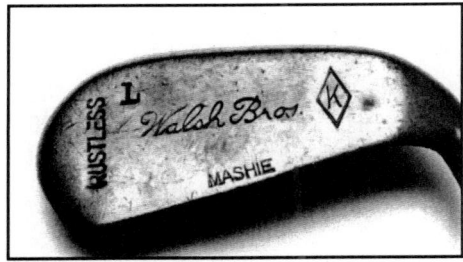

Klin-McGill mashie made from Klin Metal, a bronze alloy.

Schenectady putter. The first marketed version of the famous putter was marked "Pat Pending." Later versions carried the patent date on the back.

    Mid Iron--(D) McGill metal head, corrugated face $200
    Niblick--McGill metal head, line face, K in diamond CM ... $100
    Putter--McGill metal blade $85

Klin, Eddie
[Chicago]

    Mashie--Name in oval, dot face $30

Klin, Mike
[Chicago]
    Putter--MacGregor R model, bamboo laminate shaft $125

Knight, A.H.
[Schenectady, NY; the inventor of the original Schenectady model aluminum putter. The first production models have a "Pat. Applied For" legend on the back side, later replaced with the patent date]
*   Putter--(A) Schenectady model, center shaft, diamond face,
        "Patent Applied For" on back $600

Knight, Ben
    Mashie--(B) Vertically slotted face, open on bottom
    ('rake iron' type), Roger patent $6,000

Knox, A
    Playclub--(S) Red-orange finish $1,500
    Brassie--(S) C.1885, slightly hooked face $900
    Spoon--(S) C.1890 ....$1,500

Knox, G.P.
    Driver--Socket head, name in script $65

Knox, John
[Belfast i]
    Driver--Socket head $95
    Mashie--Line face, Gourlay moon-star CM $50
    Putter--Forgan Scotia series blade $60

Kroydon Golf Company+
[Maplewood, NJ]
    Woods--Ace model, batwing aluminum backweight ......$65 each
    Driver--Stripe top, socket head $50
    Driver--Super Kroydonite model, black finish $75
    Brassie--Hy-Power model, socket head, 2 color face insert $60
    Spoon--Model 6328, brass star in sole plate $60
    Driving Iron--H 8, dot face $50
    Mashie--N 7, dot face $45
    Mashie--NO 7, ball face $75
    Mashie--N 8, dot face $45

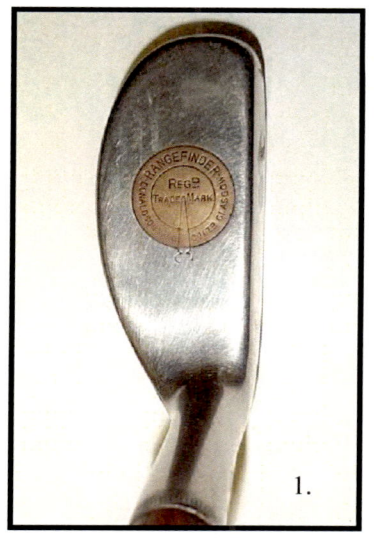

1.

2.

1. Left handed Donaldson "Bunny" model putter. (P. 93)

2. Anderson (of Anstruther) model 62 gun metal head with steel face putter. (P. 33)

3. Burke "Endgrain" putter in Schenectady shape. (P. 55)

Pete Georgiady's

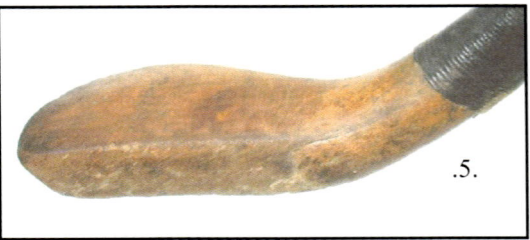

4. Willie Dunn "Unbreakable" driver. (P. 96)

5. Robert Forgan child's long nose driver. (P. 106)

6. Jack Parr bulldog brassie with red fibre face insert. (P. 209)

7. Forgan "Maxmi" driver with ivorine face insert. (P. 107)

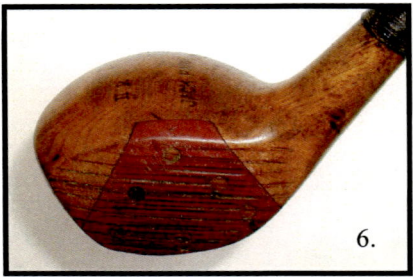

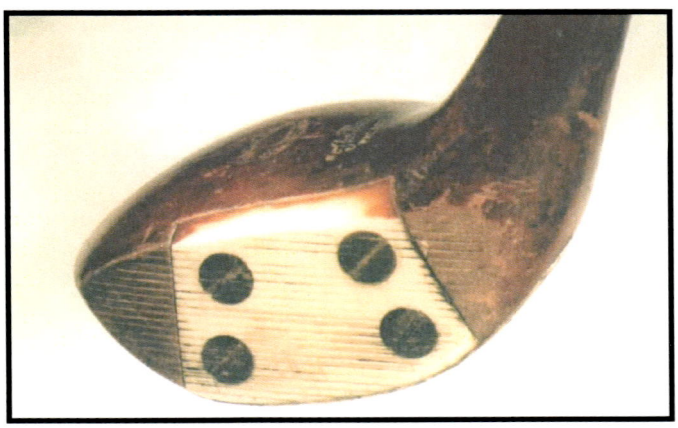

8. Frank Johnson "Eureka" model putter with steel face. (P. 147)

9. Kempshall Dunn patent pyralin putter. (P. 150)

10. Macgregor model 20 1/2 gun metal putter with mid-blade flange. (P. 172)

11.

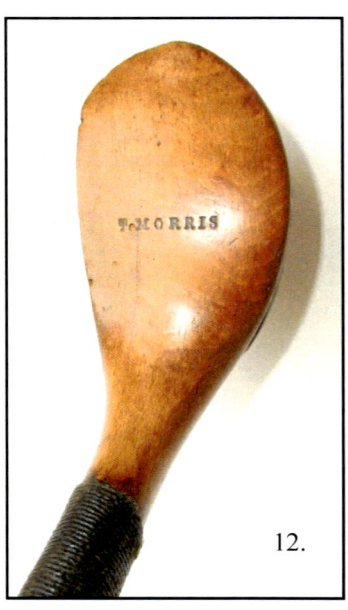

12.

11. Ben Sayers "Gruvsol" brassie. (P 227)

12. Tom Morris bulger driver. (P. 192)

13. Spalding putting baffy. (P. 248)

14. Spalding, unknown model with leather shock absorber in head. (P. 244)

14.

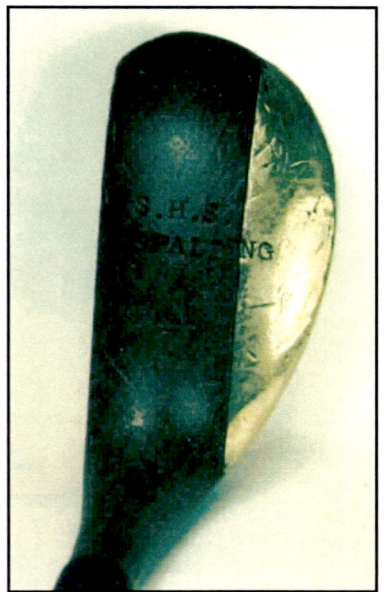

Wood Shafted Golf Club Value Guide

Mashie Iron--L 7, ball face ... $75
Mashie Iron--L 8, dot face ... $45
Mashie Niblick--P 7, tiny waffle pattern face ... $100
Mashie Niblick--PO 7, ball face pattern ... $75
Mashie Niblick--(D) Model U5, brick face ... $350
Mid Iron--J 7, ball face ... $75
Mid Iron--J 8, dot face ... $45
Mid Iron--J 9, diamond/dash face ... $50
Niblick--R 2, 50 degree, vertical lines on face ... $250
Niblick--R 7, ball face pattern ... $75
Niblick--R 8, dot face ... $50
Niblick--RO 9, diamond/dash face ... $50
Spade Mashie--P 7, ball face pattern ... $75
Spade Mashie--(D) U 5, Short Stop model, brick pattern face ... $350
Spade Mashie--U 6, tiny waffle pattern face ... $100
Jigger--M 7, ball face markings ... $100
4-Iron--MO 8, dot face ... $45
Putter--S 1, "7 degree" blade ... $80
Putter--S 7, ball face, blade ... $75
* Putter--S 8, gun metal head, dash face ... $150
Putter--SO 8, shallow blade, round back, line face ... $50
Putter--S 10, ball face blade ... $100
Putter--(A) Model B, Ray-type head, dished chamber on top $100
Putter--(A) S 30A, mallet head ... $100
Putter--(A) S 30B, Ray-Mills style with recessed

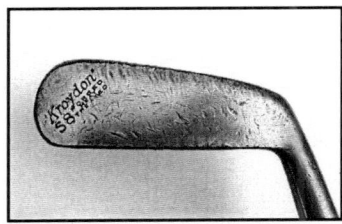

Kroydon S8 putter in a bronze alloy. The S8 was available in steel as well.

The Doerr "Top-em" putter in the broad sole model.

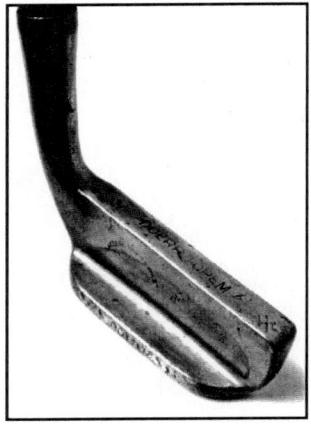

159

chamber on top $125
Putter--(A) S 31B, mallet head $75
Putter--(A) S 32, center shafted $150
Putter--(A) S 33A, center shafted $200
Putter--Panther model, iron blade, dash-diamond face $75

L

Laclede Brass Works+
[St. Louis, MO]
       Putter--(U) Doerr Topem model, stainless, top flange $150
*   Putter--(U) Doerr Topem model, phosphor bronze, negative loft, bottom flange, deeply scored line face $300

'Lakewood'
       Driver--Socket head $50

Lamino Golf Company
       Driver--(U) Laminate construction head and shaft $750
       Driver-Laminated shaft, black head, L in diamond CM $250
       Putter--(U) Laminate construction, oversized mallet head and shaft (both laminated) $1,500

Lang, Bennett*
[Perth s]
       Playclub--Beech head, light color finish $4,500

Large, William
       Putter--Offset blade, stainless $40

Lee & Underhill+
[New York retail/catalog/import company]
       Driver--(B) Split Socket model (fork splice head), leather insert $500
       Brassie--George Sargent autograph, socket head $100
       Driving Iron--Flower CM, dot face $35
       Mashie--George Sargent autograph, dot face $75

Wood Shafted Golf Club Value Guide

Putter--Kilgour Match model $150
Putter--(A) Hammer head, Schenectady style $200

Lee Company, Harry C.+
[New York retail/catalog/import company; used an acorn CM on many of their imported clubs]

Driver--Dreadnought model, socket head, name in script $100
Baffy--(A U) Schenectady shaped head but with 17-degree lofted face $2,500
Iron clubs--Neptune model, stainless, dot face, 3 chain links CM .... $35 each
Iron clubs--Script "Lee" in circle CM. line face .... $35 each
* Iron clubs-Script name, Lee+star CM .... $35 each

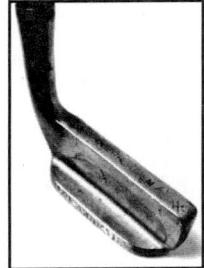

Doerr Topem putter from Laclede Brass Works.

Harry C. Lee Company house brand mid iron with acorn CM.

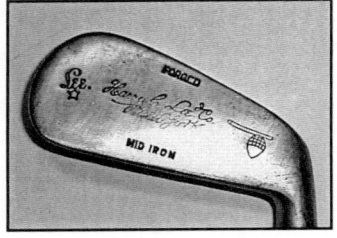

Iron clubs--Dexter series .... $30 each
Sammy Cleek--Smooth face $75
Putter--Iron blade, acorn CM $45
Putter--(A U) Schenectady model, band-crimped neck, marked 'sole licensee' $250
Putter--(A U) Schenectady model, September patent date stamped on back $125-300

◇◇Numbered irons (stainless, line face)
M-1--Mid iron $35
M-2--Mid iron, deep face $35
M-3--Mid iron, round sole $35
MA-1--Mashie, deep face $35
MA-2--Mashie, offset head $35
MM-1--Mid mashie $40
MN-1--Mashie niblick $35
N-1--Niblick, large head $45
P-2--Putter, regular blade $40

P-3--Putter, offset blade $40

Leith Golf Co.
Driver--Socket head $60

Leslie Co., R. & W.
Putting Cleek or Putter--Step down back $150

Leslie, Robert
Putter--Gun metal blade, Condie rose CM $100
Putter--Thick top of blade $350

Leslie, W.
Cleek--Smooth face, Condie rose CM $150

Letters, John*
[Glasgow]
Driver--Stripe top, socket head $80
Jigger--Newbridge series, shallow blade, dot face $75
Iron clubs--Stainless, line face, bridge CM .... $60 each

M.J. Lewis Perfect Putter with peacock CM.

Lewis, M.J.
*   Putter--(B) The Perfect Putter, peacock CM, stainless $95

Leyland (Leyland & Birmingham Rubber Company)*
Woods--L L M B in triangle CM .... $60 each
Iron clubs--L L B M in triangle, dot face .... $35 each
Niblick--Jumbo model, extra large head, dot face $150
*   Niblick--Junior Giant model $100
Numbered Irons--Century series, bear CM, line face ..... $35 each
Numbered Irons--Large 'spade' CM, line face .... $35 each
Putter--Century series, iron blade, bear CM $45
Putter--Truline series, musselback blade $45

Lillywhite's (J. Lillywhite, Frowd & Company)*+

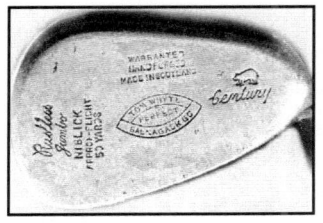 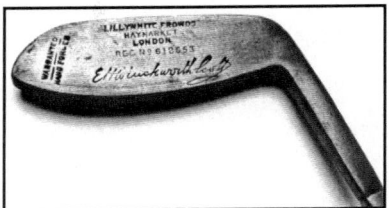

Leyland junior niblick.

Winckworth-Scott patent putter sold through **Lilliwhite's** of London.

[London]
- Driver--Butchart model, V-groove splice head $500
- Numbered irons--Whitehall series, mini-musselback, stainless, small triangle CM .... $40 each
- Putter--(B) Blade with wood insert $900
* Putter--(B) Winckworth-Scott model, autograph name stamp, square solid steel shaft $750

'Limber Shaft'
[see, Jimmy Thomson]

Lindgren Brothers+
- Putter--Adjustable, center shaft, set screw in face $750

Litchfield Manufacturing Company+
[Connecticut]
- Driving Mashie--Smooth face, deep face gun metal blade ... $300
- Iron--Smooth face, gun metal blade, name in oval mark $200

Littledale, N.
[Houghton, MI]
- Brassie--Pear shaped socket head $65

Lloyd, Joe
[1897 US Open Champion; served at clubs in England, France and US]
- Driver--Socket head $140
- Lofter--Smooth face, marked "Pau" (France) $200
- Putter--Name in straight line $150

'Lockenna'
Brassie--Socket head, red/black target face insert $100
Named/Numbered Irons--Chromed, line face $25

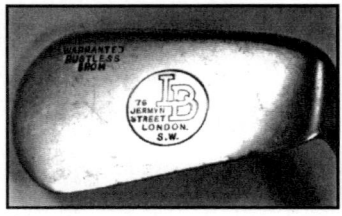

Gordon Lockhart niblick.

Spade mashie from Lockwood & Brown, London.

Lockhart, Gordon
[Gleneagles s]
Brassie--Stripe top socket head, eagle mark $100
Iron--(B)Smith model, dot face $150
* Niblick--Line face, large Eagle CM $80

Lockwood & Brown*
[London]
Approaching iron--Jungle model, beveled sole, LB CM $100
Driving Iron--Maxwell pattern $50
Mashie Niblick--(B) Smith model (anti-shank), stainless,
  Gibson star CM $150
Niblick--Giant head, dot face, "LB" on face $1,750
* Iron clubs--LB in circle CM, stainless, dot face .... $45 each
Putter--Large wood head, Gassiat style $800

Lockwood, A.G.+
[Primarily worked French Lick, IN]
Driver--Socket head, insert $100
Driver--(A) Samson face insert, socket head,
  marked Boston $150
Named Irons--Line face, pluto (devil) CM .... $55 each

Logan, Hugh*

Wood Shafted Golf Club Value Guide

[Wimbledon, St. Andrews, Glasgow, etc.; his most famous design, the Genii model iron, was manufactured by William Gibson]
    Brassie--Splice head, small lettering $150
    Named Irons--Connoisseur series, beveled sole, dot face $100

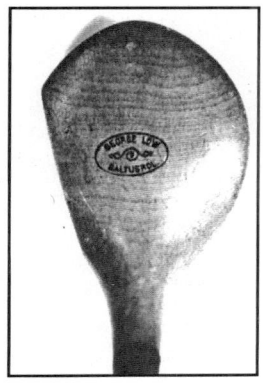

George Low persimmon head driver.

Hugh Logan "Cherokee" model aluminum putter.

                                *   Putter--(A) Cherokee, mallet head, T aiming bar $400

London Golf Company*
[London]
    Driver--Cuirass series, socket head, brass face plate $300
    Driver--Cuirass series, juvenile size $350
    Iron clubs--Name in small oval, dot face ....$60 each
    Putter--Cuirass series, wood socket head, brass face
    plate w/ 4 screws, dot face $250

Longsworth, I.R.+
[Somerset, KY]
    Putter--(A) Adjustable, boat shaped head $1,500

Lovell Arms Company, John P.+
[Boston, MA]
    Driver--Splice head $300
    Brassie--Splice head $300
    Iron--Name in block letters $150
    Mashie--Lovell Diamond series, smooth face $150
    Putter--Iron blade, gooseneck $150

Putter--Smooth face iron blade $100

Low & Hughes
[New York sporting goods house and importer]
Putter--Sure Shot model, Vaile style swan neck hosel $250

Low, George+
[predominantly Baltusrol, NJ]
* Driver--Small splice head, fiber insert $175
* Driver--Socket head $100
Brassie--Socket head $100
Mashie--Marked for Dyker Meadow, smooth face $125
Mashie--Low & Hughes brand $75
Putter--Gem model $100
Putter--(A) Mallet head, crossed clubs CM, lead face $300

Lowe & Campbell+
[Chicago, Kansas City]
Driver--Fairview series, socket head $40
Named/Numbered Irons--Ace brand,
Wilson Range series ....$30 each
Named/Numbered Irons--Special, sterling forged ....$30 each
Numbered Irons--Dot face, stainless ....$30 each

Lowe, D.
Mashie--(B) Smith model (anti-shank), made by Gourlay $150

Lowe, George*
[St. Anne's-on-Sea e]
Spoon--(S) C.1895, well dished face, honey colored head $800
Cleek--(B) Styled after the Fairlie patent (anti-shank),
made from Hawkins Never Rust Steel $275
Cleek--(B) Styled after the Fairlie patent (anti-shank) $250
Iron--(B) Anti-shank style, made by James Anderson,
serial number $200
Niblick--(B) Small head, as above, serial number $250
Putting Iron--(B) Steel blade with raised portion
along top edge $300

Set-(B) [cleek, mashie, lofter, niblick] smooth face
with matched serial numbers $1,000

Wood Shafted Golf Club Value Guide

Lumley's, Ltd.*
[Glasgow & Edinburgh]
    Driver--Dreadnought Junior model, socket head $75
    Iron clubs--Scottish Champion series, kilted soldier CM,
    dot face ....$45 each
    Iron clubs--Name in scriot, scored face ....$40 each
    Iron clubs--Cochranes, knot CM, Lumley in script ....$50 each
    Putter--Magic model,, beveled heel and toe, offset blade $75

Balfour model cleek from Lunn & Company, London retail merchants.

Lunn & Company*
[London]
    Driver--(S) C.1890, dark stain $800
*   Cleek--Balfour model, smooth face $150
    Cleek--Smooth face, short hosel $150
    Mashie--Smooth face, compact blade, heavy head $150

Lurcock, Murray
    Putter--Socket head $125

Lurie, John
    Mashie--Marked 'N Y Sport Klub', made by Burke $50

Lytton Company, The Henry
[Chicago]
    Iron clubs--Made by MacGregor, rose CM, dot face ....$45 each
    Putter--The Hub series, iron blade $40
    Putting Cleek--Juvenile $50

M

M.L. Co.
[Urbana, OH]
    Putter--Iron blade, primitive markings $25

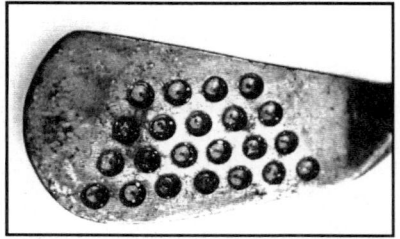

Mac & Mac dimple face back spin mashie. The indentations in the club face are large enough to accommodate a pencil eraser,

Mac & Mac Company+
[Oak Park, IL]
I 100   Mashie--(D) Back Spin model, 19 holes drilled half
        way through face $450
        Mashie Niblick--(D) Back Spin model,
        22 holes drilled half way through face $450
        Mashie Niblick--(D) Back Spin model, wide slots
        cut through face, German silver $2,000
        Putter--Brass head, lead center exposed face and back,
        square hosel and grip $450

MacDonald, The
    Putter--(A B) Long rectangular head, heel shafted,
    chamber with sliding lid housing removable weights $4,000

MacDonald, J.
[Musselburgh s]
    Mashie Niblick--Line face $45

MacFarlane, Willie
[Tuckahoe, NY; US Open Champion 1925]
    Driver--Socket head $75

Wood Shafted Golf Club Value Guide

Mashie--Name in oval, Spalding roses CM $50
Putter--Name in oval, MacGregor R model, top edge weight $75

MacGregor+

[Dayton, OH; officially called the Crawford, McGregor & Canby Co., they entered the business based on their woodworking abilities gained from 65 years in the wooden shoe-last business. Their primary CM was a rose, intended to imitate the mark of Robert Condie, the Scottish master cleek maker]

◇◇Miscellaneous clubs

    Driver--(B) Dunn one-piece, leather face insert $1,500-2,000
    Driver--Lateral fork splice $1,250
*   Driver-Splice head, deep face $250
    Driver--Model 2, dovetailed ivory face $175
    Driver--Model 3, "six-spot" ivory face insert $80-125
    Driver--Model 3 BB, red & white fiber face $75
    Driver--Model 4, "fiber lock" insert with large white dot $100
    Driver--Model 27, plain face $65-90
    Driver--Model 27-F, fiber faced $125
    Driver--Model 27-H, Samson face $275
    Driver--Model 28, plain face $75
    Driver--Model 30, plain face $75
    Driver--Model 31, plain face $75
    Driver--Model 125, short bulldog head, face insert $125
    Driver--Model 203, plain face $75
    Driver--Model 301, plain face $75
    Driver--Model 302, plain face $75
    Driver--Model 326, dreadnought, large head $125
    Driver--Model 352, plain face $75
    Driver--Model 478, steel face with 5 screws $80
    Driver--Model 478 1/2, as above $80
    Driver--MM model, plug fastened fiber face insert $60-100
    Driver--WW model, plug fastened fiber face insert $60-100
    Brassie--Short splice head, shamrock in circle CM $200
    Brassie--Short splice head, deep face $200
    Brassie--BAP model, fiber insert $65
    Brassie--BAP Bulger model 17 .... $65
    Brassie--Model 2, ivory face, 2 fiber pins $175
    Brassie--Model 4, "fiber lock" insert with large white dot $100
    Brassie--Model 4 BB, red & white fiber face $65
*   Brassie--(A) Model 17, dot face $250

Brassie--Model 27, plain face $60-100
Brassie--Model 27-F, fiber face $125
Brassie--Model 27-H, Samson face $275
Brassie--Model 28, plain face $75
Brassie--Model 30, plain face $75
Brassie--Model 31, plain face $75
Brassie--Model 203, plain face $75
Brassie--Model 225, short bulldog head, face insert $125
Brassie--Model 301, plain face $75
Brassie--Model 302, plain face $75
Brassie--Model 326, dreadnought, large head $100
Brassie--Model 352, plain face $75
Brassie--Model 479, steel face insert $80
Brassie--Model 479 1/2, as above $80
Brassie--Model MA1, 5-dot Yardsmore face inlay,
socket head $80
Brassie Cleek--Model 344, plain face $75
Brassie Cleek--Model 355, plain face, wide head $75
Brassie Cleek--Model 421. plain face $100
Brassie Spoon--Model WW, face insert, brass backweight ..$100
Spoon--Model 32, Plain face $80
Spoon--Model 312, plain face $80

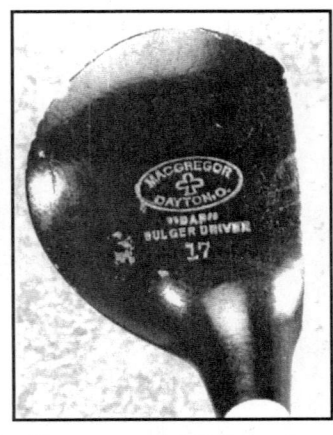

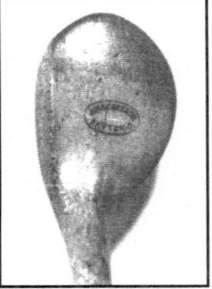

MacGregor niblick
circa 1900-1905.

MacGregor model 17 brassie
in dark finish.

MacGregor splice head driver.

Wood Shafted Golf Club Value Guide

Spoon--Model 325, bulldog style short socket head,
pegged face insert $125
Spoon--Model 373, plain face $80
Wooden Cleek-(U) Wedge shaped brass backweight $175
Approach Iron--Model 31 1/2, Em-An-Em metal, dot face .. $150
Driving Niblick--Gun metal head, name in oval, smooth face $750
Iron--Model B, smooth face, shamrock CM $75
Mashie--Model 29, thick toe, Em-An-Em metal $150
Mashie--Deep face, smooth face, shamrock in circle CM $125
Mashie--Model OA, flange sole, stagdot face $60
Mashie--Model SC1, slotted hosel, dot face $125
Mid Iron--Model OA, flange sole, stagdot face $60
* Mid Iron--Model 25, Em-An-Em metal $125
Mashie Niblick--Foulis-type, through bore hosel,
Em-An-Em Metal $250
Niblick--Model OA, flange sole, stagdot face $60
* Niblick--Smooth face, very thick head & hosel,
shamrock in circle $300
Niblick--(B) Smooth face, Fairlie style,
shamrock in circle CM $300
Niblick--Smooth face, medium head,
shamrock in circle CM $150
100 Semi-Putter--Shallow face, bent neck, thick toe $175
Semi-putter--Duralite metal, line/dot face $150
Putter--(A) Mallet head, lead face insert $350
Putter--(A) Lead face insert, square hosel, flat side shaft $400
Putter--(A) Model RA, mallet head, vulcanite T line $250
Putter--(A) Model 1, short mallet head, dot face $75
Putter--(A) Model 2, mallet head, dot face $100
Putter--(A) Model 3, Ray-Mills style, dot face $75
Putter--(A) Model 3 1/2, small Ray-Mills style $100

 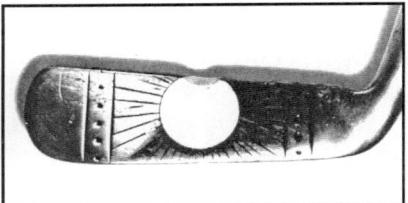

MacGregor model 52 gun metal putter.
MacGregor model B5 "Ivora" model putter with ivorine insert.

Pete Georgiady's

	Putter--(A) Model 4, Schenectady style $150
	Putter--(A) Model 11, mallet head $100
	Putter--(A) Model 12, Ray-type head $100
	Putter--(A) Schenectady-type, 4-leaf clover CM $150
	Putter--Model 20, gun metal blade $75
100	Putter--Model 20-J, swan neck, gun metal blade $250
	Putter--Model 20-W, extra wide gun metal blade $150
**	Putter--Model 20 ½, gun metal blade with raised weight ridge across center of back $300
	Putter--Model 30, gun metal gooseneck $150
*	Putter--Model 52, gun metal, gooseneck blade $125
	Putter--Model 60, gun metal, flange sole with top edge weight $100
	Putter--Model 70, gun metal dominie style, round back $225
	Putter--Model 90 gun metal, flange sole $100
*100	Putter--Model B5 Ivora, gunmetal blade with round ivorine insert, 'sunset' face markings $150-300

Putter--Model 331 Cimetric, Schenectady style wood head ..$250
Putter--Model 331 1/2 Cimetric, wide head $250
Putter--Model 486 Down-It, wood mallet head, brass face ...$250
Putter--Right Angle model, wood mallet head, black fiber insert $200
Putter--Model 486 1/2 Sink-It, 1/2 wood mallet head, aluminum face $200
Putter--Model 490 Sink-Em, wood mallet head, aluminum face, brass backweight $250
Putter--WW model, wood Schenectady style, brass face $200
Putter--Yardsmore Inlay model, wood mallet head, green fiber face $250
Putter--Model OA, flange sole, stagdot face $65
Putting Cleek--Model 33, rustless Em-An-Em metal, line face $125

◇◇Willie Dunn marked clubs

	Driver--Splice head, Willie Dunn 'bowtie' CM $350
	Cleek--Smooth face, short blade, Dunn 'bowtie' CM $175
100*	Iron--Smooth face, Dunn 'bowtie' CM $150
	Lofter--Smooth face, Dunn 'bowtie' CM $175
	Mashie--Smooth face, Dunn 'bowtie' CM $150
	Niblick--Smooth face, small head, Dunn 'bowtie' CM $450
	Putter--Iron blade, Dunn 'bowtie' mark $175

Wood Shafted Golf Club Value Guide

◇◇Early clubs (post-Willie Dunn)
- Driver--Splice head, MacGregor 'bowtie' mark $350
- Cleek--Smooth face, short blade, MacGregor 'bowtie' CM .. $175
- Iron--Smooth face, MacGregor 'bowtie' CM $150
- Lofter--Smooth face, MacGregor 'bowtie' CM $175
- Mashie--Smooth face, MacGregor 'bowtie' CM $150
- Niblick--Smooth face, small head, MacGregor 'bowtie' CM $450
- Putter--Iron blade, MacGregor 'bowtie' mark $175

◇◇"Bakspin" clubs
- Jigger--(D) Model RB, ribbed face $200
- Mashie--(D) Model 10R, Radite ribbed face $100
- Mashie--Model B4, stagdot face $45
- Mashie--(D) Model G1, grooved face $125
- Mashie--(D) Model G2, grooved face $125
- Mashie--(D) Model M1, grooved face $125
- Mashie--(D) Model R2, ribbed face $110
- Mashie--(D) Model XC, ribbed face $150
- Mashie Niblick--(D) Model 9R, Radite ribbed face $100
- Mashie Niblick--Model B, stagdot face $45
- Mashie Niblick--Model B4, stagdot face $45
- Mashie Niblick--(D) Model C2, grooved face $100
- Mashie Niblick--Model F, stagdot face $45
- Mashie Niblick--(D) Model R1, ribbed face $100
- Mashie Niblick--(D) Model R4, ribbed face $100
- Mashie Niblick--(D) Model R5, ribangled face $150
- Mashie Niblick--(D) Model R6, ribbed face $100
- Mashie Niblick--(D) Model R7, ribangled face $150
- Mashie Niblick--(D) Model RC2, ribbed face $125
- Mashie Niblick--(D) Model RZ, ribangled face $150
- Mashie Niblick--(D) Model G4, grooved face $125
- Mashie Niblick--(D) Model XA Bakspin, corrugated face ... $150
- Niblick--(D) Corrugated face $125
- Niblick--Model B4, stagdot face $45
- Pitcher--(D) Model G3, grooved face $125
- Spade Mashie--Model 11-R, Holdem series, Radite, baby waffle face $250
- Putter--(D) Model 20, gun metal blade, ribbed face $250

◇◇Edgemont series (introduced 1909)

Pete Georgiady's

MacGregor model 25 mashie made from "Em-An-Em" rustless metal.

MacGregor Edgemont series putter.

    Driver--Socket head, plain face $45
    Brassie--Socket head, plain face $45
    Approach Mashie--Dot face, shallow face $30
    Driving Cleek--Dot Face (diamond shaped pattern) $25
    Driving Iron--Dot face $25
    Lofter--Dot face $30
    Mashie--Dot face, centraject back $30
    Mashie--Dot face, thick sole, deep face $25
    Mid Iron--Dot face $25
    Mid-Iron--Juvenile $35
    Niblick--Round, medium head $30
    Putter--Gooseneck blade $40
*   Putting Cleek--Iron blade, dot face $25

◇◇Em-An-Em metal irons
    Approach Iron--Model 31 1/2, Em-An-Em metal, dot face ..$150
    Mashie--Model 29, thick toe, Em-An-Em metal $125
    Mashie Niblick--Foulis-type, through bore hosel,
    Em-An-Em Metal $300
*   Mid Iron--Model 25, Em-An-Em metal $125
    Putting Cleek--Model 33, rustless Em-An-Em metal,
    line face $150

◇◇Juvenile clubs
    Driver--Model 323, socket head $45
    Brassie--Model 324, socket head $45
    Driving Cleek--Model 304 ....$35
    Driving Mashie--Model 312 ....$35
    Lofter--Model 306 ....$35

Wood Shafted Golf Club Value Guide

Lofting Mashie--Model 305 .... $35
Mashie--Two shamrocks CM, marked "Juvenile" $25
Mid Iron--Model 309 .... $35
Mid Iron--Marked "MacGregor Junior" $30
Mid-Iron--Edgemont $35
Putting Cleek--Model 310 .... $45

◇◇Par series

Driving Cleek--Model XB, short blade, dot face $75
Driving Cleek--Model XK, long blade, dot face $75
Driving Iron--Model XA, beveled heel, dot face $75
Driving Mashie--Model XC, medium blade, dot face $75
Lofter--Model XC, centraject back $75
Mashie--Model XA 1/2, dot face $75
Mashie--Model XB, dot face, deep face $75
Mashie Jigger--Model XD, concave face $100
Mid Iron--Model XB, heavy blade, dot face $75
Mid Iron--Model XM, dot face $75
Niblick--Model XA, large head $90
Niblick--Model XW, large head $90
Putter--Model XB, narrow blade, flange sole, dash face $90
Putting Cleek--Model XA, dot face $80
Named/Numbered Irons(1-9, Putter 10)--Stainless,
"Balanced" with stars at heel ....$35 each

◇◇Peerless series

Approach Iron--Model A-1, dash face $45
Driving Cleek--Model A-1, dash face $40
Driving Iron--Model A-1, dash face $40
Jigger--Model A-1, dash face $45
Mashie--Model A-1, dash face $35
Mashie Iron--Model A-1, dash face $40
Mid Iron--Model A-1, dash face $35
Niblick--Model A-1, dash face $40
Putter--Model A-1, gooseneck blade, dash face $45

◇◇Perfection series

Driver--B4 model, plain face $60-80
Driver--Model B6, plain face $60-80
Driver--Model B8, plain face $60-80
Brassie--Model B4 .... $60-80

Brassie--Model B6 .... $60-80
Brassie--Model B8 .... $60-80
Brassie Spoon--Model B10, plain face $75-90
Spoon--Model B4 .... $60-80
Approach Iron--Model B4, Maxwell style, full stagdot face,
centraject back $75
Approach Jigger--Model B4, as above $85
Approach Mashie--Model B4, as above with straight back $75
Bobby Iron--Model B4 as above with round back $125
Driving Cleek--Model B4, as above with centraject back $75
Driving Iron--Model B4, as above $75
Mashie Iron--Model B4, as above with centraject back $85
Mashie Niblick--Model B4, Maxwell style Bakspin,
half stagdot concave face $75
Mid Iron--Model B4, as above $75
Niblick--Model B4, as above with round sole $85
Pitcher--Model B4, as above $100
Sammy Iron--Model B4, as above with round back $100
Putter--Model B4, Maxwell style, full stagdot face, flange sole $100
Putting Cleek--Model B4, as above with regular sole $100

◇◇Pilot series
Driver--Model 1, plain face $50-75
Driver--Model 2, plain face $50-75
Driver--Model L4, lady's, plain face $50-75
Brassie--Model 1, plain face $50-75
Brassie--Model 2, plain face $50-75
Brassie--Model L4, lady's, plain face $50-75
Brassie Spoon--Model 3, plain face $65-80
Driving Cleek--Model 4, line face $35
Driving Cleek--Model 104, lady's, line face $35
Driving Iron--Model 1, line face $35
Mashie--Model 8, line face $35
Mashie--Model 105, lady's, line face $40
Mashie Niblick--Model 15, Foulis style, concave face $85
Mid Iron--Model 9, line face $35
Mid Iron--Model 109, lady's, line face $35
Niblick--Model 11, line face $35
Niblick--Model 111, lady's, line face $35
Putter--Model 10S, line face $40
Putter--Model 110, lady's line face $40

Wood Shafted Golf Club Value Guide

 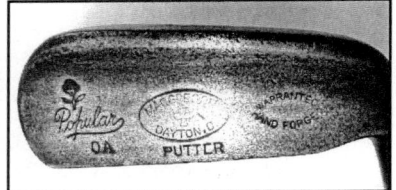

Popular series MacGregor (concave) mashie niblick in the Foulis pattern.

MacGregor model OA putter with flange sole from the Popular series.

◇◇Popular series
- Driver--Model 27, plain face $50-75
- Driver--Model 27J, plain face $50-75
- Driver--Model 31, plain face $50-75
- Driver--Model 203, plain face $50-75
- Driver--Model 492, plain face $50-75
- Brassie--Model 27 ....$50-75
- Brassie--Model 27J $50-75
- Brassie--Model 31 ....$50-75
- Brassie--Model 203 ....$50-75
- Brassie--Model 492 ....$50-75
- Brassie Cleek--Model 344, plain face $75-90
- Brassie Cleek--Model 355, plain face $75-90
- Brassie Spoon--Model 312, plain face $75-90
- Approach Cleek--Model G, musselback, dot face $60
- Approach Iron--Model A 1/2, straight back, dot face $50
- Approach Iron--Model B, round back, dot face $50
- Approach Mashie--Model AA, Carruthers hosel $75
- Approach Mashie--Model E, centraject back $50
- Approach Mashie--Model G, thick toe $75
- Approach Mashie--Model J, diamond back $60
- Approach Mashie--Model S, slightly round back $50
- Driving Cleek--Model A, straight back, short blade, dot face $35
- Driving Cleek--Model B, round back, dot face $40
- Driving Cleek--Model C, diamond back, dot face $45
- Driving Cleek--Model D centraject back, short socket, dot face $45
- Driving Iron--Model A, straight back, dot face $40

Driving Iron--Model A 1/2, centraject back, dot face $40
Driving Iron--Model B, round back, dot face $35
Driving Iron--Model C, diamond back, dot face $45
Driving Mashie--Model A, straight back, dot face $40
Driving Mashie--Model B, weighted on top edge, dot face $50
Driving Mashie--Model C 1/2, diamond back, dot face $50
Jigger--Model A, straight back $50
Jigger--Model A 1/2, concave face $100
Jigger--Model B, centraject back $50
Jigger--Model 8-B, notch hosel $75
Lofter--Model A, straight back $50
Lofter--Model B, round back $50
Lofter--Model C, centraject back $50
Lofting Mashie--Model F, extra wide blade $60
Mashie Iron--Model A, straight back, dot face $50
Mashie Niblick--Model A, straight back, wide toe $45
Mashie Niblick--Model B, round back, concave face $100
Mashie Niblick--Model C, Foulis style, dot face $75
* Mashie Niblick--Model E, Foulis style, concave face $150
Mid Iron--Model A, straight back, dot face $35
Mid Iron--Model A 1/2, diamond back, dot face $50
Mid Iron--Model AA, Carruthers hosel $75
Mid Iron--Model C, centraject back, dot face $45
Mid Iron--Model E, straight back $40
Mid Iron--Model F, heavy blade $45
Mid Mashie--Model C, "Bull Dog", dot face $75
Niblick--Model A, dot face, straight back $45
Niblick--Model B, small head, smooth concave face $300
Niblick--Popular series, Model B, medium size head,
concave face $150
Niblick--Model C, large head, dot face $50
Niblick--Model G, large heavy blade $50
Sammy Jigger--Model C 1/2, beveled heel and toe $75
Putter--Model A 1/2, wide back, beveled edge $45
Putter--Model H, slight gooseneck, dot face $50
Putter--Model HH, gooseneck $75
Putter--Model K, gooseneck, narrow blade $60
Putter--Model M, shallow face $50
Putter--Model R, top edge weight $60
* Putter--Model OA, flange sole $60
Putting Cleek--Model H 1/2, long blade, dot face $50

Wood Shafted Golf Club Value Guide

Putting Cleek--Model A, straight back, dot face $50
Putting Cleek--Model B, diamond back, dot face $60
Putting Cleek--Model BB, musselback $50
Putting Iron--Model A 1/2, deep face, beveled top edge $60
Putting Iron--Model C, back and face have same loft $50

Named/Numbered Irons (1-9, putter 10)--Line face,
small club pip CM $35

◇◇Superior series
    Driver--Model 7, plain face, brass backweight $75-90
    Brassie--Model 7, plain face, brass backweight $75-90
    Approach Iron--Model S-C-1, stagdot face, slotted hosel $100
*   Bobbie Iron--Model S-D-1, round sole, stagdot face,
    slotted hosel $150
    Cleek--(U) Model S-D-1, stagdot face, slotted hosel $100

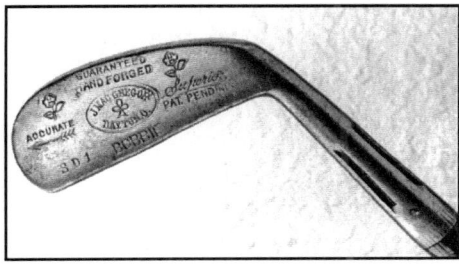 

MacGregor model SD1 Bobbie iron
with slotted hosel from the Superior series
                                  MacGregor Chieftain series driver
                                         with ivory backweight

    Driving Iron--(U) Model S-C-1, diamond back, slotted hosel,
    stagdot face $125
    Jigger--Model S-B, stagdot face, slotted hosel $125
    Jigger--Model S-C-2, stagdot face, slotted hosel $125
    Mashie--Model S-C-1, stagdot face, slotted hosel $100
    Mashie--Model S-C-2, stagdot face, slotted hosel $100
    Mid Iron--Model S-C-1, stagdot face, slotted hosel $100
    Mid Iron--Model S-C-2, stagdot face, slotted hosel $100
    Mid Mashie--Model S-C, stagdot face, slotted hosel $100
    Mashie Niblick--Model S-C-1, stagdot face, slotted hosel ... $100

Pete Georgiady's

Niblick--Model S-C-2, stagdot face, slotted hosel $100
Putter--Model S-C-2, blade, stagdot face, slotted hosel $125
Putter--Model S-X-B, Orion style, broad sole, stagdot face,
slotted hosel $150
Putter--Model S-B-V, Brown-Vardon style, rounded back,
stagdot face, slotted hosel $150

◇◇Airway series irons

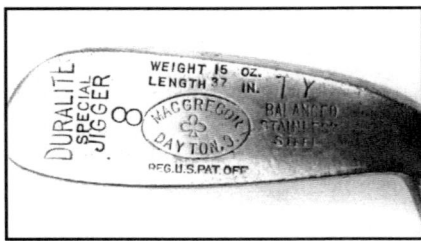 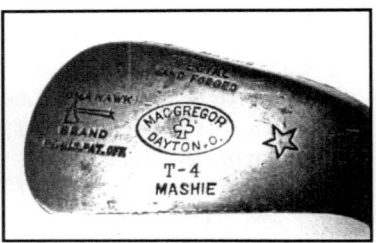

MacGregor #8 Duralite jigger.

MacGregor Tomahawk model mashie.

Named irons--Dot face, slightly concave ....$65 each

◇◇Chieftain model
*100   Woods (driver, brassie, spoon)--Ivory backweight,
        inlay on top of head ....$750-1,200 each
        Set of 3 matched woods $3,000-4,000

*Chieftain woods with **steel or coated steel** shafts ... $200-400 each*

◇◇Duralite series irons
*   Named Irons--Stainless ....$35 each
        Numbered Irons--Stainless ....$30 each
        Semi Putter--Duralite metal, line/dot face $150
        Set of six or more consecutively numbered clubs ....$40 each

◇◇Go-Sum series irons
        Numbered Irons--Stainless ....$30 each

◇◇Lady Mac series irons
        Numbered or named irons--Stainless ....$25 each

◇◇Nokorode series irons

Wood Shafted Golf Club Value Guide

        Numbered or named irons--Stainless ....$30 each

◇◇Premier series irons
        Named irons--Line face ....$35 each
        Mashie--(D) Corrugated face $125

◇◇Radite series irons
        Numbered or named irons--Stainless ....$30 each
        Set of six or more consecutively numbered clubs ....$45 each

◇◇Tomahawk series irons
*   Named Irons--Soft steel, shield design in dots on face,
        tomahawk and star CMs ....$65 each

◇◇Yardsmore series
        Woods--Black & white ivorine face insert ....$85 each
        Numbered Irons--Stainless ....$30 each
        Set of six or more consecutively numbered clubs ....$45 each
        Putter--Yardsmore Inlay model, center shaft wood mallet head,
        green fiber face $250
        (The Yardsmore putter was produced in a limited edition replica by MacGregor in the late 1990s)

MacKay, D.
[North Berwick s]
        Driver--Socket head $75
        Brassie--Stripe top, socket head $75

Mackie, Isaac
[Staten Island, NY]
        Brassie--Socket head, name in oval $100

Mackie, J.
        Mid Iron--Stewart pipe CM, line face $50

Mackrell & Simpson
        Mashie--Line face, Stewart pipe CM $50

Mackrell, James+
[Aiken, SC]
        Brassie--(U) Very l large head, signature name stamp $100

Mashie--Model 20, flange sole, line face, Winton
diamond CM $65
Niblick--Medium head, smooth face $150

MacNamara, Dan
[Boston, MA, et al]
Driver--Socket head $75

Macnamara, W.
[Lahinch i]
Driver--Longish socket head $100

MacPherson, A.F.
Niblick--Dot face $40

MacPherson, Duncan*
[Manchester e]
Spoon--Bulldog style short socket head, fiber face insert $90
Approaching Putter--Terrier Brand, model 17 blade $75
Putter--Terrier Brand, model 7, dog CM, line face $60
Putter--Terrier Brand, musselback blade $60

MacPherson, J.
Niblick--Arrow & Heart CM, line face $60

Macy Company, R.H.
[New York City department store]
Woods--all models .... $50 each
Riverside brand irons, stainless, dot face $35
SupreMacy brand irons, stainless, line face $35

Maiden, Jimmy+
[Nassau, NY; Atlanta, GA]
Putter--Stewart pipe CM, bent neck $80

Maiden, Stewart+
[Nassau, NY; Atlanta, GA]
Brassie--Dalglish pattern, rounded sole, face insert $300
Mashie--Diamond back, line face, Pipe CM $65

◇◇Stewart Maiden series by Hillerich & Bradsby

Wood Shafted Golf Club Value Guide

    Numbered Irons--Stainless $40
    Putter--# 10, stainless blade $75
    Numbered Irons--Stainless with B-Bow shaft $60
    Putter--# 10, stainless blade with B-Bow shaft $90

'Majestic'
[see Burr-Key]

Malpass, Harry
[Detroit, MI, et al]
    Driver--Ivorine face with five black pegs, socket head $90
    Mashie--Dot face, 3 bar CM $35

'Malvern, The'
    Putter--(A B) Braid-type head $80

'Marathon'
[Chicago; brand name from the Montgomery Ward Company department store]
    Numbered Irons--Stainless, line face ....$25 each

Marling, Alex
[Aberdeen s]
    Putter--Magic model, bent neck blade, broad sole $75

Marling & Smith*
[Aberdeen s]
    Driver--Splice head $150
    Mashie Niblick--Dot face, Cochrane knight CM $50

Marriott & Ransome
    Putter--(B) Triangular gun metal head,
    three hitting faces $2,500

Marsh & Co., Jordan
[Boston, MA]
*   Putter-Model 18, Avona brand $60

Marshall, William
[Onwentsia, Chicago]
    Lofter--Smooth face, long blade $125

Martin & Kirkaldy*

Jordan Marsh "Avona" model putter.

Martin & Kirkaldy "Ellite" series pitcher.

[Edinburgh]
    Driver--Andrew Kirkaldy autograph model,
    dreadnought socket head $175
    Brassie--Pug model, short socket head with thick toe $125
    Brassie--Sovereign model, socket head $75
    Spoon--Superb series, ivorine insert, socket head $125
    Spoon--Splice head, name in script $175
    Baffy--Splice head, full sole plate $225
    Mashie--Elite model, dot face $60
    Mid Iron--Kirkaldy autograph model, dot face $75
    Niblick--Elite series, large head, line face $75
*   Pitcher-Elite series, Kirkaldy autograph $75
    Putter--Elite series, Andrew Kirkaldy Excelsior,
    triangular backweight, line face $100

Martin & Patrick*
[Edinburgh]
    Driver--Sovereign model, socket head $75

Martin, R.B.
[Edinburgh and Kirkaldy, Fife s]
    Mashie--The Golf Depot, dot face $75
    Niblick--Smooth face, small head $150

Martin's Velometer Golf Clubs
[Herne Bay e]
    Driver--(B) Velometer model, socket head $450

Wood Shafted Golf Club Value Guide

    Brassie--(B) as above $450

Martin, W.
    Irons--(U) Step back design, matched set..........................$60 each

Massy, Arnaud
[Open Champion 1907; worked several locations in France]
    Named Irons--Autograph model, Gibson star CM ....$75 each

May & Malone
    Iron clubs--Bogey model, M+M in shield CM ....$45 each
    Putter--Bogey model, dash face blade $50
    Putter--80P, Eagle series, flange sole, eagle head CM $50

May, Dick
[Newcastle e; later U.S.]
    Putter--(B) Bulge face blade, line face $175

Mayo, Charles*
[Southampton, Long Island]
    Driver--Socket head $50
    Putting Cleek--Premier model, hosel notch $80

McAndrew, J.
[Aberdeen s]
    Brassie--Splice head, narrow head $175

McAndrew, Robert
    Mashie--Smooth face, name stamp in italics $125

McDaid, Martin*
[Edinburgh]
    Driver--Small splice head, horn slip $200
    Driver--(A) Mills style compact head $250

McDermott, John J.
[Atlantic City, NJ, et al; US Open Champion]
    Brassie--Jumper model, socket head, fiber face insert $150
    Mid Iron--Diamond back, arrow CM dot face $80
    Iron--Little Johnny model, 6-pointed star CM $100
*   Jigger--Little Johnnie model, notched hosel,

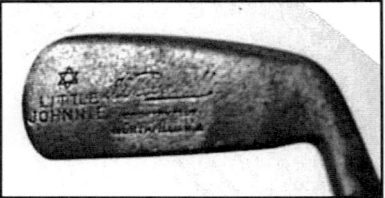

John McDermott "Little Johnny" jigger.

McEwan late model playclub
probably from the
Douglas McEwan II era, circa 1890.

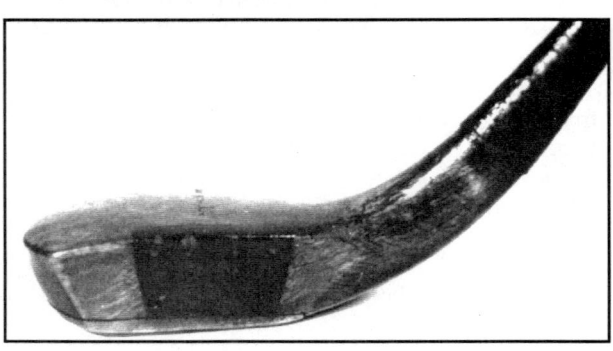

    narrow blade, dash face $100
    Putter--Little Johnny model, mallet head $125

McDonald, C.
[Glengarry s]
    Putter-Glengarry bonnet (cap) CM $50

McDonald, William
    Driver--Short splice head $150

McDonald, W.*
    Driving Putter--(L) Slender thorn wood head $6,000

McDowall, J.
    Mashie--Spalding anvil CM $40

McEwan & Sayner
    Brassie--Short socket head $75
    Niblick--Smith model anti-shank, stainless, Ayres CM $200

McEwan & Son*
[Bruntsfield (Edinburgh) & Musselburgh s; this firm founded in 1770 worked

Wood Shafted Golf Club Value Guide

continuously until 1895. Six generations of McEwans made golf clubs up to WWII]

◇◇Feather ball period clubs
    Playclub--(L) C.1780, large thistle stamp $25,000-50,000
    Playclub--(L) C.1840, dark finish $10,000-20,000
    Long Spoon--(L) C.1850, dark finish $7,500-10,000
    Putter--(L) C.1840, slightly hooked face $10,000-20,000

◇◇Guttie ball period clubs
    Playclub-(L) C.1860, leather face insert $3,000-6,000
    Playclub--(L) C.1880, leather face insert $2,500-4,500
*   Playclub--(L) C.1890, slightly shorter head $1,000-2,500
    Driver--(S) C.1895, short head, leather face insert $750-1,000
100*   Long Spoon--(L) C.1880, dark finish $2,500-4,000
    Short Spoon--(L) C.1880, broad, dark colored head $2,500-4,000
    Baffing Spoon--(L) C.1880, well lofted face $3,500-5,500
    Brassie--(S) C.1895, shorter head $750-1,000
    Cleek--C.1895 smooth face, oval stamp, Stewart serpent CM $125
    Cleek--Smooth face, Condie fern CM $150
    Iron--C.1890, smooth face, straight line name stamp $200
    Lofter--C.1895, smooth face, oval stamp, Condie rose CM . $150
    Lofting Iron--Smooth face, Condie fern CM $225
    Mashie--C.1890, smooth face, straight line name stamp $150
    Niblick--C.1890, small head, oval name stamp $400
    Niblick--C.1895, medium size head, Stewart pipe CM $200
    Niblick--C.1895, very small head, Stewart serpent CM $600

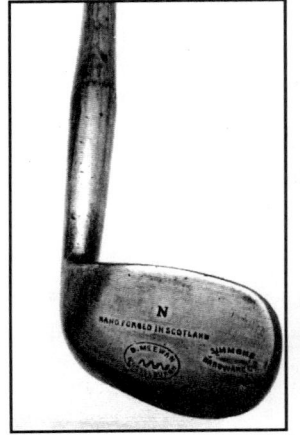

McEwan niblick marked for Douglas McEwan, Musselburgh.

Fred McLeod autograph mashie niblick.

Pete Georgiady's

>Niblick--Medium head, smooth face, Stewart serpent CM ...$200
>Putter--(L) C.1880, long slender head $1,500-3,000
>Putter--(L) C.1890, shorter, broader head $1,000-2,000
>Putter--(S) C1895, short head $750-1,000
>Putter--C. 1895, gun metal blade, straight name stamp $150
>Putter--C.1895, bent blade style, oval name stamp $150
>Putter--C.1900, regular iron blade, oval name stamp $125

McEwan, David*
[Birkdale]
>Driver--Birkdale model, small socket head, name in oval $100

McEwan, Peter*
[Nairn s]
>Iron clubs--Line face, name in script $50

McEwan, Stewart
[Harrisburg, PA]
>Driver--Socket head, steel face insert with screws $100
>Mashie--Smooth face $75
>Mashie--Dot face, 3 bar CM $35
>Mashie--Dot face, centraject back, 3 bar CM $40

McEwan, William*
[Formby e]
>Driver--(B) Dunn patent $1,500-2,000
>Driver--Socket head $125

McGregor
[see MacGregor]

McGill Golf Co.
[Valparaiso, IN]
>Mashie Niblick--(D) Klin Klub, deep hyphens only
>on middle 1/3 of face $200

McIntosh, David
>Driving Iron--Smooth face, Stewart pipe CM $75
>Pitcher--Smooth face, Celtic oval head $150
>Putter--Gun metal blade $80

McKenna, J.
Brassie--Splice head $100

McLeod, Fred
[Chicago, IL, et al; US Open Champion]
Brassie--Very short splice head $250
Mashie Niblick--Autograph model $80

'Meadowlark'
[MacGregor store brand]
Iron clubs--Dot face, 2 club pips CM .... $25 each

Meaker, R.H.
Driver--Splice head $100

Melville, Jack
Driver--Stripe top, socket head $45

Metal & Alloy Specialty Co.
[Buffalo, NY]
Niblick--RadiName model, circular dot face pattern $65

'Metropolitan'
Putter--Blade, made by JH Williams, W in
diamond on hosel $175

Mieville-Lancier

Mieville-Lancier mid iron. The salient feature of this brand was its laminated bamboo shafts.

[England]
*   Numbered Irons-Flanged sole, bamboo shaft,
        house CM .... $100 each

Miles, A.
Brassie--Handkraft brand, socket head $50

Millar, Charles L.*
[Glasgow; also proprietor of the Glasgow Golf Company and the Thistle Golf Company]

    Driver--Socket head, thistle CM, patent training rubber grip .$300
    Iron--Smooth face, small thistle (Reg'd.), smooth face $90
    Lofter--Smooth face, round back, marked 'C L Millar' $100
    Mashie--Smooth face, short blade, small thistle CM $150
    Mashie--Thistle Brand, thistle in circle CM $50
    Putter--Gun metal blade, thistle CM $100

Miller & Taylor*
[Glasgow]

    Mashie--(B) D & T Spinner Mashie, concave face, half dots $250
    Mashie Niblick--(B) Concave face, half dot face,
    curling stone CM $250

Milne, John*
[Neasden, London]

    Driver--Socket head $80

Minton
[Barbourville, KY]

    Putter-Steel blade, thumb-groove handle (like Huntly) $150

Mitchell & Ness+
[Philadelphia, PA]

    Driver--Socket head, stripe top $60
    Mashie Niblick--Stewart pipe CM, line face $50
    Mid Iron-Flange sole, Monel $65

Mitchell & Weidenkopf+
[Cleveland, OH]

    Brassie--Socket head, circular ivorine insert $125

Mitchell, Joe+
[Cleveland & Jacksonville, FL; also see P.G. Manufacturing Co.]

    Driver--Socket head, palm tree CM $65
    Mid Iron--Smooth face, anvil CM, made for P.G. Mfg. Co. ...$65

Mitchell's
[Milwaukee, WI]

Wood Shafted Golf Club Value Guide

Iron clubs-Name in oval, boxing gloves CM .... $45 each

'Monarch'
[Great Lakes Golf Company brand]
Iron clubs--Dash face, crown CM ....$25 each
Putter--Iron blade, crown CM $30

Monk, Arthur
Mashie--Stainless, dot face $30

Morehead Golf Company+
[Milwaukee, WI]
Driver--Socket head, crescent shaped vulcanite face insert .. $250
Jigger--Model S, dash face, swastika CM $45
Mashie--Ship's wheel CM, stainless, dot face $40
Mid Iron--Swastika CM, line face $80
Putter--Glen Eagle series, flange sole, eagle head CM $50

Morgan, E.
Mashie Niblick--Dot face, oval head $50

Morris & Youds*
[Hoylake e]
Mashie--(B) Smith model (anti-shank), Spence &
Gourlay club pip CM $250
Mashie-Pipe brand, name in double outline oval, line face $85

Morris, John (Jack)
[Hoylake e; nephew of Old Tom, he was professional and club maker to the Royal Liverpool G.C. for over 60 years]

Jack Morris niblick circa 1900.

Tom Morris Broadclair model putter

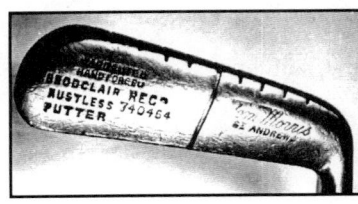

	Driver--Splice head	$200
	Driver--Socket head	$90
	Cleek--Smooth face, Stewart pipe CM	$90
*	Niblick--Medium size head, smooth face	$150
	Named Irons--John Morris model, Stewart pipe CM, scored face	$75 each
	Named Irons--Name in oval, no other marks	$65 each
	Putter--Wood transitional splice head	$850
	Putter--Iron blade, mark in oval	$80
	Putter--Wood mallet head, stork CM	$300

Morris, Tom*

[St. Andrews; he was four times Open Champion in the 1860s and his moniker became The Grand Old Man of Golf. Originally trained as a ball maker, he opened his club making business in 1867 though his popular Autograph series was not introduced until several years after his death]

◇◇Long nose (guttie ball) period clubs

	Playclub--(L) C. 1870, thin narrow head, light color	$10,000-15,000
	Playclub--(L) C.1875, narrow head	$2,500-5,000
*	Playclub--(L) C.1885, wider head than above	$1,500-3,500
	Driver--(L) C.1895, leather face insert	$1,000-2,000
**	Driver--(S) C.1900, as above	$600-1,000
	Spoon--(L) C.1875, narrow head	$3,500-6,000
	Spoon--(L) C.1885, wider head than above	$1,500-3,500
100*	Brassie--(L) C.1895, leather face insert	$1,500-3,000
	Brassie--(S) C.1900, shorter head, thicker neck	$500-1,000
	Baffy--(L) C.1890, well spooned face, stamped shaft	$1,500-2,500
	Putter--(L) C.1880, wide shallow head, large lead backweight	$1,500-3,000
	Putter--(L) C.1895, more compact head, deeper face	$1,000-2,000
	Putter--(S) C.1900, transitional shaped head	$400-800
	Cleek--Smooth face, Stewart pipe CM, oval stamp	$300
	Cleek--(B) Smooth face, round sole	$400
	Mashie--Smooth face, Stewart pipe CM, oval stamp	$250
	Niblick--(B) Concave face	$500
	Niblick--Smooth face, medium size head	$300
	Niblick--Smooth face, small head	$500

Wood Shafted Golf Club Value Guide

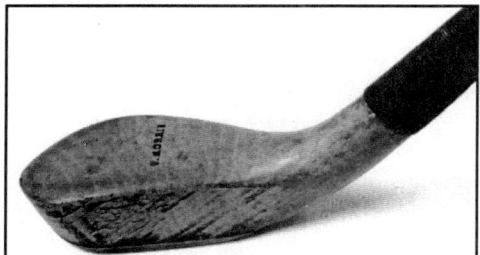

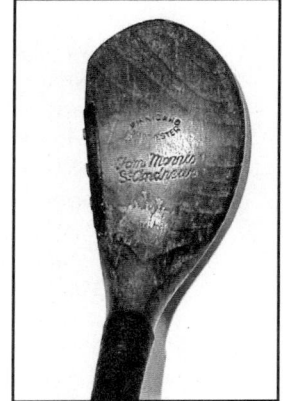

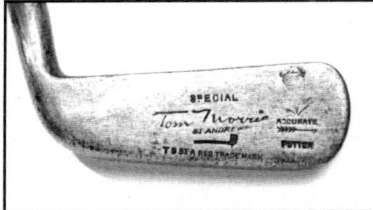

Tom Morris clubs:

Top L—**Playclub circa 1885.**
Top R—**Autograph series splice head driver.**
Mid L—**Stewart Autograph series putter with large head CM.**
Lower L—**Brodie made Autograph series "Monarch" cleek.**

Putter--Gun metal blade, Stewart serpent CM $200
Putter--Cylindrical iron head, 'drainpipe' model $3,500

◇◇20th century clubs

     Driver--Short splice head, long scare $300
     Driver--C.1910, short splice head $250
*   Driver--Elongated splice head, Autograph series, fibre insert $200
     Driver--Socket head, stripe top, Autograph series $150
     Brassie--Socket head, Autograph series $125
*   Cleek-Monarch series, beveled toe $100
     Driving Iron--Autograph series, dot face, pipe CM $75
     Iron--Autograph series, dot face $60
     Iron--Autograph series, juvenile $100
     Iron--Monarch series, Brodie CMs $125
100* Jigger--Autograph series, Stewart pipe CM, dot face $75
     Mashie--Autograph series, line face, Condie rose CM $75
     Mashie--St. Andrean series, musselback, Old Tom CM,

        stainless $75
        Mashie--(D) Dedum model, Brodie triangle CM $175
        Mashie Niblick--Autograph series, line face,
        Condie rose CM $75
        Mashie Niblick--'Morris Model', Stewart pipe CM, dot face ..$150
        Mashie Niblick--Autograph series, stainless, triangle/BS&A &
        Tom Morris CMs, line face $75
        Niblick--Autograph series, Old Tom CM $75
        Niblick--Autograph series, Stewart pipe CM $75
        Spade Mashie--Autograph series, Old Tom CM,
        line face, stainless $75
        Spade Niblick--Autograph series, head of Old Tom &
        Brodie CMs, dreadnought size head $150
        Putter--(B) Straight Line model, Old Tom and Brodie CMs ..$150
        Putter--Autograph series, Stewart pipe and arrow CMs $75
        Putter--Autograph series, Wellington model, Old Tom CM $125
        Putter--Socket wood head, Autograph series $250
*   Putter--Autograph series, Stewart large Old Tom CM $150
        Putter--The Davie model $125
*   Putter-(B) Broadclair model, round back blade, grooved sole $250
        Numbered Irons-Elect series, line face, Brodie CMs .... $60 each

Motion, J.G.
[Minneapolis, MN]
        Driver--Splice head $250

Mules, W.*
[Penarth w]
        Driver--(B) Leather cushion behind metal face plate $800
        Iron--(B) Leather cushion behind metal face plate $1,200

Munro, Alexander*
[Aberdeen s]
        Playclub--(L) Thornwood, light finish $4,000-5,000

Munro, Robert*
[Wimbledon, Chislehurst e]
        Driver--Bulger splice head, leather face insert $150
        Driver--Large socket head $100
        Putter--(S) C.1895, large splice head $600

Murray, Albert
[Montreal, QUE]
    Iron clubs--Diamond back, Moosehead CM ....$75 each

David Myles model "Nipper" iron showing patent mark on face. Albert Murray diamond back mashie with moosehead CM.

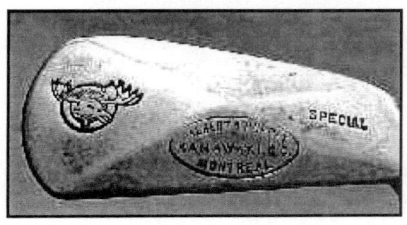 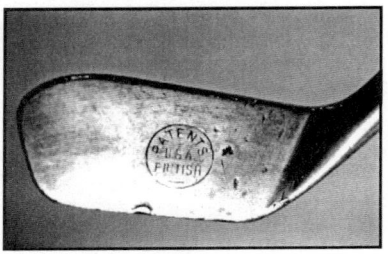

Murray, Charles+
[Montreal, QUE]
    Driver--Socket head $75
    Mashie Niblick--Spalding Gold Medal, right angle face lines $75
    Mid Iron--Blade with maple leaf CM $75
    Putter--Iron blade, offset head, name in oval $60

Murray, D.
    Brassie--Splice head $100

Murray, J.
[Pitlochry s]
    Brassie--Socket head $75
    Putting Iron--Iron blade, line face $45

Murrie & Sons*
[Methven s]
    Mid Iron--Smooth face, Joe Anderson OK CM $75
    Putter--Concentric back, dash face $60

Murton, J.
[Newcastle e]
    Niblick--Smooth face, heavy medium size head $100

'Mutt'

Niblick--X-23, smooth face, dog head mark $45

Myles, David*
[Dundee s]
* Driving Iron--(B) Nipper model, circle on face $400
Driving Iron--(B) Placer model, circle on face $500
Driving Iron--(B) Paxie model, circle on face $400
Driving Iron--(B) Rexor model, circle on face $500

N

'Nassau'
[Brand name from New York Sporting Goods]
Putter--Gun metal blade $150

National Golf Company+
[Chattanooga, TN]
* Named Irons--Moccasin series, line face ....$30 each
Putter--Homer model, blade $35

Neaves, Charles*
[Leven & Lossiemouth s]
Driver--Splice transitional head $200
Driver--Socket head, fiber insert $80
Driver--Long Tom model, large socket head $85
Spoon--Splice head, full sole plate $225
Cleek--Smooth face, marked for Leven $80
Mashie Niblick--(B) Genii model, smooth face $75
Mid Iron--Smooth face, name in oval $50
Putter--Large socket wood head $200

Neilson, Robert*

Wood Shafted Golf Club Value Guide

[Musselburgh s]
- Driver--Splice head $150
- Driver--Socket head $80
- Cleek--Line face $60
- Iron--Condie rose CM, dot face $60
- Niblick--Smooth face, Condie rose CM $80

'Nesco'
- Putter--Brass head with aiming fin, aluminum insert $1,800

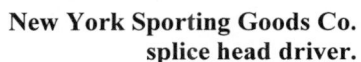

National Golf Co. Moccasin mid iron.

New York Sporting Goods Co. splice head driver.

New York Sporting Goods Company+
[New York]
* Driver--Splice head, stag over shield CM $275
- Cleek--Running stag CM, dot face $125
- Lofter--Smooth face, oval mark $125
- Mashie--Running stag CM, dot face $125
- Niblick--Small head, concave, name inside Maltese cross, smooth face $500
- Putter--Gun metal blade, "N.Y.S.G." $150
- Putter--Hillside model, name in decorated oval $125

Ness, O.M.
- Putter--MacGregor R model, top weight $150

Newbery, Ernest*
[Strawberry Hill e and Italy]
- Sammy--Stewart pipe CM, line face $75

*   Named Irons--(B) Half-moon model, crescent-shaped weighted portion on back .... $400 each

Niblett-Flanders
Iron clubs--Life Saver model, stainless, dot face .... $50 each

 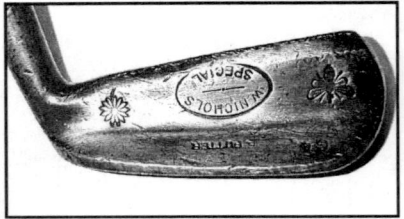

Ernest Newberry 'Half Moon" model niblick.
W. Nichols gun metal putter made by Burke.

Nicholls Brothers+
[The firm of F. Bernard (Ben) Nicholls and Gilbert Nicholls, English professionals working around Boston, MA C.1900. Clubs were marked Nicholls Brothers or Nicholls Special]
Driver--Splice head $200
Driver--Special bead splice head $350
Driver--Socket head, steel face insert $150
Driver--Socket head $95
Cleek--Smooth face, nickel plated $75
Cleek--Yellow rustless metal, smooth face $100
Lofter--Short round back blade, smooth face $70
Mashie--Concentric back, smooth face, name in oval $75
Niblick--Name in oval, smooth face, Hunt Co. shaft stamp .. $500
Putter--Gun metal blade $85
Putter--Iron blade, marked "Nicholls Special" $60

Nicholls, F. Bernard "Ben"+
Iron clubs--Smooth face, name in block letters .... $75 each

Nicholls, Gilbert "Gil"+
Mashie--Name in oval, Spalding Gold Medal $45

Nichols, W.
*   Putter--Gun metal, Burke model G4, flower & bee CMs $125

Nicholson Brothers
[Anstruther s]
    Iron clubs--Nicoll hand CM, stainless .... $60 each

'Nicola'
    Putter--(A B) Two faced hammer head with
    semi-circular cut-out for bridging ball $1,200
    Putter--(B) Two faced hammer head in gun metal with
    semi-circular cut-out for bridging ball $1,500

Nicoll, George*
[Leven s; founded in 1881, this firm was one of the premier cleek making companies, making only metal headed clubs. Their CM was a hand, which came in several versions over the years]

◇◇Clubs made prior to use of hand CM (1898)
    Cleek--Smooth face, small circular name stamp $175
*100   Cleek--(B) Leather face insert $2,000
    Cleek--(B) Gutta percha face insert $2,250
    Iron--Smooth face, name in arc $200
    Lofter--Smooth face, long blade $300
    Mashie--Smooth face, round back $200
    Niblick--Small head, name in arc $350
    Putter--(B) Nicoll patent model $250
    Putter--Swan neck model $350

◇◇Irons with Hand CM
    Cleek--F.G. Tait model, dot face $125
    Driving Iron--Nap model, line face $50
    Driving Iron--Precision series, flange sole, stainless $30
    Iron--Smooth face, name in arc, small hand CM $100
*   Iron--Clinker series, oval head $60
    Iron--Nap model, concave face $75
    Iron--San Souci series $50
    Jigger--Musselback, hand CM, dot face $75
    Mashie--Braid model, musselback, dot face, hand CM $80
    Mashie--Recorder series, dot face $40
100   Mashie--Fairlie's patent, small hand CM $175
*   Iron--Nicoll autograph, made for Donald Ross $150

Mashie Niblick--Marked Playklub, small diamond &
hand CMs, chromed $40
Mashie Niblick--(D) Name in script, corrugated face $75
Mashie Niblick--Zenith series, dot face, oval head...................$60
Mashie Niblick--Big Ball series, stainless, deep face $35
Mashie Niblick--Big Shooter series, stainless, line face $35
Mashie Pitcher--Zenith series, line face $80
Mid Iron--Sure series, dot face $40
Niblick--Able series, line face $40
Niblick--Indicator series, dot face $50
Pitcher--(D) Corrugated face $125
Pitcher--(D) Zenith series, corrugated face $125
Putter--Trusty model, musselback blade $75
100   Putter--Gem style head $75
Putter--Whippet model, long hosel $60
Putter--Gray series, line face $50
Putter--Nap model, beveled heel and toe $75
Putter--The Gray, model name in script, long blade $100
Putter--Zenith series, long blade $75
100   Putter--F.G. Tait model $100-150
Putter--Park model, bent neck $150

Nicoll Clinker model iron.

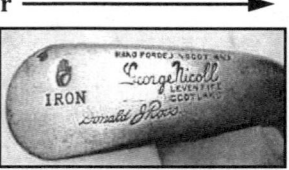

Back & face of a **George Nicoll patent leather face cleek.** →

Nicoll iron with Donald Ross autograph.

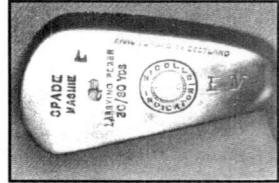

Nicoll Indicator model spade mashie.

Nicloo Precision flanged niblick.

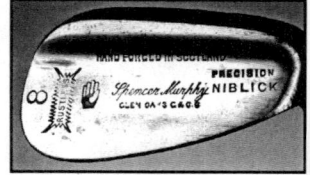

Putter--Recorder series, long blade, dot face $50
Putter--Philp model, beveled heel and toe $95
Putter--Indicator series steel mallet head $275

Set--Indicator model, 8 matched irons and putter $1,000
Named Irons--George Nicoll in script ....$45 each
Numbered Irons--George Nicoll name in script,
stainless, line face ....$35 each
Named Irons--Big Ball series ....$35 each
Named Irons--Big Shooter series ....$35 each
Numbered Irons--Cracker Jack series, Carruthers hosel,
dot face ....$40 each
Numbered Irons--Compaction Blade, dot face ....$35 each
Numbered Irons--Akurasy series, musselback, line face .$40 each
*   Named/Numbered Irons--Indicator series, dial CM ....$45 each
Set (1-9, Putter)--Indicator series $600-700
Named/Numbered Irons--Mac Smith Duplicate Set,
stainless ....$50 each
*   Named or Numbered Irons--Precision series, stainless,
flange sole ....$35 each
Named/Numbered Irons--Recorder series, name in script,
hand CM ....$45 each
Numbered irons--Viking series, Viking ship CM ....$35 each

Nicolson, T.*
[Pittenweem s]

Iron--Line face $75
Mashie--Smooth face, Edinburgh Gold Medal stamp $125
Putter--Bent neck, Edinburgh Gold Medal CM $150
Putter--Juvenile, marked B, Gold Medal CM $100

Noirit, E & A
[Walsall e]

Putter--(A) Model 123, round back with lead face insert $175
Putter--(A) BMR model, lead face insert $250
Putter--(A) TTS model, Ray-type with three plateaus
and spider web face $250

Norrie, R.*
[Johnstone s]

Putter--(B) Cochrane Castle model, overspin-type, gooseneck hosel

$125

Northwestern Golf Co.
[Chicago, IL]
*   Iron clubs--Ace series, winged propellor CM, line face .. $35 each

Norton, Tom

Northwestern Golf Company mid iron.

Willie Norton mashie.

[Llandrindod w]
         Lofter--Ariel series, smooth face $60

Norton, William
[New Jersey]
         Driver--Short splice head $150
*   Mashie--Dot face, two pine cones CM $75
         Mashie--Dot face $40
         Mashie--(U) 2 star CMs, Spalding Lard 'whistler' shaft $4,000
         Niblick--Small round head, smooth concave face $350

Novak, Joe
[San Francisco]
         Adjustable Iron--(U) Novakclub, line face $1,000

         [Similar Novakclub with steel shaft .... $100-150]

Noyes Brothers
[Boston, MA retail store]
         Driver--Transitional splice head $250

O

'O-V-B'+
    Driver--Model 571, socket head $75
    Brassie--Model 531, socket head $75
    Cleek--Model 731, Carruthers hosel $100
    Mashie--Model 781, 1/2 dot concave face $85
    Mashie--Model 841, line face $50
    Mid Iron--Model 831, line face $50
    Mashie Niblick--Model 852 .... $50
    Niblick--Model 711, line/dot face $60
    Putter--931, gun metal blade $75
    Putter--Model 931, initials in shield, flange sole $60
    Putter--Model 932, iron blade $60

O.W.C.+
[see Overman Wheel]

Ockenden, James
[Raynes Park, London, et al]
    Driver--Socket head $50

Ogg, Willie
[Worcester, MA, et.al.]
    Spoon--Socket head, bull dog-type, fiber insert $100
    Mashie--Spalding Dedstop 6, waffle face $300

Ogilvie, Dave
[Morris County, NJ and Augusta, GA, et.al.]
    Brassie--Pick-up model, sole protrudes from face $300
    Spoon--Pick-up model $400
    Irons--Stewart pipe models, line face .... $60 each
    Niblick--Extreme gooseneck anti-shank type hosel, round sole $350

Oke, J.H.*
[Sutton Coldfield e, et al]
    Mashie--Smooth face $75
    Putter--Offset blade $45

Oke, W.G.*
[Honor Oak, London, et al]
    Mashie--Oak Brand, oak tree CM, dot face $50
    Putter--Staynorus stainless head, long thin hosel $100
    Putter--Oak Brand, oak tree CM $80
    Putter-Oak Brand, oak tree CM, extra long hosel $175

Ollarton, R.
    Brassie--Small splice head $100

'Olympia'
[MacGregor store brand]
    Putter--Line face, 2 club pips CM $25

Ornum Putter Company
[St. Andrews]
    Putter--(B) Round wood mallet socket head, brass face plate $250

Osborn
    Mid Iron--"Osborn's Rustless", tiny hand & heart CM $60

Ouimet & Sullivan

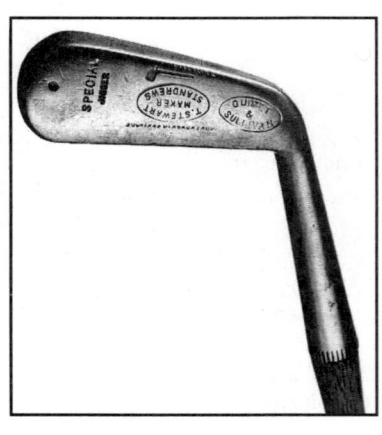

Tom Stewart jigger made for the Boston firm of Ouimet & Sullivan. Francis Ouimet's limited involvement with this firm almost cost him his amateur status.

[Boston]
    Driver--Socket head $250
*   Jigger-Stewart pipe brand, line face $150
    Niblick-Stewart pipe brand, line face $150

Wood Shafted Golf Club Value Guide

Outing Goods Manufacturing Company+
    Driver--(S U) Brooklawn Special model, splice head,
    markings in red paint, fiber face $1,250

Overman Wheel Company+
[Springfield, MA; also see Victor-O.W.C.]
    Cleek--Smooth face $250
    Niblick--Smooth face, small gun metal head $2,000

PGA model mid iron made by MacGregor.
                              PGA model iron made by Spalding.

PGA model iron made by Spalding.
                              PGA Manufacturing Company mid iron.

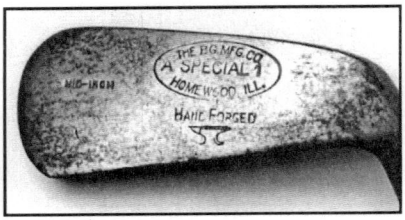

P

P.G.A. or 'Professional Golfers Association'+
[Clubs made by Spalding and MacGregor marked "P.G.A." were sold by member professionals of the P.G.A. of America. The P.G.A. acted as a co-op and obtained volume discounts, passing the savings on to pros with smaller shops]

Driving Iron--P 10, line face $40
Jigger--P 81, crossed clubs CM, line face $40
Mashie--Kro-Flite CM, dot face $30
Mashie Iron--P 41, dot face $35
Mashie Iron--P 40, line face $35
Mashie--P 50, line face $40
* Mashie--Acorn & hammer CMs $45
Mashie Niblick--P 60, line face $40
Mashie Niblick--P 61, Dedstop ribbed face $100
* Mid Iron--P 22, deep cut line face, crossed clubs CM $35
Niblick--P 91, line face $40
* Numbered Irons--Spalding roses, arrow and long
golf club CMs $30
Numbered Irons--Kro-Forged model, crow CM $30
Putter--Kro-Flite series, long golf club CM $40
Putter--P-1, crossed clubs CM $40
Putter--P-3, blade, crossed clubs & shamrock CMs $40

P.G. Manufacturing Company+
[Homewood, IL; marketing co-operative for several Midwestern club makers of Scottish descent]

Mashie--Made for Joe Mitchell, anvil CM $65
Mashie Niblick--Marked "Genuine Foulis Mashie Niblick",
smooth concave face, anvil CM $200
* Mid Iron--Dot face, anvil CM, Homewood, IL $60
Niblick--Homewood model, smooth face, anvil CM $60
Putter--Birdie series, iron blade, anvil and trophy CMs $60

Park, John "Jack"+
[Essex County, NJ; young Willie Park's younger brother]

Driver--Socket head $125

Park, Mungo*
[Alnmouth e; Open Champion 1874, younger brother of Auld Willie Park]

Playclub--(L) Dark head $3,500-5,000
Putter--(L) C.1880, beech head $3,000-4,000

Park & Son, William*
[Musselburgh s; founded by Open Champion Old Willie, the firm had very small output until Young Willie assumed leadership in 1885. Then the firm became one of the largest in Scotland]

 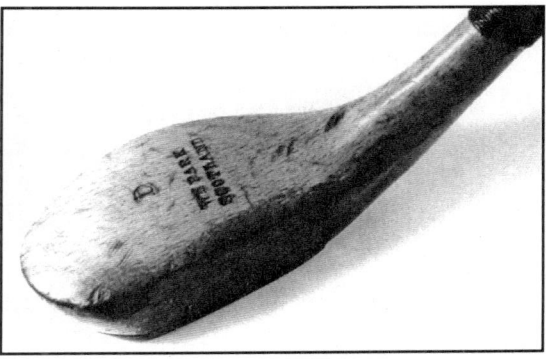

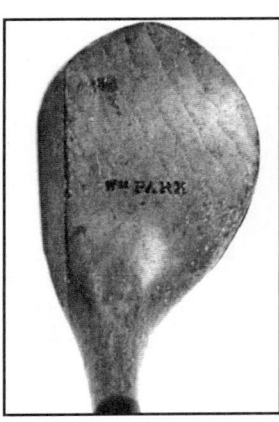

Park Compressed Patent driver (upper left)

Park late model long nose driver (upper right)

Park splice head driver (lower left)

Park transitional head driver (lower right)

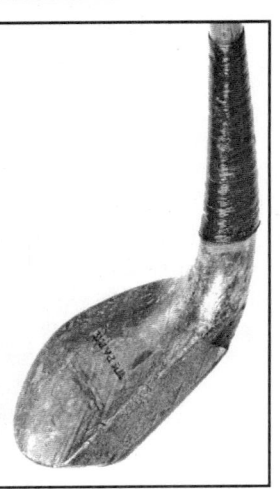

◇◇Early clubs made by Willie, Sr.

       Playclub--(L) Long head $5,000-15,000
       Spoon--(L) Long head $6,000-15,000
       Putter--(L) Long head $5,000-15,000

◇◇Clubs made during the time of Willie, Jr.
*   Playclub--(L) Late long nose, stamped "D" for driver $1,250
*   Driver-(S) Transitional splice head $1,000
       Driver--(S) Bulger head, bowed face, shaft stamp .. $1,500-2,500
*   Driver--Splice head, straight face $250-350
       Driver--Short socket head, shaft stamp $150-200
       Brassie--(S) Bulger head, bowed face, shaft stamp . $1,500-2,500

*100   Brassie--(B) Compressed patent splice head $300-500
Brassie--(B) Pik-up model, grooved sole $450-600
Baffy--Transitional splice head $700
Putter--(S) Transitional head, shaft stamp $1,000-2,500
Putter--(S) Wood head, modern manufacture C. 1970 .... $75
Cleek--Smooth face, oval stamp $200
Driving Cleek--(B) Smooth face, round back $200-300
Driving Mashie--Extra deep face, small oval stamp $750
Iron--Smooth face, oval stamp $125
Iron--Line face, line stamp $75
Lofter--(B) Smooth concave face $300-600
Lofter--Smooth face, oval stamp $150-200
Lofter--Smooth face, straight name stamp $200
Mashie--Smooth face, oval stamp $100
Mashie--Smooth face, name in oval with outline $125
Mashie--Stock exchange model, thick heavy blade,
smooth face $175
Mashie Niblick--(B) 'Step Face', made by Spalding $3,500
Niblick--Small head, smooth face, straight name stamp $400-500
Niblick--Medium head, smooth face, oval stamp $250-350
Niblick--Large diamond back head $150

100   Putter--(B) Bent neck, "patent" marking,
shaft stamp $150-300
Putter--Marked "Original Bent Neck Putter" $85
Putter--Iron blade, oval stamp $100
Putter--Gun metal blade, oval stamp $150

Park & Son
[Mungo and Son; Gullane s]
    Putter--(A) Mallet head $150

Parker, William
[Carnoustie s]
    Mid Iron--Royal Crown model, crown CM, dot face $60
    Mashie--Defiance Brand, lion CM, Maxwell pattern $65
    Putter--Blade, eye CM $75

'Parlor Putter'
[See Wellington-Stone Company]

Parr, Jack

Wood Shafted Golf Club Value Guide

**   Spoon--Socket head, fiber insert $85
          Mashie--Dot face $35

Parr, Tom*
[Heswall e]
    Driver--Superb model, socket head, face insert $65
    Putter--Centre-Balance model, gun metal blade $80

Parr, S.
    Mashie--Stainless, line face $30

Partridge Company, Horace
[Boston, MA]
    Brassie--Socket head $60
    Mashie--Diamond back, line face $40
    Mashie Niblick--Foulis-type, monogram CM, concave smooth face $85

Patrick & Son, A.*
[Leven s; this firm was actually founded by Patrick's father, John in 1847. It continued in business until the 1930s]

◇◇19th century clubs
    Playclub--(L) Dark head, shallow face $2,500-4,500
    Driver--(S) Bulger head $1,250-2,000
    Driver--Splice head, leather face insert $300-400
    Brassie--(S) Transitional head $1,000-1,800
    Spoon--(L) C.1880, dark head $2,500-4,000
    Putter--(L) Beech head $2,000-3,000
    Putter--(S) Semi-long nose splice head $1,250-1,750
    Putter--Gun metal blade, thick hosel $150

◇◇20th century clubs
    Driver--Short splice head $200-300
    Driver--D.J.S. model, socket head $80
    Driver--The Robbie model, socket head, aluminum
    face insert $150
    Brassie--Short splice head $200-300
    Brassie--(B) Perfector model, triangle face insert $250
    Brassie--Popular model, socket head, fiber insert $50
    Brassie--Acme model, fiber face insert with 5 pegs $100

Pete Georgiady's

Spoon--Apex model, bulldog style short head,
6 peg fiber face insert $125
Spoon--"Est'd 1847" markings, socket head $85
Approach Mashie--Own Model, Welmade horseshoe CM $45
Driving Iron--Half musselback, spur CM, line face $100
Driving Iron--Tivoli series, thick toe, spur CM $125
* Iron--Juvenile with gun metal head, spur CM $75
Mashie--Diamond back, spur CM, line face $75
Mashie--The Bass Rock model, dot face $60
Mashie Niblick--Nicoll hand CM $50
Niblick--Popular series, "P" CM, "Est'd 1847" markings $80
Numbered Irons--Blade marked "Est. 1847" .... $50 each
Numbered Irons--Own Model, Welmade horseshoe CM,
line face .... $35 each
Putter--Gun metal mallet head, steel face insert $300
Putter--The Robbie model, wood socket head, steel
face plate $300
Putter--Welmade series, stainless dot face blade,
horseshoe mark $60
Putter--Welmade series, stainless dot face blade,
gooseneck hosel $75

 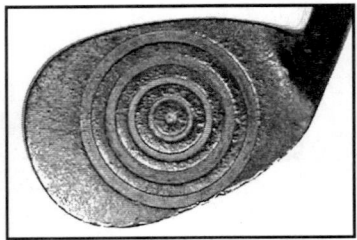

Alex Patrick juvenile iron in gunmetal.

      J. Patrick niblick with deep ringed face marks.

Patrick Brothers
    Iron--Smooth face, name in oval $75

Patrick, Alex
[New York]
    Driver--(S) Bulger shaped head, leather face insert $350

Patrick, D.M.
[Leven s]
    Driver--Socket head $100
    Brassie--Splice head $300
    Putter--(B) Foster's model, wood socket head $650
    Putter--Iron blade $80

Patrick, David
[Leven s]
    Jigger--Pefector series.. $75

Patrick, John
[Leven s; brother of Alex Patrick, Sr.]
    Spoon--(L) Beech head $2,500-5,000

Patrick, John
[Tuxedo, NY]
    Iron--Smooth face, pipe CM $90
*   Niblick--Large head, circular deep grooves on face $600
    Putter--Deep face blade, gun metal $150

Paxton, James*
[Romford e, et al; nephew of Peter Paxton]
    Brassie--Socket head, Paxtonite insert $150

Paxton, Peter*
[Raised in Musselburgh, Paxton was a fine golfer who preferred business to competitive golf. His firm was located in several English towns and his clubs were highly sought]
    Playclub--(L) C.1885, long head $1,500-3,500
    Driver--(S) Transitional head $900-1,500
    Driver--Ealing model, socket head $150
    Brassie--(S) Bulger head, crown CM $1,000-1,500
    Brassie--(S) Bulger head $600-1,200
    Brassie--(S) Transitional head $750-1,500
    Short Spoon--(S) Medium short head,
    well lofted face $1,000-1,500
    Putter--(S) Short transitional head $750-1,000
    Cleek--Smooth face, Eastbourne address,
    made by W. Wilson $600

	Iron--Smooth face, Tooting address	$300

        Iron--Smooth face, Tooting address $300
        Lofter--Smooth face, Eastbourne address,
        made by W. Wilson $750
        Mashie--Smooth face, short heavy blade,
        made by J. Anderson $400
*   Mashie Iron--Smooth face, oval name stamp $300
        Putter--Long iron blade $275
        Putter--Gun metal blade $150

Peacock, J.M.
        Putter--Gun metal blade $75

'Peacock'
        Mashie--Line face, large bird CM $25

Pearson, J.S.
[Southall, London]
        Mashie Niblick--Slots cut through face $2,200

Pederson+
[New York]
        Mashie Niblick--(U) Convex face, line face $250
        Niblick--(U) Convex face, line face $300
        Putter--(A) Own Model, 2 dials on top of head $250

Peeples, Thomas
[Pittenweem s]
        Cleek--Name in circle, smooth face, Masonic compass CM ..$250
        Mashie--Name in circle, smooth face $200

'Pegasus'
[see Seales Allen]

Penick, Harvey
[Austin, TX]
        Semi-Putter--MacGregor rose CM, Penick name in script $200

Philp, Hugh
[St. Andrews; possibly the most famous club maker of all time. His clubs were prized as collectibles by the end of the 19th century. The wide price range reflects demand for clubs in varying states of condition. Clubs in fine or ex-

Wood Shafted Golf Club Value Guide

cellent condition are rare and extremely valuable]
100   Playclub--Long head, straight face $5,000-25,000
         Putter--Long head, slight hook face $5,000-25,000

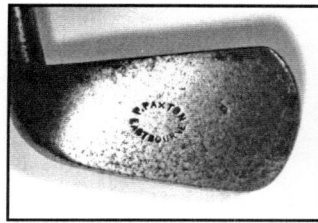 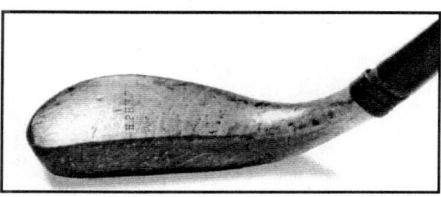

Peter Paxton deep face mashie iron.

                                       Hugh Philp playclub.

Phosphor Bronze Smelting Company+
[Baltimore, MD]
       Putter--(A) Kismet model, rectangular head,
       shafted at heel $150-250

'Piccadilly'
[W.T. Grant Company (New York) brand name]
       Iron clubs--Chrome head, line face .... $25 each
       Putter--Model P-2, twin diamond mark $30

Playgolf, Inc.+
[Cleveland, OH]
       Iron clubs--Chrome head, "P G" on face .... $25 each

'Playwell'
       Iron clubs--Chrome head, line face .... $25 each

Pope, W.R.
[Chorlton-cum-Hardy, Manchester e]
       Putter--Short headed blade $125
       Putter--(A B) Center shafted, square head $300

Potts, W.H.
[Briarcliff, NY]
       Mashie--Line face, small Spalding thistle CM $40
       Putter--Gun metal mallet head, cork face insert,

made by Spalding $1,250

Premier Golf Company, Ltd.*
[Battersea, London]
        Driving Iron--Dot face, 3 crowns CM $75

Premier Golf Club Company*
[Glasgow]
        Cleek--Rustless, dot face $50
        Putter--The Premier model, name in script,
        bar shaped blade, oval hosel $100

'Prestwick'
[There were several users of this name, most notably Burke and J. & D. Kinnell]

'Pro-Made'
[B.C. Leather & Findings Co., Vancouver]
        Driver--Socket head, stripe top $75

'Pro-Made'
[Leather Parts & Golf Manufacturing Co., Detroit, MI]
*   Iron clubs-Peacock mark, line face .... $25 each

 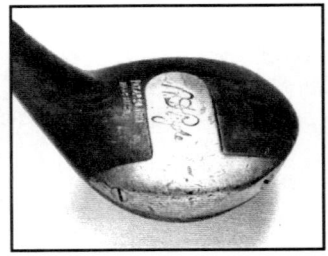

Pro-Made mid iron.
                          R.D. Pryde brassie with patent backweight.

Pryde, R.D.
[Hartford, CT]
        Driver--Bull Dog model, bulldog head CM, socket head $50
*   Brassie--(U) Socket head, one piece aluminum sole plate &
        head weight $300

Iron--Dash face, Nicoll hand CM $40
Brassie--Dash face, bulldog head CM $50

Pulford, George
[Hoylake e]
Brassie--Splice bulger head $200

Purkess, J.
Niblick--Excelsior model, eye CM, line face $60

R

R.G.C. Co.+
[see Rustless Golf Club Company]

Ramsbottom, Robert*
[Manchester e]
*   Driver--(A B) Wood face dovetailed into head, horn slip $900
Iron--(B)Smooth face, claw hosel $800
Lofter--Smooth face, slightly concave $300

Randall, John*
[Sundridge Park, London]
Driver--Short splice head $100
Driver--(B) Grand Slam model, socket head,
grass fiber insert $125
Iron clubs--Stewart pipe CM, dot face .... $45 each
*   Putter--(A B) Long mallet head, lead filled plug holes $250
Putter--(A) Flallie model, mallet head $100

Randall, Robert*
[Herne Bay, Kent e]
Driver--(B) Velometer model, large socket head $350
Mashie Niblick--Asp model, line face $60
Pitcher--Line face, hatchet CM $75
Putter--(B) True Sight model, iron blade, oval hosel $150
Putter-(B) True Sight model, square grip with
thumb depressions, broad sole, name in script $100

Pete Georgiady's

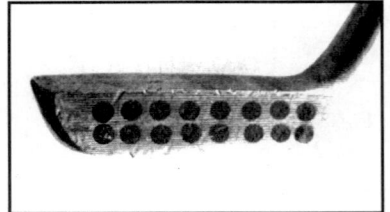

Ramsbottom patent aluminum driver.

John Randall patent aluminum putter.

Rawlings Sporting Goods+
[St. Louis]
    Brassie--Small socket head $100
    Putting Cleek--Dot face blade $60
    Putter—Target model, bronze, Chicopee-style head $80
    Numbered Irons--Siege Gun series, line face,
    cannon CM .... $50 each

Rawlins, Horace+
[U.S. Open Champion 1895, worked at various east coast clubs]
    Driver--Horace Rawlins stamp, deep face splice head,
    Spalding Special shaft $350
    Driver--Socket head $250
    Brassie--Splice head $250
    Iron--Smooth face, hand struck name stamp $300

Ray, Edward (Ted)*
[Open Champion 1912, US Open Champion 1920; professional at several important English clubs]
    Driver--Socket head $100
    Driver--(B) Steel face insert, socket head $300
    Driving Iron--Autograph model, marked for Oxhey GC $60
    Mashie Niblick--Everbrite brand, stainless $75
    Named Irons--E. Ray model, Stewart pipe CM,
    scored face .... $65 each
    Named Irons--Autograph series, made by Wilson Co. ... $60 each
    Putter--(A) Schenectady style, marked for Ganton $250

'Rayl, The'
    Irons or putter--Heather model, offset blade $50

Wood Shafted Golf Club Value Guide

Reach Company, A.J.+
[Philadelphia sporting goods company owned by the Spalding Company]
Driver--Model 56R, splice head, keystone CM $125
Driver--Socket head, double stripe top $50
Driver--Model X95, long socket head $85
Driver--Fairway series, socket head, keystone CM $50
Woods--Model 598, black/white diamond pattern fancy face,
bamboo shaft ....$100 each
Wood Set--Model 598 .... $350
Woods (dr, br, sp)--Warwick series, socket head,
keystone CM ....$75 each
Wood Set--Warwick series $275
Mashie--Red Brand, stainless, line face $35
Mashie--Superior Grade series, dot face $35
Mashie Niblick--(D) Chek-Rite model C92R,
corrugated face $100
Mashie Niblick--(D) Dedstop model C51R, corrugated face $100
Mid Iron--Model 1R, large keystone CM $40
Mid Iron--Line face, hammer & anvil CM $35
Mid Iron--Reach series, keystone CM $35
Niblick--(D)Check-Rite model C98R, corrugated face $100
Niblick--(D) Hammer brand, corrugated face $100
Named Irons--Warwick series, keystone CM $30
Putter--Hammer & anvil CM $40
Putter--Willie Mack model, iron blade, line face $50
Putter--(A) Model R4. keystone CM $90
Putter--Model 8P, Super Grade series, flange sole $60
Putter--Warwick series, blade, keystone CM $35
Putter--Eagle Grade series, line/dot face $50
Numbered Irons--Eagle Grade, Expert Model,
eagle CM ....$40 each

Read Golf Company
[Boston, MA]
Spoon--(U) Barnes-Read model, brass face insert $150
Spoon--(U) Read Balanced model, bulldog socket head $150
Irons--Name in diamond, scored face ....$40 each

Read, William

Pete Georgiady's

    Driver--Splice head, diamond monogram CM $150
    Brassie--Read model, socket head, diamond CM $60
    Putter--Bent neck blade, broad sole $65

Redpath & Co.
[Glasgow]
    Mashie--Dot face $35

Reekie, Tom
[Elie s]
    Driver--Socket head, plain face $60
    Iron--Brodie triangle/BS&A CM $50
    Mashie--Line face, Stewart pipe CM $40

Reflex Manufacturing Company
[Cincinnati, OH]
    Driver--(U) Socket head, special rotating grip $400

Reid, John
[Atlantic City, NJ]
    Brassie--(U) Compressed, bulger splice head $400
    Mashie--Smooth face, short head, name in arc $150
    Niblick--Atlantic City model, medium face $300
    Putter--Gun metal blade $100

Reid, Wilfred
[Banstead, London, later Detroit, MI]
    Driver--Pear shape socket head $80

Reith, W.R.
[Eltham e]
    Brassie--(S) Splice bulger head $300

Remson Company+
[Erie, PA]

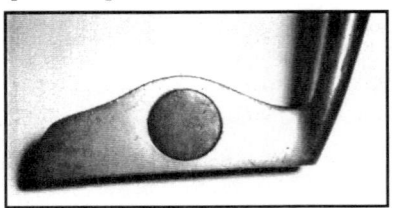

The Remson putter had a sweet spot insert made of black hard rubber set into the bronze club head.

Wood Shafted Golf Club Value Guide

  *100   Putter--Gun metal head, hump in center of blade, plastic face inlay at sweet spot $400

Renouf, T.G.*
[Manchester e]
- Driver--Stripe top, socket head, ivorine face insert $75
- Cleek--Diamond face $65

'Rev-O-Noc'
[Conover (spelled backward) Hardware Co., St. Louis, MO]
- Driving Iron--Smooth face, Carruthers hosel $85
- Mashie--Model 36, line/dot face $55

Rhino Cupples Company
[St. Louis, MO]
- Iron clubs--Scored face, rhinoceros CM $40
- Putter--Blade, rhinoceros CM $45

Rhodes, F.
- Baffy--(B) Shoebury patent, cup face $400

Rigden, F.E.
[Garden City, NY]
- Driver--Short splice head $150
- Mid Iron--Smooth face $80
- Niblick--Perfect model, smooth face, two stars CM $100
- Putter--Bent neck blade $125

Righter, Walter "Turk"
- Putter--(A U) Center shaft pendulum style, special finger bar in grip $800

Ritchie, W.L.*
[Addington, London]
- Driver--Socket head, signature stamp $85
- Mashie--(D) Stopded model, flower CM, concave face, dot punched $125
- Mashie Niblick--Own Model, WLR Brand, flower CM $60
- Putter--The Uncanny model, round topped blade, notched at hosel $75
- Putter--The "Uncanny," prism shaped blade sloped back $175

Pete Georgiady's

    Putter--Gem model, flower CM $75

'Rob Roy'
[MacGregor economy series]
    Mashie--Dot face, name in arc $25
    Mid Iron--Line face, name in arc $25

Robertson, Andy
[Burr-Key series]
    Iron clubs--Autograph series, Burr Key Bilt, line face ... $30 each

Robertson, Fred
[Cooden Beach e]
    Driver--Socket head $60
    Mashie--Stainless, line face, "PROJ" CM $50

Robertson, Peter
[Oakmont, PA, et. al.]
*   Brassie, Spoon--Socket head, one piece sole plate/
    backweight $225
    Cleek--(U) Notched at hosel, Nicoll hand CM $250

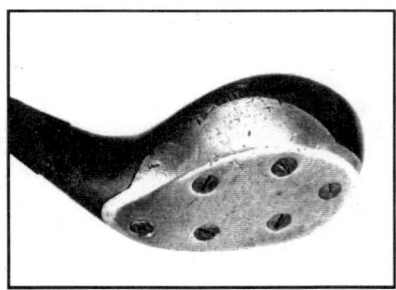

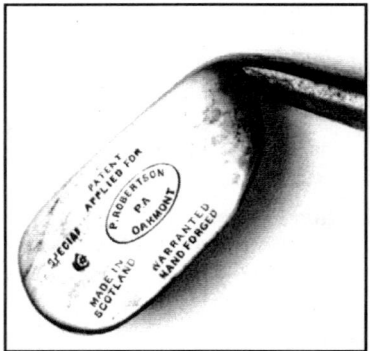

Peter Robertson patent brassie with weighted sole plate.

Peter Robertson patent mashie with deeply notched hosel joint.

Peter Roberston niblick with hand CM.

*   Mashie--(U) Notched hosel joint, dot face $250
        Niblick--Large head, line face, Nicoll hand CM $80
*   Niblick-Line face, hand and spade CMs $100
        Putter--Wood Schenectady-type $200

Robertson, William
[Oakmont, PA]
Brassie--(U) The Leader model, socket head,
one piece sole plate-backweight $225

'Robo'
Putter--(A) Mallet head with notch cut out of toe $300

Robson, Fred
[Cooden Beach e, and other locations]
Brassie--Splice bulger head $200
Mashie--Proj model, stainless head, dot face, sold by Harrods $50

Rodwell & Company, Charles*
[London]
Mashie--Flange sole, offset blade $50
Niblick--(B) Fairlie model (anti-shank), diamond/dot face $200
Putter--(A) Rodwell model, mallet head with aiming
dial on top $175

Rogers Peet Company
[New York City]
Iron clubs--Scored face, RPCo monogram CM .... $40 each
Putter--Offset blade $25

Rollins & Parker*
[Redditch e]
Mashie--Maxwell pattern, line face $75
Mashie--(B) Smith model (anti-shank), line face $200
Mashie Niblick--Excelsior series, eye CM, round back $60
Niblick--Excelsior series, round back, eye CM $80
Putting Cleek--Dash face blade, eye CM $75

Rolls, A.E.
Mashie--Dot face $40

Ross, A.M.*
    Putter--(B) Negative loft, thickened sole $250

Ross, Alex (or Alec)
[U.S. Open Champion 1907; Donald's younger brother]
    Driver--Socket head, marked Pinehurst $100
    Mashie--Spalding hammer CM, name in oval $50
*   Iron clubs--Burke fleur-de-lis CM, dot face $50

Ross, Donald

Alex Ross mashie niblick made by Burke.
        Donald J. Ross putter made in Monel Metal.

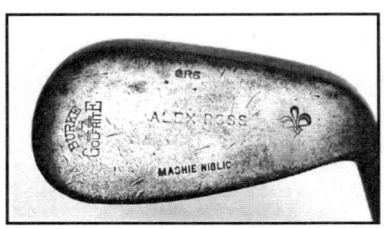 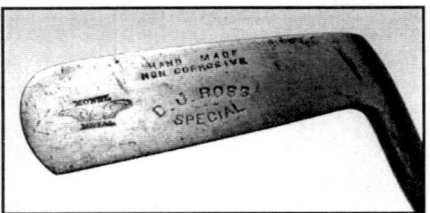

[Oakley (Boston), MA & Pinehurst, NC]
    Driver--Socket head, name in script $200
    Brassie--Socket head, crossed clubs CM $150
    Spoon--Small splice head $500
    Spoon--splice head, stripe top, name in script,
    Spalding Reach patent model date marking $200
100   Cleek--Smooth face, Dornoch stamp $300
    Iron--George Nicoll, lie face, Ross nema in script $100
    Mashie--Smooth face, name in arc $100
    Mashie--Name in oval, Stewart pipe CM, dot face $85
    Mashie--Straight line name stamp, dot face $100
    Mashie--(D) Bakspin model (MacGregor), slotted face $150
    Mashie--Smooth face, MacGregor rose CM $100
    Mashie Niblick--Smooth face, name in arc $125
    Mashie Niblick--Kro Flite model, Ross name in script $100
    Mid Iron--Line face, crossed clubs CM $125
    Mid Iron--Line face, Burke scales CM $90
    Niblick--Small head, smooth face $500
    Niblick--Medium head, smooth face name in arc $150

Wood Shafted Golf Club Value Guide

Chipper--Pinehurst model run-up iron, line face
(like semi-putter) $250
Putter--Iron blade, name in oval $125
* Putter--Spalding Monel blade $150
Putter--Wood Schenectady-type, brass face $300

Ross, John

St. *[various locations including*

Jack Ross mashie with shore bird CM.

Andrews]

Driver--Splice head, face insert $150
* Iron--The Creek model, shorebird CM $60

Rowe, Jack*
[Ashdown Forest e]

Driver--Small splice head $200
Driver--Splice head, extra long fishing rod shaft $300
Mashie--Pipe brand, dot face $60
Mashie Niblick-Aero model, bi-plane CM, rustless $65
Putter--Wood socket head $200

'Royal'

Mashie--Line face, chrome head $25
Iron clubs--Chrome, shield CM .... $25 each

'Ruso'

Driver--Socket head, rooster CM $45
Iron clubs--Line face, rooster CM $40

Rustless Golf Club Company+
[Chicago]

Mashie--Thick toe, sun CM $90
Mashie Iron--Smooth face, face CM $75
Mashie Niblick--Rustless, marked "Genuine Foulis",
concave smooth face, sun CM $200

S

S.B.F.
[Stix, Baer & Fuller, St. Louis, MO department store]
    Brassie--Socket head, S.B.F. in shield CM $75
    Mashie--Smooth face, company crest mark $65
    Putter--Gun metal, company crest CM $95

S.D. & G.+
[Schoeverling, Dailey & Gales, Boston, MA retail store]
    Driver--(B) Compressed model, made by R. Simpson $350
    Brassie--Splice head $150
    Brassie--Socket head, flag stick CM $80
    Cleek--Smooth face, marked "Best Quality" $80
    Iron--Name in box, smooth face $75
    Mashie--Smooth face $75
    Mashie--Model 1, Ringer series, flag CM $35
    Pitcher--S D & G trademark, dot face $50
    Pitcher--Rounded sole, line face $60
    Iron clubs--Ringer series, flag in hole CM, dot face .... $35 each

S.G.C.M. Co.
(see Scottish Golf Club Mfg. Co.)

S-V-B +
[Scruggs, Vandervoort & Barney, St. Louis, MO hardware and sporting goods retail store]
    Iron Clubs--Scored face, made by Spalding .... $45 each
    Putter--Gun metal, MacGregor model 60, flange sole $100

St. Andrew Golf Company*
[Glasgow, later Dunfermline s]
    Driver--Synchrometric series, socket head $60
    Driver--Name in variable height letters $60
    Driver--HBC model, stripe top, ivory face and backweight ..$200
    Driver--Bobby model, juvenile socket head $40
    Driver--Kiddy model, juvenile socket head $40

Wood Shafted Golf Club Value Guide

Brassie--Scottie, juvenile socket head $40
Brassie--Super Stag series, stripe top $65
Brassie--Socket head, patented Grypta grip $350
Cleek--Super Stag series, stainless, line face $35
Driving Iron--Smooth face, stag head CM $60
Iron--Stag head CM, smooth face $60
Mashie--Scottie brand, stainless, line face $35
Mashie--Standard series, line face $40
Mashie Niblick--Challenge series, Maxwell pattern,
stainless, sun CM $40
Mashie Niblick--(D) Straight name stamp,
leaping stag CM, corrugated face $100
Mid Iron--Stag head CM, dot face $50
Mid Iron--St. Andrew in variable height letters, line face $40
Niblick--Model 32, Maxwell pattern, leaping stag CM $50
Niblick--Thick sole, medium head, leaping stag CM $40
Niblick--(B) Fairlie model (anti-shank), line face $150
Spade Mashie--Suxes series, stainless $40
2-Iron--Choix series, stainless, line face $30
Putter--Dick May model, convex face $150
Putter--Bobby model, juvenile gun metal blade $40
Putter--(A) XXX model, black sight line $75
Putter--Jupiter model, heavy iron blade $50
Putter--Standard series, bent neck, line face $50
Putter--Hawkins Never Rust steel, flange back,
running stag CM $60
Putter--Gun metal mallet head, steel face insert $250

'St. Andrews Special'
[MacGregor store brand]

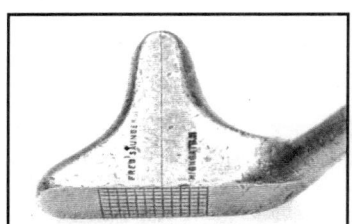
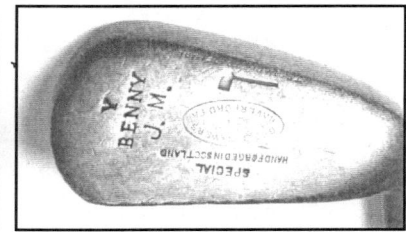

Fred Saunders "Striaghtline" aluminum putter.

Ben Sayers "Young Benny" iron.

Jigger--Convex back, crown CM, name in arc $40
Putter--Iron blade, crown CM, name in arc $40

'St. Regis'
Irons--Chrome head, shield CM $25

Sales, Ernest
Putter--(S) Wood socket head $125

Sandison, Ludovic*
[Aberdeen s]
Putter--(L) Thorn head .... $15,000 or more

'Sandy Mac'
Putter--Lion CM, made by Burke $40

Saunders, Fred*
[Birmingham and Highgate, London]
Driver--Red fiber face insert, socket head $60
Mashie--Diamond back, dot face $40
*100 Putter--(A) Straightline model, large back lobe $800
Putter--Long iron blade $50

Saville Company, Ltd., J.J.*
[Sheffield e]
Iron Clubs--Saville model, stainless, dot face $50

Sayers, Bernard (Ben)*
[North Berwick s; Sayers was a fixture in N. Berwick for over 50 years. His son Ben, Jr. ran the firm after Ben Senior's retirement]
Driver--(S) C.1885, light colored head $500
Driver--Splice transitional head $200
Driver--Autograph model, socket head $75
Driver--Socket head $75
100 Driver--Dreadnought model, large socket head $150
Brassie--(B) Domex model, rounded sole, stripe top $150
Brassie--Socket head, stripe top $75
Spoon--Small socket head, wooden cleek $150
Baffy--(B) Masta model, splice head with protruding sole front edge $500
Spoon--(B) Gruvsol model with grooved sole plate,

Wood Shafted Golf Club Value Guide

	socket head	$150
**	Spoon--(B) Socket head, stripe top, marked for the N-B Exhibition	$200
	Wooden Cleek--Autograph model, socket head	$125
	Wooden Cleek--(B) Gruvsol model, socket head, grooved sole plate	$175
*	Benny--Stewart pipe CM, dot face, Stewart pipe CM	$75-110
	Benny--Spalding Anvil CM	$65-100
	Cleek--Redan model, Maxwell hosel	$100
	Iron--Tweenie model, round sole, Stewart pipe CM	$100
	Lofter--Special Benny, Stewart pipe CM	$75-100
	Lofter--Smooth face	$85
	Mashie--(D) Stop um model, corrugated face, H & B mitre CM	$200
100	Mashie--Maxwell pattern, holes in hosel	$60
	Mashie Iron--Dunedin series, dot face	$70
	Mashie Niblick--(D) Stop um model, corrugated face	$200
	Mid Iron--Redan model, Maxwell pattern	$80
	Niblick--Large stainless head, line face	$50
	Niblick--Digger model, thick top edge, thin bottom	$150
	Young Benny--Smaller Benny iron, line face, Stewart pipe CM	$85-125

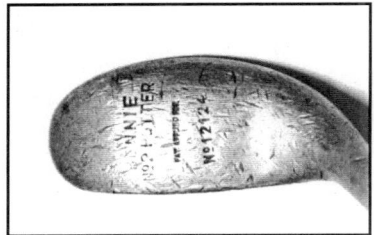 

Two versions of the Benny Putter. The aluminum head (left) and the more common stainless, low-profile blade with grooved sole.

Named Irons--Ben Sayers model, Stewart pipe CM, scored face	$70
Named Irons--Waverley series, flange sole, line face, robin CM	$60 each
Numbered Irons--Autograph series, stainless	$50 each
Numbered Irons--Craig series, robin CM, pointed toe, line face	$50 each

Numbered Irons--Crest series, stainless, line face .... $35 each
Numbered Irons--Domesole series, stainless .... $40 each
Numbered Irons--Regent series, stainless .... $35 each
Numbered Irons--Target series, bull's eye on sweet spot $40 each
Numbered Irons--Waverley series, stainless .... $35 each
Putter--(L) Late period, long head $450
Putter--(S) Splice head, brass sole $300
Putter--Wood mallet head $300

*100   Putter--(B) Benny model, grooved sole, stainless $100-175
Putter--(A B) Benny model, mallet head $150
Putter--Wood socket head, fiber sole slip $80
Putter--Straight gun metal blade, name in block letters $150
Putter--Gun metal blade $125
Putter--(B) Gassiatt-style wood putter $450
Putter--Gun metal mallet head, steel face insert $250
Putter--Gun metal blade, name in block letters $75

Sayers, Ben Jr.
[Cuckfiend, Royal Wimbledon, e; son of Ben Sayers, left Wimbledon in 1911 to join his fathers firm]
Driver--Dreadnought, socket head $125

Sayers, George
[Merion, Philadelphia, PA; old Ben Sayers' son]
Brassie--Stripe top $125
Benny--Stewart pipe CM, dot face $75-110
Mashie--(D) Stop um model, corrugated face,
H & B mitre CM $200
Niblick--Dot face, Stewart pipe CM $50
Putter--Blade, 2 Spalding rose CMs $50

Saynor, Cedric
[Duffield e]
Putter--(A B) Raised face and rounded back toe and heel,
back shaped like Mickey Mouse ears $1,000

Schenectady Putter Company
[Schenectady, NY]
*100   Putter-(A U) Center shaft, patent legend on back $300
(photo under 'Knight')

Wood Shafted Golf Club Value Guide

F.A.O. Schwarz Company juvenile niblick from the Clan series.

A.H. Scott Monarch iron with weight ridge.

Schmelzer's
[Kansas City hardware company]
    Iron--M-12, Pilot Series, diamond back, dash face $35
    Mashie--Dot face $30
    Mashie--Anderson arrow CM, dash face $45
    Putter--P-1, Pilot series, Burke model 69 .... $75

Schoverling, Daly & Gales+
[see S.D. & G.]

Schwarz, F.A.O.
[New York toy store]
    Driver-Clan series, bell CM, juvenile size socket head $60
    Mid Iron--Clan series, bell CM, juvenile size $45
    Mashie-Clan series, bell CM, junior size $40
*   Lofter--Clan series, bell CM, juvenile $55
    Putter--Clan series, bell CM, juvenile $75

Scott, A.H.*
[Elie s; Scott was appointed club maker to the Prince of Wales in 1901 and obtained a royal warrant just as Robert Forgan had for an earlier prince]
*100   Driver--(B) Fork splice head $300-500
    Driver--Socket head, lion over crown CM $80
    Brassie--(B) Fork splice head $300-500
    Cleek--Signature, plume of feathers CM, smooth face $150
*   Iron--Monarch model, ridge on back $85
    Mashie--The Midget model, short blade $150
    Lofter--Line face, lion over crown and Brodie triangle CMs . $75
    Spade Mashie--Line face, lion over crown CM $50

Pete Georgiady's

Stymie Mashie--Lion CM, concave face $125
Putter--(A) Monarch model, mallet head $100
Putter--(B) Straight-Line model, blade with top edge weight $150
Putter--(B) The Leslie model, two level back $75
Putter-(B) Broadclair model, round back,
groove sole, lion/crown CM $250
Putter--Stymie model, concave face $150
Putter--Park model, lion and (Hewitt's) heart CMs $100

Scottish Golf Club Manufacturing Company, Ltd.*
[Edinburgh]

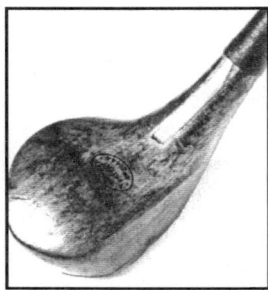 

A.H. Scott Unbreakable model ('fork splice') driver.

James Sherlock driver with cleek mark on sole plate.

Driver--Splice head, face insert $250-400
Driver--(S) Transitional splice head, fishing rod style grip ...$750
Driver--Socket head $150
Cleek--Smooth face $150
Iron--Round back, thick hosel $200
Lofter--Smooth face, long blade $200
Mashie--Smooth face, monogram w/ arrowheads CM $125
Putter--(S) Wood splice head $400
Putter--Iron blade $200
Putter--Gun metal blade $250

'Scotty'

Driver--Name in diamond, socket head $30

Seales Allen

Mashie--Pegasus model, winged horse CM, diamond back,

> line face $30

Sellars, Robert J.
[London]
> Iron clubs--Horseshoe shaped CM, dot face .... $100 each
> Putter--Gun metal blade, horseshoe CM $125

Sellars, W.
> Putter--Wood mallet head, aluminum face insert $175

Shaler Company+
[Waupun, WI]
> Woods--Marked with fancy Shaler S $40
> Named Irons--Overbrook series, chromed .... $25 each
> Named Irons--Tailor Made series, line face .... $30 each
> Numbered Irons--Tailor Made series, line face,
> S in circle CM .... $30 each

Sheffield Steel Products, Ltd.
[Sheffield e]
> Iron clubs--Name in large oval, club weight
> stamped on head .... $50 each

Shelly, W.H.
[Anstruther s]
> Brassie--Socket head $60

Shepherd, Alex*
[Inverness s]
> Iron clubs--Line face, hand holding
> shepherd's crook CM .... $75 each

Sherlock, Ray & Turner*
[Abingdon e]
> Brassie--(B) Metal face, SRT in circle CM $300
> Mid Iron--Stainless, line face SRT in circle CM $60

Sherlock, H.G.
[Worlington & Newmarket e]
> Brassie--Socket head, triangular insert $75

Sherlock, James*
[Oxford, Stoke Poges & Hunstanton e]
*   Driver-Socket head, aluminum sole plate, Oxford CM $100
            Brassie--Socket head $60
            Spoon--Small splice head $300
            Iron--Montmorencie model, Gibson star CM $75
            Mashie--Smooth face, Stewart pipe CM $75
            Semi-Putter--Shallow face chipper, Oxford CM.....................$125
            Putter--Small bar shaped head, Oxford CM $125

Sherratt, B.
[Saddleworth e]
            Iron clubs--Riding saddle cleek mark .... $50 each

Silverite Company
            Iron clubs--High nickel stainless, arm CM $40

'Silver Ace'
[Robert E. McClure patent]
            Putter-(A) Round center shaft head with front blade $400

Simmons Hardware Company
            Brassie--Socket head, oval name stamp $35
            Approach Iron--Model S/18, swastika CM $75
            Mashie--(D) Model S/33, corrugated face $75
            Mid Iron--Line face $30

'Simplex'
[Clubs with this name were produced by Francis Brewster, Robert Simpson and others; see Brewster, Simpson]

Simpson, Alex*
[Maidenhead e]
            Putter--(B)Maidenhead model, iron blade, square hosel $250

Simpson, Archie*+
[Aberdeen s; various locations in U.S.]
            Driver--Small splice head, ash shaft $300
            Brassie--Socket head, marked for Aberdeen $100
            Niblick--Small head, smooth face $350
            Putter--Offset blade $75

Wood Shafted Golf Club Value Guide

Robert Simpson "Ivorex" model **driver** with ivorine face insert.

Robert Simpson semi-long nose wood with leather face.

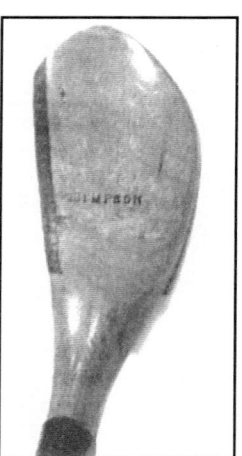

Simpson, G.O.
    Mashie--(D) 'Stop em' model (Spalding), corrugated face .. $100

Simpson, J. & A.*
[Edinburgh]
    Cleek--Full musselback, Carruthers hosel, mitre CM $125
    Iron--Name inside oval, smooth face $65
    Putter--Maxwell pattern, star/moon CM, line face $50

Simpson, Robert*
[Carnoustie s]
    Playclub--(L) C.1885, medium length head $1,500-2,000
    Long Spoon--(L) Lancewood shaft $1,500-2,000
    Driver--Short splice head, face insert $200
*100   Driver--(S) Bulger splice head, ash shaft $900
    Driver--Socket head, straight name stamp $100
    Driver--(B) Marked 'Compressed' $400
    Driver--H H model, socket head, face insert $125
    Driver--Perfect Balance model, brass backweight,
    socket head $100
    Driver--Paragon model, socket head $75
*   Driver--Ivorex model, socket head, ivorine face insert $100
    Driver--Matchless series, socket head $75
    Driver--Malinka model, socket head $75
    Driver--(B) Celluloid splice head $2,500

Pete Georgiady's

Simpson "Premier" model iron putter.
Balingall's patent flange sole iron made by Robert Simpson.

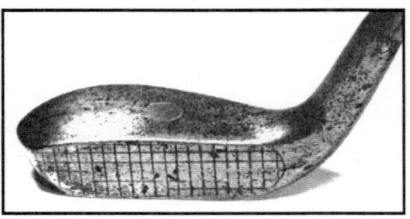 

     Brassie--(S) Bulger splice head $750
     Brassie--(S) Transitional splice head $600
     Brassie--(B) Laminated splice head $750
     Brassie--Ivorex model, ivorine face insert $100
     Brassie--Medalist model, socket head, aluminum face insert $100
     Brassie--(B) Reliance model, socket head $100
     Spoon--Simplex model, socket head, brass backweight $65
     Bunker Mashie-Line face, anchor CM $100
     Driving Iron--Line face, anchor CM $60
     Driving Mashie-Line face, anchor CM $75
     Iron--(B) Perfect Balance model, large bulge on back
     of sweet spot $450
*   Lofter--(B) Ballingall's model, smooth face, flange sole $300
     Mashie--(B) Ball face model, oversized round
     sweet spot on face $1,250
     Mashie--Concentrated model, V-shape thickened back $150
     Mashie--(B) Malinka series, faceted back $80
     Niblick--(B) Malinka series, faceted back $100
     Putter--(S) C.1890, transitional head $800
     Putter--(S) C.1900, fiber sole slip $350
     Putter--(S) Wood socket head $300
*   Putter--(B S) Premier model, hollow steel head $450
     Putter--Gem model, vertical line face $80
     Putter--Teacher model, offset head, hump on top $150
     Putter--(B) Perfect Balance model, large bulge
     in center of back,
     S in circle CM $500
     Putting Cleek--Iron blade, S in circle CM $65
     Putter--Low profile blade, pointed nose $125
     Putter--Teacher model, offset gem-type $100

Wood Shafted Golf Club Value Guide

Simpson, Robert S.
[Chicago, Memphis, Milwaukee, Kenosha, San Diego, et.al.]
    Iron--Smooth face, Gibson star CM, marked for St. Louis $60
    Mashie--Marked "Champion", name in double oval, dot face $100

Simpson, Tom
[Southport e]
    Mid Iron--Stainless, VK CM, dot face $40

Slater, F.
    Mashie Niblick--Propellor Brand, propeller CM, line face $45

Slazenger & Sons*+
[London and New York]
    Driver--(B) Demon model, patent face insert $950
    Driver--(B) One piece, leather face insert $1,500-2,000
    Driver--(B) Screw socket head (#682960) $200
    Driver--(B) Screw socket head in large dreadnought size $300
    Driver--Splice head $175
*   Driver--Socket head, pear shape, New York address $125
    Brassie--(S) Elongated socket head $100
    Brassie--Vardon model, small splice head $300
*   Cleek--Smooth face, 6 point star CM $125
    Cleek--The Ball Model, thick toe, smooth face,
    large circular CM $250
    Iron--Centraject series, thick blade $150
    Iron--Smooth face, name in oval, rose CM, Condie
    name in oval $100
    Iron--Line face, Craigie rifle CM $80
    Mashie--Boodie series, smooth face $125
    Mashie--Smooth face, St. Andrews series, name in arc $150
    Mashie Niblick--dot face, Gourlay moon/star CM $60
    Niblick--Tiny concave head, centraject back,
    6 point star CM $600
    Niblick--Small head, smooth face, Stewart serpent CM $300
    Niblick--Concave face, thick sole, stainless,
    6 point star CM $200
    Putter--Iron blade, Stewart pipe CM $60
    Putter--Iron blade, Condie rose CM, NY address $75
    Putter--Oak Brand (W.G. Oke), extra long hosel $175
    Putter-Gem style, Nicoll hand CM, dash face $75

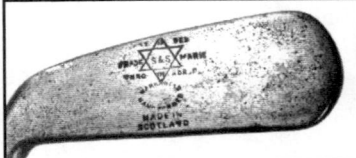

Slazenger left hand cleek with star CM.

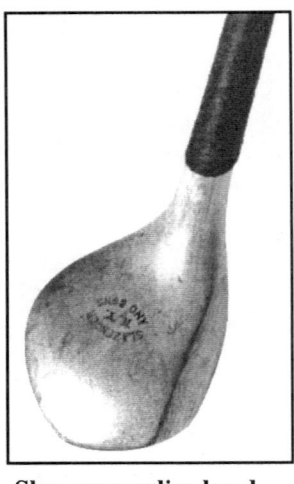

Alex Smith jigger.

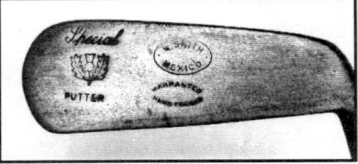

Willie Smith putter from Mexico.

Slazenger splice head driver with New York markings.

```
Putter--Gun metal blade, marked "Slazenger & Sons" ..........$175
Putter--Centraject series, gun metal blade ................$175
Putter--(A U) Triangular head with center shaft .....................$550
Putter--(A) Mallet head, cross hatched face ...........................$100
Putter--Wood socket head, swan neck bent hosel,
  marked Slazenger on toe .........................................................$600
Putter-Center Balance model, head marked "gun metal" .......$150
```

Smalldon, W.G.
Niblick--Tru-Flite model, stainless, line face, swallow CM $35

Smart, J.
[Chicago]
Putter--Smooth face iron blade, Stewart pipe CM $50

Smethwick Golf Company*
[Smethwick Birmingham e]
Cleek--X 33, smooth face, shield CM $75
Mid Iron--Valor series, line face, bench wheel CM $75

Smith, Alex+
[Nassau, later Wykagyl, NY; US Open Champion]

Wood Shafted Golf Club Value Guide

      Driver--Socket head, Nassau mark $100
*   Jigger--Smooth face, name in circle $60
      Mashie--(D) Baxpin, made by Wilson $150
      Named Irons--Alex Smith irons, name in oval,
      scored face .... $50 each

Smith, C. Ralph
[W. Middlesex e; later U.S.]
      Mashie--Pipe brand, line face $45
      Lofter--Center shafted anti-shank style, smooth face $750
      Putter-(A,B) Medalist model, tapered back, square grip $125

Smith, E.
[Halifax e]
      Mashie--(B) Smith model (anti-shank), name in small oval,
      smooth face $150

Smith, G.F.
[Amateur golfer and patentee of the goose neck anti-shank iron]
      Mashie--(B) G.F. Smith model (anti-shank), hollow back,
      line face, made by D. Anderson $200

Smith & Sons, J. C.*
[Monifieth s]
      Named Irons--Line face, Stewart pipe CM $45

Smith, Willie+
[Chicago, Mexico, et. al.; US Open Champion]
I   Putter--Marked 'W. Smith, Mexico', Millar thistle brand CM $150

Smith, W.B.
      Sammy--Approach Eagle model, dot face $60
      Putter--Long blade and hosel, pointed toe, shallow face $150

Smith, W.P.*
[London]
      Putter--(A) Maxmo model, mallet head $125

Smith, Herd & Yeoman
[Chicago]
      Iron-Stewart pipe model, name in arc, smooth face $150

'Southern Cross'
[Australian made]
    Mid Iron--Stainless, dot face, constellation CM $75

Somerville, Andrew
[Dunbar s]
    Driver--(S) Transitional splice head $500
    Cleek--Smooth face $200

Spalding & Brothers Company, A.G.*+
[Chicopee, MA, London e and Dysart s; Spalding quickly became the leading supplier of golf equipment in the US due to their established sports marketing network. They entered the British market about 1900. Spalding produced a seemingly infinite number of combinations of markings and club types not all of which can be itemized here]

◇◇Spalding (block letters) series
*   Driver-(S) Bulger type splice head $400
    Cleek--Smooth face $150

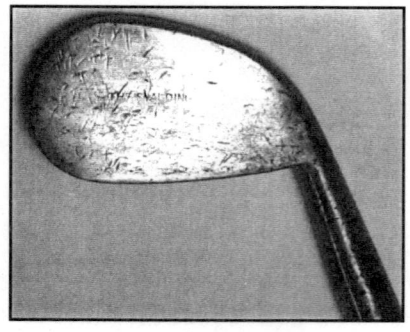

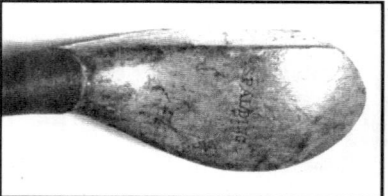

Driver from the earliest 'Spalding' series.

The Spalding driving niblic.

    Iron--Smooth face $125
    Mashie--Smooth face long blade $150
    Niblic--Small head, smooth face $850
    Putting Cleek--Iron blade $200

◇◇'The Spalding' series
    Driver--Splice head $150-300
    Brassie--Splice head $150-300

Wood Shafted Golf Club Value Guide

*100	Cleek--Smooth face, Carruthers hosel $150
	Cleek--(U) Cran model, wood face $600-900
	Cleek--Diamond back, gun metal, smooth face $125
	Driving Mashie--Smooth face $100

    Cleek--Smooth face, Carruthers hosel $150
*100 Cleek--(U) Cran model, wood face $600-900
    Cleek--Diamond back, gun metal, smooth face $125
    Driving Mashie--Smooth face $100
*   Driving Niblic--The Spalding series, large oval head,
    smooth face $2,750
    Iron--Convex back, smooth face $125
    Lofting Mashie--(U) Center shafted, round head $3,250
    Mashie--Short heavy blade, smooth face $100
    Niblic--Smooth concave face, medium size round head $500
    Niblic--Large head, smooth face $150
    Putter--Extra deep face, gun metal blade $250
    Putter--Gun metal diamond-back blade $175
    Putting Cleek--Gooseneck iron blade $175

◇◇'Spalding Special' series
[Name can appear in block letters or more infrequently in a more stylized font, almost script]

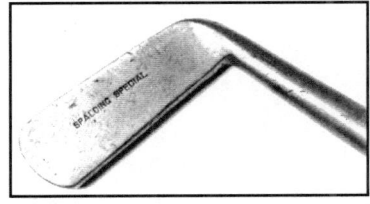 

Gun metal putter from 'Spalding Special' series.

                                    Mashie from the "Vardon' series.

    Driver--Splice head, name in script $300
    Driver--Horace Rawlins stamp, deep face splice head,
    Spalding Special shaft $350
    Cleek--Name in block letters $125
    Driving Iron--Name in script $250
    Iron--Name in arc, smooth face $250
    Mashie--Name in block letters $250
    Lofter--Name in block letters $275
    Putter--Name in script, gun metal blade $225
*   Putter--Name in small block letters gun metal blade $200

◇◇Vardon series

Pete Georgiady's

    Driver--Small splice head $250-400
    Brassie--Short splice head $250
    Cleek--Name in small oval, diamond (X) face scoring $125
    Driving Mashie--Smooth face $125
    Jigger--Smooth face $100
    Lofting Mashie--Smooth face $125
    Mashie Iron--Smooth face, short blade $125
100 Mashie--Line face $75
    Mid Iron--Line face, shaft stamped with Vardon autograph ..$150
    Mid Iron--Smooth face $125
    Mid Iron--Line face $75
    Niblic--Small heavy head, smooth face $500
    Putter--Iron blade $150
    Putting Cleek--Offset iron blade $100

◇◇Other Early Club model lines

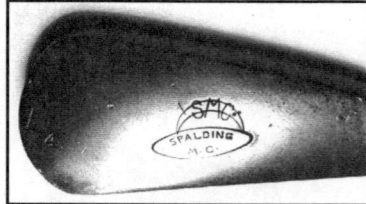 

Mashie from the 'S.M.Co.' series showing both marks.

Putter from the series with the oldest 'baseball' mark.

◇Clan series
    Driver--Splice head $450
    Driver--Socket head $200
    Cleek--Juvenile model, smooth face, stamped shaft $250
    Lofter--Smooth face, stamped shaft $300
    Mashie--Smooth face, name in block letters $300
    Niblick--Smooth face, medium size head $500
    Putter--Iron blade $400

◇'Spalding' in a horseshoe shaped mark
    Brassie Niblick--Splice head, horseshoe CM $1,250
    Spoon--"A.G. Spalding & Bros." in horseshoe $750

Wood Shafted Golf Club Value Guide

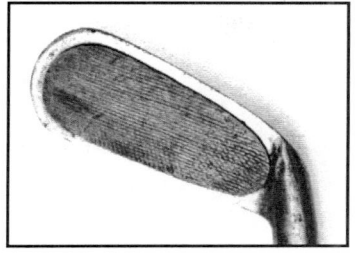 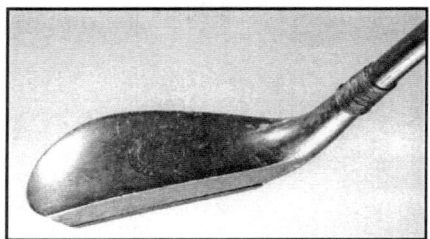

The Cran patent cleek with wood face.

Long head wood putter (with baseball mark on crown of head).

Iron--Smooth face, "Syracuse" in arc shaped CM $125
Iron--Spalding name in horseshoe $250

⬦S.M.Co. series
    Driver--Splice head $400
    Brassie--Splice head $400
    Cleek--Smooth face, short hosel $300
    Iron--Smooth face, long hosel $300
*   Mashie--Smooth face $250
    Niblic--Smooth concave face $650
    Putter--Iron blade $300

⬦Single outline 'baseball' mark
    Cleek--Smooth face, shaft stamp $200
    Mashie--Smooth face, shaft stamp $250
    Lofter--Smooth face, knurled hosel $300
*   Putter--Gun metal blade $250

⬦Doubleline 'baseball' mark

 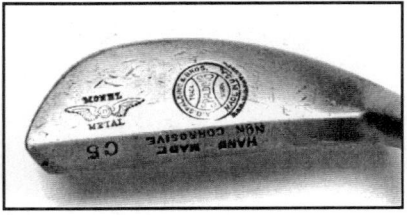

Deep face gun metal putter from the Crescent series.

Monel metal putter with baseball mark.

Pete Georgiady's

	Driver--Model F, socket head	$90
	Cleek--(U) Cran model, wood face	$600-900
	Cleek--Flat diamond back shape, 'baseball' CM, smooth face	$150
100	Iron--(U) Spring face	$750-1,000
	Jigger--Model A 17	$65
	Lofter--Model B 3, deep smooth face, short blade	$100
	Mashie Niblic--Model N4, Monel	$55
	Mid Iron--Model V, heavy line face	$50
	Putter--Model D, bent neck	$60
*	Putter--(L) Long slender splice head	$1,650

◇◇Crescent series

Brassie--Socket head, 'ball' CM $80
Cleek--Flat diamond back shape, 'baseball' CM, smooth face $150
Lofter--Baseball CM, smooth face $80
Mid Iron--Smooth face $45
* Putter--Deep face, gun metal blade, 'baseball' CM $250
Putter--H model, small steel head, similar to BV model $175

◇◇Morristown series

Driver--Bulger spliced head $275
Driver--Morristown series, splice head $175
Brassie--Small splice head $175
Cleek--Morristown series, 'ball' mark, smooth face $60
Driving Mashie--Morristown series, smooth face, shaft stamp $100
Niblic--Morristown series, round head, smooth concave face, shaft stamp $500
Putter--Morristown series, gun metal blade $95

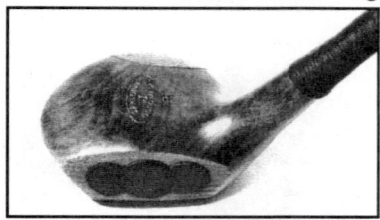

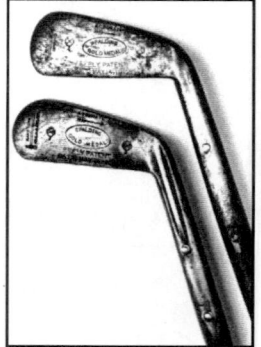

The Jacobus Rigden patent driver with three wood plugs in the face.

The two hosel styles found on **Seely patent irons.**

Wood Shafted Golf Club Value Guide

◇◇Gold Medal series
      Driver--Model C, shaft stamp $60
      Driver--(U) Model J, compressed socket head $400
      Driver--(U) Model J, socket head, 3 wood plugs in face $275
*100   Driver--(U) Model JR, Rigden backweight,
      3 circular Jacobus wood face blocks $300
      Driver--(U) Model R, brass backweight $125
      Driver--(U) Model RN, brass backweight $125
      Driver--Model 7, real ivory insert, 2 screws $400
      Driver--Model 18, splice head, oval stamp $150
      Driver--Steel face insert, 4 screws $150
      Cleek--Carruthers hosel, centraject back $100
      Driving Iron--Model B93, flange sole, dash face $200
*100   Iron--(U) Seely model, with reinforcing ridge $650-850

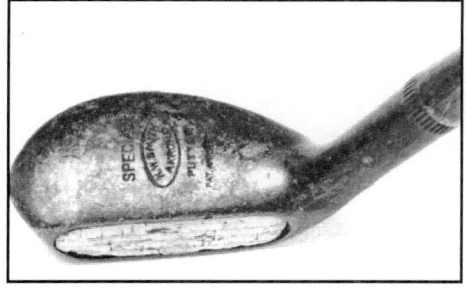

Model G putter with cork face from the 'Gold Medal' series.

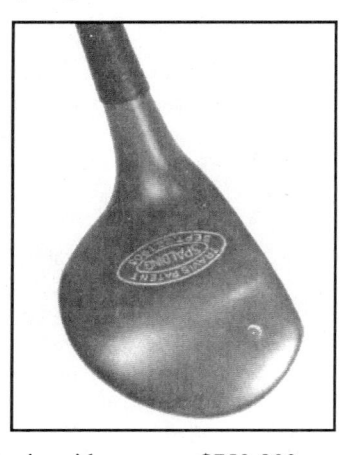

Travis model socket driver.

*100   Iron--(U) Seely model, without reinforcing ridge $750-900
      Iron--RS model, rounded sole $125
      Mashie--(U) Model DF, angled two surface face $600
      Mashie--(D) Model 1 Dedstop, corrugated face,
      2 roses CM $100
      Mashie--Right angled face lines (90 degree) $65
      Mashie--Hammer CM near toe $50
      Mashie Niblic--(U) Park's 3-step face $3,250
      Mashie Niblic--Model 3, Foulis model with patent date $250
      Mashie Niblic--Model series, Foulis style concave face $125
      Mid-iron--(U) Leitch patent with raised ridge on

	center of back, dash face	$150
100	Mid Iron--(U) Fitted with Lard perforated metal shaft	$2,000-4,000
	Mid Iron--Model F, hammer CM, smooth face	$60
	Mid Iron--Model 2, dot face, hammer & roses CMs	$45
	Niblick--Model D, smooth face	$75
*	Putter--(U) Model C, brass mallet head, cork face insert	$1,250
	Putter--Model BV, Brown-Vardon style, oval hosel, rounded top to back, dot face	$250
	Putter--Model G, gun metal blade, oval stamp	$75
	Putter--Model H, rounded back	$150
	Putter--Model LW, broad sole, 2 roses CM	$150
	Putter--Model 2, 2 roses and hammer CMs	$45
	Putter--Model 6, 2 roses and hammer CMs	$45
	Putter--Model 9, gun metal, flange sole, oval stamp	$65
	Putting Cleek--Model C, straight stamp, hammer CM	$65

◇◇Miscellaneous clubs

**	Driver--Socket head, leather insert slotted into head	$500
*	Driver--(U) Travis patent, "P", "S" or "R" stamped on sole	$175
	Driver--(U) Duncan model, one piece sole plate & backweight, socket head	$85
	Driver--S925W model, socket head	$65
	Driver--Autograph, Maltese cross insert, stripe top	$65
	Driver--Spalding Autograph, stripe top	$50
	Driver--Model F, small socket head	$50
	Driver--Fire Brand, arm holding torch CM	$150
	Brassie--Socket head, Cyril Walker autograph	$100
	Brassie--Model C, socket head, straight line stamp	$50
100	Brassie--(U) Model EM three piece splice	$200-400
	Brassie--(U) Duncan model, one piece sole plate backweight	$125
	Brassie--(U) Skooter model, brass sole edge plate	$275
	Brassie--(U) Barrel sole, Dalgleish pattern, fiber face insert	$300
	Brassie--(U) Model R925, Autograph, Rigden brass backweight	$75
	Brassie--Autograph marked head, raised ring shaft (looks like pseudo bamboo)	$1,500
	Spoon--(U) Model EMS, three piece splice	$425
	Spoon--Model 16, socket head	$55
	Driving Mashie--Deep face, two roses & hammer CMs,	

dot face $200
Iron--Indian head CM $80
Mashie--Model 3, bronze head, 2 roses & hammer CMs,
circle dot face $300
Mashie--Model M3, Monel, winged ball CM $60
Mashie Niblic--Model C 4, smooth concave face,
boat shaped head $250
Mashie Niblic--Model G-3, Monel, round sole,
super gooseneck hosel $400
Mashie Niblic--Name in block letters, Foulis style in bronze. $350
Mid Iron--Model Irons series, Autograph, hammer CM,
dot face $40
Niblic--Fire Brand 9-H, hand holding torch CM, line face $50
Niblic--Heather series, line face, 2 roses CM $40
Sky Iron--Model M-8, two roses & hammer CMs,
wide line face $75
Putter--Model 1-H, Fire Brand, hand holding torch CM $75

◇◇Aluminum clubs

Driver--(A S) Model D $250
Driver--(A U) Vehslage patent, marked "The Spalding",
wood face $2,500
Brassie--(A S) 1U model, fairway club $300
Brassie--(A) 3 U model, fairway club $300
Brassie--(A S) B model, fairway club $250
Cleek--(A S) C model, fairway club $250
Cleek--(A) CC model, ... $750-1,000
Cleek--(A) Gold Medal series, spring face $750-1,000
Driving Iron--(A S) Model 2, fairway club $250
Lofter--(A S) L model, fairway club $250
Mashie--(A S) M model, fairway club $200
Mid Iron--(A) Fairway club $175
Putter--(A U) American Putter model, Schenectady style,
Dysart anvil CM $250
Putter--(A) CK model, offset mallet head, 'ball' mark $250
Putter--(A) Model 4, 2 roses CM, mallet head $125
Putter--(A) Gold Medal 5 model, mallet head,
lead face insert $300
Putter--(A) HH model, Schenectady style head $150
Putter--(A) RM model, Ray-Mills style head $100
Putter-(A) Fownes-type, long mallet with heel $400

◇◇Deep Groove irons
    Mashie Iron--(D) Forged Model, ribbed face $100
    Mashie--(D) Gold Medal 1 Dedstop, ribbed face,

 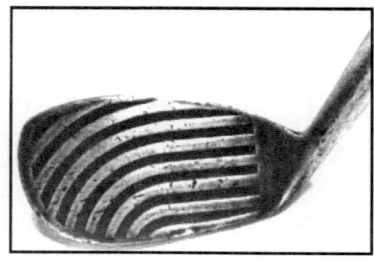

Model 1 Dedstop series mashie niblic with 'waffle' face markings.
Kro-Flite series model F-6 with 'waterfall' pattern deep grooves.

	2 roses CM $100
	Mashie--(D) Gold Medal M 1 Dedstop, ribbed face $100
	Mashie--(D) Stop'Em model, ribbed face $125
	Mashie--(D) Dedstop model C91, ribbed face $100
	Mashie Niblick--(D) Jock Hutchison, Pittsburgh in double oval $150
	Mashie Niblic--(D) Stop'Em model, ribbed face $125
*100	Mashie Niblic--(D) Dedstop 1, waffle face $300
100	Mashie Niblic--(D) Dedstop 6, waffle face $300
	Mashie Niblic--(D) Medal C51, Dedstop, corrugated face $100
	Mashie Niblic--(D) Dedstop model C54, ribbed face $100
	Mashie Niblic--(D) Dedstop model C67, ribbed face $100
	Mashie Niblic--(D) Dedstop model C69, ribbed face $100
	Mashie Niblic--(D) Dedstop model C92, ribbed face $100
	Mashie Niblic--(D) F 6, double waterfall face, crow CM $3,000-4,000
100	Mashie Niblic--(D) F 6, waterfall face, crow CM $250-400
	Mashie Niblic--(D) F 6, corrugated face, crow CM $150
	Mid Iron--(D) Forged Model, ribbed face $100
	Niblic--(D) Medal C98, Dedstop, corrugated face, 2 thistles CM $100
	Niblic--(D) Stop'Em model, ribbed face $175
	Pitcher--Model M 7, ribbed face $125
	Pitcher--(D) Dedstop Kro-Flite, ribbed face $100

Wood Shafted Golf Club Value Guide

    Pitcher--(D) F 7, waterfall face, crow CM $250-400
    Pitcher--(D) F 7, corrugated face, crow CM $150
    Pitcher--(D) F 17, waterfall face, crow CM $250-500
    Sky Iron--(D) Dedstop Kro-Flite, ribbed face $150

◇◇Putters not belonging to other model series
    Putter--A.G. Spalding 10, Schenectady style, wood head,
    brass face plate $200-350
    Putter--(A) Model 4, 2 roses CM, mallet head $125
    Putter--(A) Gold Medal 5 model, mallet head,
    lead face insert $300
*   Putter--Model C5, small Monel mallet head with
    peaked crown, Monel and 'baseball' CMs $400
    Putter--Model BV, Brown-Vardon style, oval hosel,
    rounded top to back, dot face $250
    Putter--CH (Chicopee) model, iron, center shaft, dot face . $250

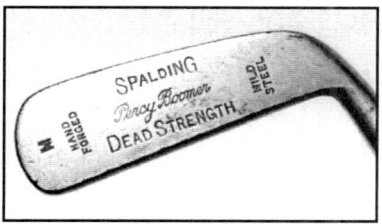
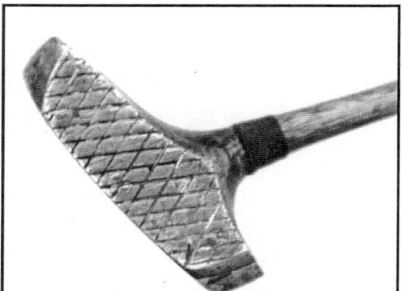
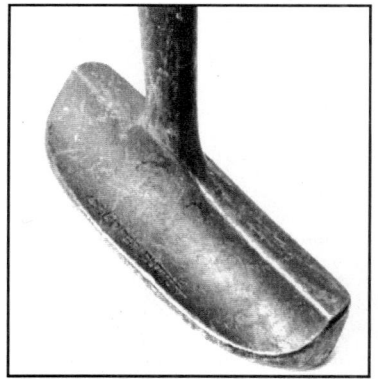
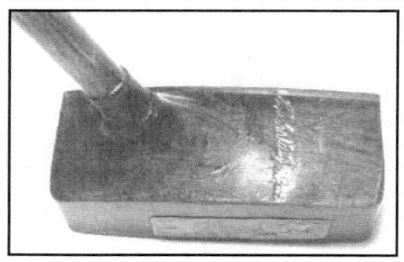

Dead Strength model putter.   **Model R wood Schenectady putter.**
Chicopee model putter.   **'Travis model' (WT) putter.**

	Putter--CH model, bronze center shaft, dot face $300
	Putter--(A) CK model, offset mallet head, 'ball' mark $250
	Putter--Crescent series, H model, small steel head, similar to BV model $175
*	Putter--Dead Strength model, blade, slightly rounded face $125
*	Putter--HB model, center shaft, dot face $200
	Putter--(A) HH model, Schenectady style head $150
	Putter--LF model, mallet head, 2 roses CM $250
	Putter--LW model, broad sole, 2 roses CM $150
100	Putter--O 'Olympic' model, pointed toe, curved top edge, square solid steel shaft $600-1,000
*	Putter--R model, wood Schenectady-type, brass sole plate, wide boat shape $200-350
	Putter--(A) RM model, Ray-Mills style head $100
*	Putter--WT (Walter Travis) model, square wood Schenectady-type head, brass face................................. $250-350
	Putter--Travis model, extra-long square wood head, brass face $450
	Putter--(A U) American Putter model, Schenectady style, Dysart anvil CM $250
**	Putting Baffy--Mallet head with large brass backweight ... $ 675

◇◇Forged Model series

Cleek--Forged Model, Carruthers hosel, name in script $100
Mashie--Forged Model L9, heavy line face $60
Mashie Iron--(D) Forged Model, ribbed face $100

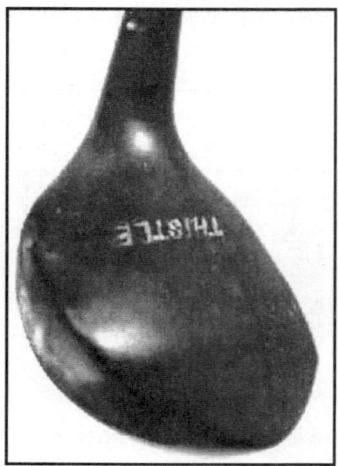

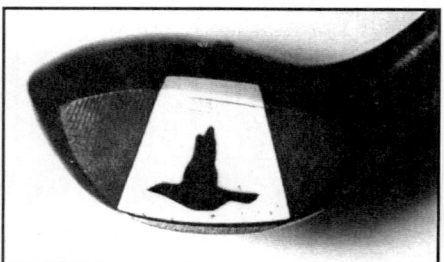

Thistle model driver.

Kro-Flite series driver with black and white flying crow face insert.

Wood Shafted Golf Club Value Guide

    Mid Iron--(D) Forged Model, ribbed face $100
    Niblic--M 9 model, line face $40
    Sky Iron--M 8 model, line face $60

◇◇Dundee series
    Woods--Socket head, plain face .... $50 each
    Iron clubs-Dot face .... $35 each
    Putter--Iron blade $35

◇◇Thistle clubs
*   Woods--Socket head, "Thistle" italicized .... $40 each
    Driver--As above, brown composition head,
    wood pin through neck $400
    Iron clubs--Line face, "Thistle" italicized between 2
    thistle sprig CMs .... $35 each
    Putter--Line face, "Thistle" italicized between
    2 thistle sprigs CM $35
    Mid Iron--Thistle series, made in Australia,
    dot face $50
    Cleek--Name in block letters, thistle plant CM,
    circular dot face $50
    Mashie--Dot face, small thistle plant CM in name oval $65
    Mashie Niblic--Foulis style, small thistle plant CM,
    concave face $150
    Mid Iron--Medal 2, thistle plant CM $40
    Putter--Steel blade, Spalding name in block letters,
    thistle plant & hammer CMs $50

◇◇Symetric Set irons
    #1 through 9-Irons--Stainless, trophy CM .... $30 each
    #10 (Putter)--Stainless blade, offset head $35
                                     Matched Set--7 or more irons

 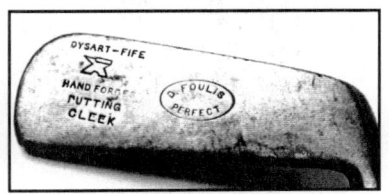

Sky iron (in Standard Spalding OEM markings).

        Dysart-Fife putter from the Spalding plant in Scotland.

Pete Georgiady's

in sequence .... $45 per club

◇◇Kro-Flite "F Series"
    Driving Iron--F 1, 4-line face $40
    Mid Iron--F 2, 4-line face $35
    Mid Mashie--F 3, 4-line face, crow CM $40
    Mashie Iron--F 4, 4-line face $40
    Mashie--F 5, 4-line face, crow CM $35
    Mashie--F-5, marked "Junior" $50
    Driving Iron--F 1, 4-line face $40
    Mashie Niblic--(D) F 6, double waterfall face,
    crow CM $4,000
    Mashie Niblic--(D) F 6, waterfall face, crow CM $400
    Mashie Niblic--(D) F 6, corrugated face, crow CM $80
    Pitcher--(D) Dedstop Kro-Flite, ribbed face $75
    Pitcher--(D) F 7, waterfall face, crow CM $250-400
    Pitcher--(D) F 7, corrugated face, crow CM $150
    Pitcher--(D) F 17, waterfall face, crow CM $250-500
    Sky Iron--F 8, 4-line face, crow CM $75
    Niblic--F 9, 4-line face, crow CM $40
    Putter--F 10, 4-line face, crow CM $45

◇◇Kro-Flite series
*100   Driver--Socket head, flying crow insert $200
        Brassie--Socket head, fancy face insert of flying crow $200
        Spoon--Socket head, flying crow insert $200
*   Sky Iron--(D) Dedstop Kro-Flite, ribbed face $150
        Sky Iron--K 8, line face $65
        Putter--Kro-Flite series, RF model, long hosel $50
        Putter--Juvenile, marked J $40

        Nos. P1 through P9-Irons--PGA brand (large letters),
        line face, crow CM .... $35 each
        Nos. P10 (Putter)--PGA brand (large letters), thick
        soled blade, crow CM $40
        Putter--9, PGA brand, crow & long golf club CMs, dot face $40

        Numbered Irons--Stainless, flying crow CM,
        marked "Pat. Applied For" .... $30 each
        Numbered Irons (1-9)--Stainless, dot face,
        flying crow CM $25

Wood Shafted Golf Club Value Guide

#10 (Putter)--Stainless, dot face, flying crow CM $40
#19 or 29-Iron--Stainless, extra-large head,
flying crow CM .... $65 each
Matched Set--6 or more clubs in sequence .... $40 per club

#1 through 9-Iron--Stainless, Sweet Spot Irons, dot face,
 flying crow CM, registration number .... $25 each
#10 (Putter)--Stainless blade, offset head $30
#19 or 29-Iron--Stainless, Sweet Spot Irons, dot face,
extra-large head, flying crow CM, registration number . $45 each
Matched set--6 or 9 clubs in numerical sequence
with matching registration numbers .... $50 per club

[Robert T Jones, Jr. iron clubs were produced for almost four decades. Wood shaft clubs were made only in 1932. Jones model clubs with wood grain coated steel shafts are frequently found by collectors. They have minimal value because they are not wood shafted but collectors will continue to seek them simply because of their name association. Collector value: $5-15 per club]

100   #1 through 9-Iron--Stainless, Robert T. Jones,
        Jr. signature, dot face, registration number ....$100-200 each
        Matched Set--6 or 9 clubs in sequence with
        matching registration numbers .... $250 per club

[Calamity Jane putters were made from 1932 well into the 1960sthere are at least six design variations from the several manufacturers that copied Jones's famous putter. The two models shown below are most common models with Kro-Flite markings]

100   Putter--Calamity Jane model, 3 bands of

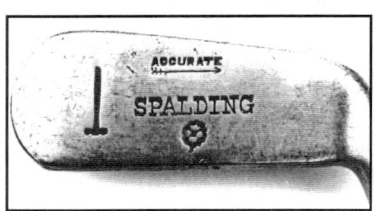

Junior niblic with Spalding script name.

Juvenile iron with single rose and hammer CMs.

whipping on shaft, crow CM $150-300

Calamity Jane steel shaft putter $75-150

◇◇Clubs produced in Britain
- Cleek--(A S) Model CI, fairway club $250
- Driving Iron--Tong brand, tongs CM, line face $100
- Iron--Gold Medal series 'push iron', anvil CM $90
- Lofter--Tong brand, tongs CM $125
- Mashie--Crescent series, hammer CM $60
- Mashie--Gold Medal series, anvil CM, roses CM $50
- Mid Iron--Large thistle CM, dot face $50
- Sammy--Marked "Dysart Fife", weighted back $90
- Putter--Anvil CM, iron blade $50
- Putter--Anvil CM, deep face iron blade, name in script $125
- Putter--Crescent series, iron blade 'ball' CM $75
- Putter--(A U) American Putter model, Schenectady style . $250
- Putter--Parputta model, iron blade, reverse (hollowed) musselback, anvil CM $300
- Putter--Dead Strength model, blade, slightly rounded face $125
- Putter--Argyle series, anvil mark, bent neck blade $50
- Putter--SR model, round sole, anvil CM $125
- Putting Cleek--Tong Brand, iron tongs CM $150
- Putting Cleek--Dysart series, iron blade $50

◇◇Juvenile and Junior clubs
- Driver--Name in block letters $35
- Brassie--Name in block letters $35
- * Iron--Dot face, hammer & single rose CMs $40
- Mashie--Smooth face, hammer & single rose CMs $40
- Mashie--Model C, smooth face, name in arc $45
- * Niblic--Line face, junior $60
- Putter--Hammer & single rose CMs $50
- Putter--Kro-Flite series, juvenile, marked J $50

Sparling, George
- Putter--Gun metal blade, laminated bamboo shaft $200

Spence & Gourlay*
[St. Andrews]
- Iron--Model 1, shamrock CM, dot face $60

Wood Shafted Golf Club Value Guide

    Lofter--Small oval head, face scoring in shape of daisy $150
    Mashie--Model 12, shamrock CM, dot face $60
    Mashie--Smith-style (anti-shank), made for
    Morris & Youds, line face $200
    Mashie Niblick--(D) Varsity model, corrugated face $125
    Niblick--Heavy medium head, shamrock CM, dot face $60
    Niblick--Dreadnought size head, club pip and acorn CMs,
    dot face $100
    Niblick--Model 10, diamond back, dot face $75
    Putter--Dot face, Forgan crown CM $50

Spence, James*
[St. Andrews; successor to the Spence & Gourlay firm, he sold out to Forgan in 1920]

    Mashie--Line face, flagstick CM $50
    Mashie Niblick--Oval head, line face, flagstick CM $50
    Niblick--Giant model, flagstick CM $125
    Numbered Irons--Line face, JS in oval CM $40
    Putter--Blackwell model, iron blade $75
    Putter--Giraffe model, long thin hosel and blade $125
    Putter--Blackwell model, flagstick CM $75
    Putter--100 model, dot face, flagstick CM $65

Spittal, David
    Driver--(U) Socket head, half metal, half wood shaft $750

'Sport-Mart'
    Numbered Irons--Chrome, line face $20

Sports & Games Association, Ltd.
[London]
    Iron clubs--Royal Ajax series, line face .... $60 each

'Sports Depot'
[Liverpool e]
    Iron clubs--Royal series, stainless, dot face $45

Sportsman's Emporium, The*
[Glasgow & Edinburgh]
    Putting Cleek--Long smooth face blade, Gibson star CM ... $75

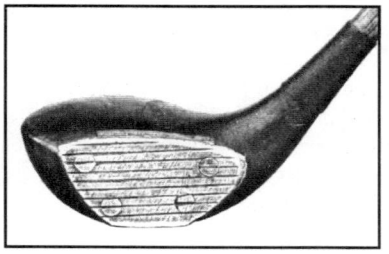

Sprague steel face driver.

Stadium Golf Company Wonder model putter.

Stadium Golf Company Korecta series iron.,

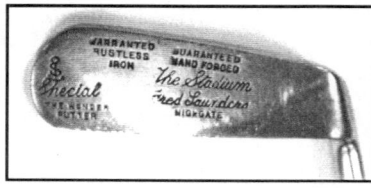

Sprague, C.S.
[Boston, MA]

	Driver--Socket head, steel plate over face w/ 4 screws, insert underneath $250
	Driver--Socket head, patent Kempshall Pyralin face $300
	Mashie--Standard series, deep face, line face $60
	Mashie--Stewart pipe CM, dot face $65
100	Putter--(A U) Block shaped head with ball-in-socket adjustable hosel $2,500
	Putter--Stewart bar back model, dash face $125

Stadium Golf Company*
[Bermondsey, London]

	Brassie-(B) Loft-em model, concave sole $200
	Brassie-Baffy--(B) Dunlewy model, pointed sole $350
	Mid Iron--Model 21, stainless, line face, anchor-S CM $50
	Mid Iron--(B) Mystic model, round sole, highly offset hosel $300
	Mashie Niblick--Model 60, dot face $50
	Niblick--(B) Dunlewy model, dot face, pointed sole $250
	Niblick--Korecta 8 model, anchor-CM, target face $250
	Niblick--Model P8, oversize head, line face $80
100	Scuffler--(B) Rivers-Zambra model approach putter $150-200
	Putter--(B) Per Whit model, round blade, solid back $500
	Putter--(B) Korecta model, raised top edge with aiming

Wood Shafted Golf Club Value Guide

    notch, line face anchor CM $250
    Putter--Model 5, offset blade, square handle, anchor-S CM $60
    Putting Cleek--Model 55, steel blade, anchor-S CM $50
    Putting Cleek--Model 2, steel blade, anchor-S CM $60
    Numbered Irons--The Nacky model .... $50 each

'Standard'
[Model name used on certain Spalding series and B.G.I. series irons]
    Cleek--Juvenile smooth face, made by B.G.I. $75

Standard Golf Company*
[Sunderland e; founded by an engineer adept at working in metal, this company strictly produced aluminum clubs. The fame of their creator, Sir William Mills, caused these clubs to be known throughout the world as Mills clubs and they were the one of the first brands to be offered in "matched sets"]

All clubs are made from <u>aluminum</u> and, except for the 1896 Standard model, have a serial number stamped on the crown of the head. Fairway-type clubs are listed here as 'brassies' although Mills catalogs and advertisements randomly describe them as brassies, spoons or by the names of the iron clubs they emulated.

    ◇◇Drivers, brassies and baffies
*   Driver--(B) Standard model, 3 wood blocks in face,
         weight markings on crown of head, no serial number $600-800
    Driver--DA model, wood face $350
    Driver--DB model, wood face $350
    Driver--WD model, wood face $300
    Brassie--BA model, wood face $350
    Brassie--BB model, wood face $350
    Brassie--WB model, wood face $300
    Brassie Spoon--BGS, wood blocks in back $275
    Baffy--BSX, hook face $500
    Baffy--BSX2, hook face $450
    Baffy--BSZ model $300

    ◇◇BS series semi-long nose clubs
*100   Brassie--BS1 model $350
    Brassie--BS2 model, ... $350
    Brassie--BSD1 model, ... $200

Brassie--BSD1 1/2 model $225
Brassie--BSD2 model $200
Brassie--BSD2 1/2 model $225
Brassie--BSD3 model $300

◇◇CB and MSD series short headed clubs
    Brassie--CB1 model $200
    Brassie--CB1 1/2 model $200
    Brassie--CB2 model $250
    Brassie--CB3 1/2 .... $500
*   Brassie--MSD1 model $100-200
    Brassie--MSD1 1/2 model $125-225
    Brassie--MSD2 model $125-175
    Brassie--MSD2 1/2 model $150-200
    Brassie--MSD3 model $175-250
    Brassie--MSD3 1/2 model $300-400
    Brassie--MSD4 model $300-400

◇◇Miscellaneous clubs
*   Niblick--NK model $350-500
*100   Duplex Club--RL1 model, 2 sided head $400-600
    Duplex Club--RL1 1/2 model, 2 sided head $400-600
    Duplex Club--RL2 model, 2 sided head $400-600
    Duplex Club--RL2 1/2 model, 2 sided head $400-600

◇◇Putters
    Putter--AK model, rectangular head $200-300
    Putter--(S) Braid-Mills model $100-150
    Putter--Braid-Mills-1915 model, mallet head $45-75
    Putter--CS model, Schenectady style $175
    Putter--CSI model, Schenectady style head $200
    Putter--CSA model, Schenectady style head
    with rounded top $200
    Putter--CSD model, duplex Schenectady style head $500

1. Mills 'Standard' driver with wood face.
2. Model BSD1 along side a Model MSD1 (right).
3. Model KL extra long putter
4. Model RL duplex club.
5. Model RBB putter.
6. Model NK niblick.
7. Model Y putter.
8. Model RNG putter.

Wood Shafted Golf Club Value Guide

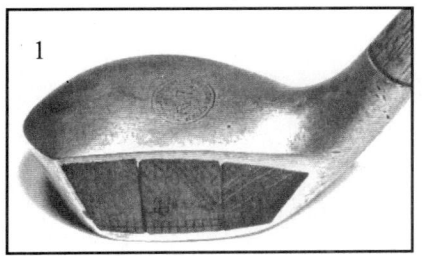
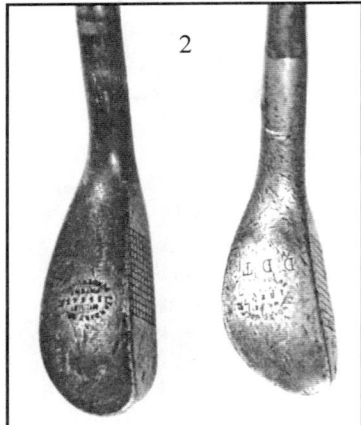
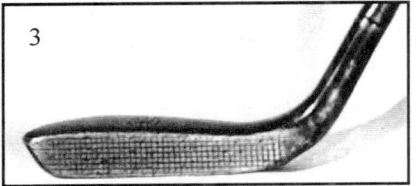
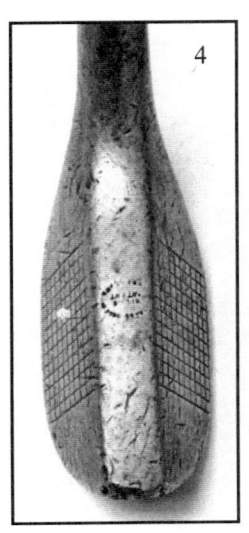
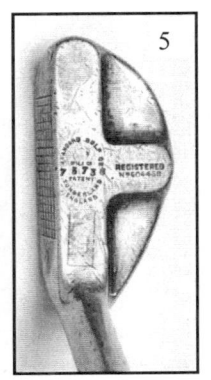
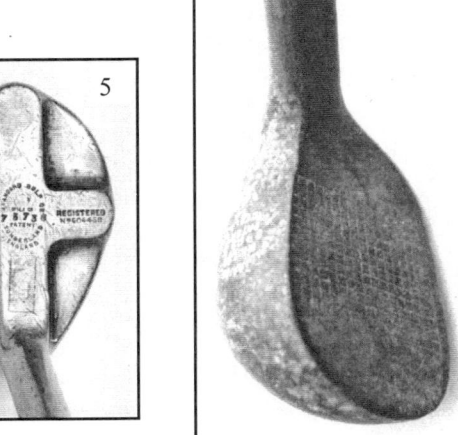
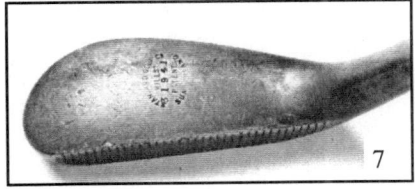
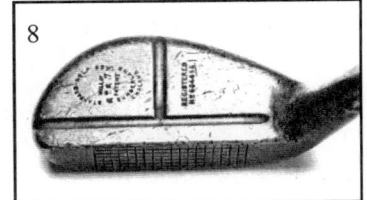

	Putter--CSRA model, Schenectady style head with right angle shaft $600
	Putter--Collins model, Braid-type mallet head $125
	Putter--Cotton-Mills model, mallet head $80
	Putter--Edgar-Mills model, tiny mallet head $100
	Putter--JM model, bent neck, small mallet head $100
	Putter--(L) K model $250-400
*	Putter--(L) KL model, extra long nose $300-500
	Putter--(S) KS model $250
	Putter--(L) L model $250-400
	Putter--MNB model, offset mallet head, truncated back $125
	Putter--MNG model, mallet head $75
100	Putter--Ray-Mills model $45-75
	Putter--RRA model, aiming rib $125
*	Putter--RBB model, top aiming rib $125
	Putter--RBB model, 3 rubber aiming dots (2 red, 1 green) on crown $125
	Putter--RM model, bent neck $100
	Putter--RMG model, gooseneck Ray style $150
	Putter--RMR model, aiming groove $100
	Putter--RNB model, top aiming rib $100
*	Putter--RNG model, top aiming groove $100
	Putter--RRA model, raised aiming T $100
	Putter--RR model, Ray style with raised rib $150
	Putter--RSB model, Ray style with slant back $150
	Putter--RSR model, top aiming groove and bevel $150
	Putter--Rodwell model, large mallet with circular aiming disc $150
	Putter--(S) SB model $300
	Putter--(S) SS model $200
	Putter--WM model, bent neck $100
	Putter--(L) X model, Harold Hilton style $150-250
*100	Putter--(L) Y model $175-250
	Putter--(S) YS model $175-250
	Putter--(L) Z model $200-300
	Putter--Mallet model, cylindrical hammer head $1,250
	Putter-(L) WF model, wood face insert $1,250
	Putter--Steel blade, Birmingham address $125

Steer, J.A.*

Wood Shafted Golf Club Value Guide

[Blackpool]
    Brassie--Large head, fiber face insert $75

Stein, Joseph
[Nashua, NH]
    Spoon--(U) Wooden cleek, marked 'Pat. Pending' $125

Stephens, Fred
[Liverpool e]
    Iron clubs--The Liver model, stork CM, Maxwell pattern, stainless, dash face .... $50 each

Stephens, James
[Liverpool e]
    Mashie--Huyton brand, stainless, dot face $40

Stewart, Rufus
[Australia]
    Niblick--Map of Australia on club back, line face $75

Stewart, Thomas*
[St. Andrews; Stewart was the dean of Scottish iron club makers with a world-wide reputation for excellence. The prime characteristic of all Tom Stewart irons is the pipe cleek mark though a few early ladies and juvenile irons bear a serpent mark]

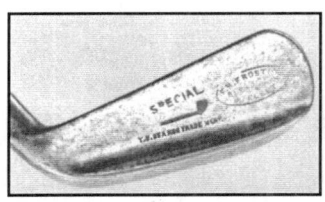 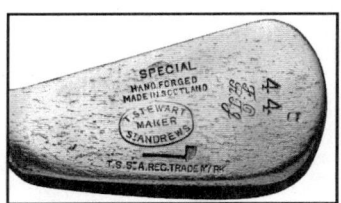

    Stewart flange sole putter.   **Stewart FO/RTJ model iron.**

◇◇Pipe CM with no registration legend underneath; also serpent CM
    Cleek--Extra long heavy blade, smooth face 4 1/2" hosel . $250
    Cleek--Smooth face, short blade, serpent CM $125
    Cleek--Smooth face, Carruthers hosel $175
    Cleek--Smooth face $75

Pete Georgiady's

Iron--Smooth face $65
Iron--(B) Fairlie model (anti-shank) $250
Lofting Cleek (Jigger)--Smooth face $125
Lofting Iron--Smooth face $90
Mashie--Smooth face $90
Niblick--Small head, smooth face, serpent CM $400
Niblick--Small head, smooth face, pipe CM $500
Niblick--Medium head, smooth face $50
Putter--Iron blade $50-90
Putter--Long shallow blade, serpent CM $100
Putter--Gun metal blade $125
Putter--Gun metal blade, serpent CM $125
Putter--Iron blade, bent hosel $50-150

◇◇Pipe CM with trademark registration legend
    Approaching Cleek--Line face, long blade $60
    Bobbie--Banana shaped blade with round sole,
    line face, pipe CM $90
    Cleek--Line or dot face, short Carruthers hosel $100
    Cleek--Scored face $50
    Driving Mashie--Line face $60
    Iron--Smooth face $65
    Iron--(B) Fairlie model (anti-shank), scored face $175
    Iron--Smooth face, musselback $100
    Iron--Dot face $45
    Iron--Diamond back, line face $60
    Jigger--Smooth face $80
    Jigger--Dot face $65
    Jigger--Freddie model, dot face $75
    Lofting Iron--Dot face $60
    Lofting Mashie--Dot face $80
    Mashie--Smooth face $75
    Mashie--(B) Smith model (anti-shank), line face $200
    Mashie--Dot face $45
    Mashie--Flange sole, line face $100
    Mashie--Vardon model, Vardon autograph, line face ... $100
    Mashie--Maxwell pattern, dash face $75
    Mashie--(D) Corrugated face $150
    Mashie Iron--Line face $50
    Mashie Niblick--Oval head, line face $50
    Mashie Niblick--Foulis-type, line face (not concave) $85

Wood Shafted Golf Club Value Guide

Mashie Niblick--(D) Corrugated face $150
Mid Iron--Smooth face $60
Mid Iron--Dot face $45
Mid Mashie--Dot face $60
Mongrel Iron--Rounded head, musselback $100
Mongrel Mashie--Line face $80
Niblick--Giant head, line face $1,500-2,000
Niblick--Medium head, line face $50

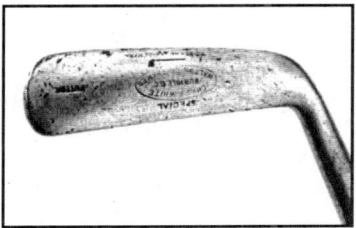

Stewart concentrated back putter.

Stewart "Bassackward" putter.

Niblick--Large head, line face $75
Pitcher--Oval head, line face $65
Push Iron--Line face $85
Sammy--Dot face $75
Spade Mashie--Deep line face $60
Spade Mashie--(D) Corrugated face $175
1-Iron--Dot face, laminated bamboo shaft $100
1-Iron--Dot face, pipe CM $50
2-Iron--Dot face $40
2-Iron--Dot face, 'reject' mark $80
3-Iron--Dot face $40
4-Iron--Dot face $40

*100   #1 through 9-Iron--RTJ model, pipe CM .... $90-140 each
#1 through 9-Iron--RTJ/FO model, pipe CM .... $90-140 each
Putter--(B) Stewart patent, hollow back $350
Putter--Bar back model, bent neck style, dash face $150
Putter--Iron blade $50
Putter--Park style bent neck blade $100
Putter--Offset blade, accurate/arrow CM $65-85

	Putter--Gun metal blade	$75
	Putter--Gem style iron head	$100
*	Putter--Concentrated back	$90
	Putter--Long iron blade, beveled heel and toe	$80
	Putter--Small iron mallet head	$600
*	Putter--Long shallow blade, flange sole	$125
	Putter--Sarazen model, blade	$100
•	Putter--'Bassackward' model, hosel bent backward	$500

[Tom Stewart produced thousands of iron heads for most of the top club makers or maker/professionals of the day. The following list is a general guideline for named clubs from these most common makers or series. Sometimes, smooth face irons can be found from these makers although, on 20th century clubs, this only reflects in only marginally higher value. Numbered irons, as opposed to those with names, from the same makers are worth slightly less.]

Anderson & Blyth irons, scored face	$60 each
D & W Auchterlonie irons, scored face	$60 each
Tom Auchterlonie irons, scored face	$60 each
Alex Campbell irons, scored face	$60 each
Alex Herd irons, line or dot face	$75 each
Herd & Herd irons	$60 each
Herd & Yeoman irons, scored face	$60 each
Jock Hutchison autograph series irons, scored face	$75 each
Robert T Jones, Jr. autograph series irons	$600-1,000 each
Willie Kidd irons, scored face	$60 each
Jack Morris irons, scored face	$85 each
Tom Morris autograph series irons, scored face	$50-100 each
Ray, E (Ted) irons, scored face	$75 each
Ben Sayers irons, scored face	$50-80 each
Alex Smith irons, scored face	$60 each
Alex Taylor irons, scored face	$55 each
Harry Vardon autograph series irons, scored face	$100-150 each
Tom Vardon irons, scored face	$75 each
William Yeoman irons, scored face	$60 each
Jack Youds irons, scored face	$60 each

Stilton, Robert

Driver--(S) Transitional splice head, fiber insert $300

Wood Shafted Golf Club Value Guide

Stirling & Gibson*
[Edinburgh s; forerunner to the firm of William Gibson & Company]
- Cleek--Smooth face, short blade $150
- Mashie--Smooth face, deep face, name in arc $100
- Niblick--Smooth face, medium head $150
- Putter--Bent blade style, 2 small stars and Masonic compass CMs $200

Stoddard, W.
- Niblick--Splice head $100

Stoddart, W.E.
[Various clubs in New York]
- Mashie--Pandy model, 2 flags CM, bottom weighted round sole $100
- Putter--Stoddart model, reverse musselback, thicker on top, flags CM $125

Stoker, J.
- Putter--Triumph model, offset musselback $300

Stokes & Company*
[London]
- Putter--Smith model, smooth face $60

Strachan, W.
- Spoon--(S) Transitional splice head, leather face insert $400

Strauss Toy Store
[New York]
- Iron--Midget size $100

Strath & Beveridge
[New York]
- Playclub--(L) Beech head $8,000

Strath, David*
[St. Andrews]
- Playclub--(L) Dark stain $4,000-6,000
- Spoon--(L) Dark stain $7,500-10,000

Strath, George*+
[St. Andrews, Troon s, later US]
    Playclub--(L) Beech head $6,000
    Driver--(L) Beech head with grassed face $4,000
    Driving Iron--Spalding Gold Medal series, smooth face ... $100
    Mashie--Spalding Gold Medal, deep dot face $100
    Putter--(L) Beech head $4,000
    Putter--Center shaft, crescent shaped head,
    moon/star CM $1,600

Stream-Line Company+
[St. Louis, MO]
    Driver--Melhorn No. 50 model, metal head
    with sole plate $250
    Putter--(A) Melhorn model 10P, rail sole $150

Strong, Herbert
    Iron clubs-Line face, arm holding hammer CM .... $45 each

Stuart, J.G.
    Driver--Socket head $50

Sunderland Golf Company
[Sunderland e]
    Putter--(A) Mills "Mallet" (hammer head) model $1,250

'Supreme'
    Mid Iron--Matched, reg'd, chromed $20

'Sure Winner'
[also see Union Golf Company]
    Driver--Socket head, stripe top, jockey on
    running horse CM $60

'Sure-Thing'
    Putter--(A) Triangular shaped head $100

Sutton, H.L.
[Rhyl w; Sutton Coldfield e]
    Driver--Socket head $75
*   Putter--(A B) Mallet head with 3 rollers in sole $2,500

Swank, David
Mid Iron--Model 7, musselback, line face $35

Sweny, H.R.+

H.L. Sutton aluminum putter with three roller bars in the sole. The rollers were included to prevent 'stubbing.' This club is now illegal.

[Albany, NY]
Driver--(U) Center shafted splice head $2,500-4,000
Driver-Simplex-type, long head $900
Driver--Splice head, heel shafted, marked
Sweny Sporting Goods $200
Cleek--Smooth face, name in block letters $150
Niblick-Smooth face, small head $300

Sykes, William*
[Horbury e]
Mid Iron--The Select, Gourlay moon/star CM, dot face $60

T

Tait, T.
[Leven s]
Driver--Socket head $100
Mid Iron--Smooth face, Millar thistle CM $65
Putter--Thick blade, thistle CM $75

'Taplow'
[John Wanamaker Co., Philadelphia proprietary model name]
Driver--Socket head $60
Pitcher--(D) Corrugated face, hand CM $125

Taylor Brothers

Jigger--Line face $45
Putter--Convex back, bottom half sculpted out $150

Taylor Company, Alex+
[New York retailer; additional clubs listed under ATCO]
Driver--Autograph model, juvenile socket head $60
Mashie--Ravisloe model, smooth face $60
Mashie Niblick--Atco Brand, dot face $40
* Niblic--Model 25, crown CM, large head, flange sole,
dash face $50
Named Irons--Alex Taylor model, Stewart pipe CM,
scored face .... $50 each

Taylor, Josh*
[Richmond, Surrey e; J.H. Taylor's younger brother]

Brassie--(B) 'Bombe model, crossed sabers CM,

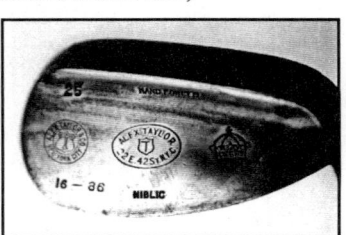

A Burke model 25 niblick marked for **Alex Taylor & Company.**

bulged sole $400
Iron clubs--Mascot model, running greyhound CM ..... $60 each

Taylor, J.H.
[see Cann & Taylor]

Taylor, Thomas
[Chicago]
* Driver--(U) Streamline shape pointed at back $3,000
Mashie--(U) Comb style sole, line face,
Anderson arrow CM $4,000

Tedder, Walter*

Wood Shafted Golf Club Value Guide

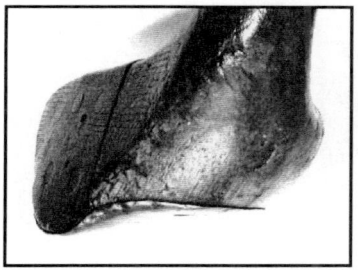 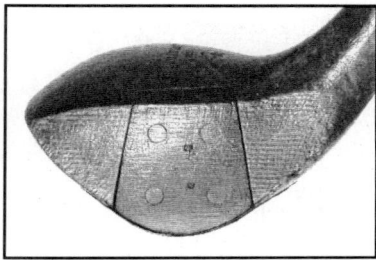

Josh Taylor round sole brassie ("bombe").

[Nottingham e]
    Driver--Socket head $70

Teen & Company, A.*
[Blackheath, London]
*   Driver--(B) Claude Johnson patent, round head $2,000
    Driver--(S) Angus Teen, Maltese cross CM $1,000
*   Cleek--Bar back model, horizontal weight along back ... $1,000
    Approaching Putter--Roundback blade made
    in nickel bronze alloy $400

'Thistle'
[Clubs named Thistle were produced by many makers. Also see George Bussey, Charles Millar, Spalding, Edward Tryon, J. Winton]

'Thistle Brand'
[Made by Charles Millar]
    Brassie--Socket head $75

Thistle Golf Company
[Glasgow; made by Charles Millar]
    Spoon--Marked "Baffie", splice head, face insert $450
    Putter--Thistle Brand, gun metal blade, thistle CM $75

Thistle Putter Company+
[New York]
    Putter--(A U) McDougal T Square model, mallet head
    with aiming T on top $150

    Putter--(A U) McDougal T Square model,

removable weights in head $600

Thistle Special
[also see Edward K. Tryon]
    Jigger--Smooth face, name in oval $75

Thom, Charles
[Shinnecock Hills, NY]
    Driver--Socket head $125
    Approach Iron--Dot face, Spalding accurate mark $100

Thompson Valve Company
    Named Irons--Thompson Valve Steel, line face $45

Thompson, James

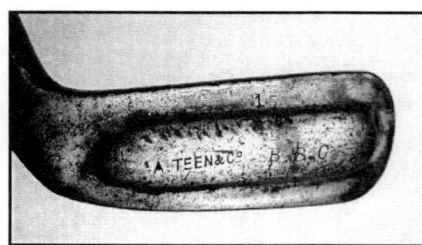

A. Teen & Company "Bar Back Cleek."

A. Teen & Company "Claude Johnson Patent Driver."

Thomas Taylor patent driver.

Wood Shafted Golf Club Value Guide

[St. Andrews]
    Driver--Socket head, hollow back model $225
    Putter--Accurate model, iron blade, bent neck $60

Thompson, J.
    Driver--(S) Transitional splice head $350

Thomson, A.
    Brassie--Socket head $100

Thomson, Jimmy
*100   Woods--(U) Big Ball model, socket head with patent
       extra whippy Limber Shaft .... $300 each

Thornton & Company, Ltd.*

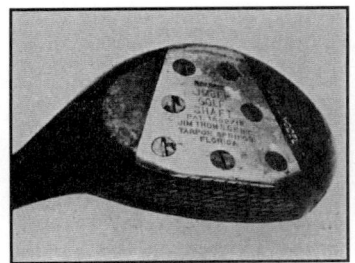
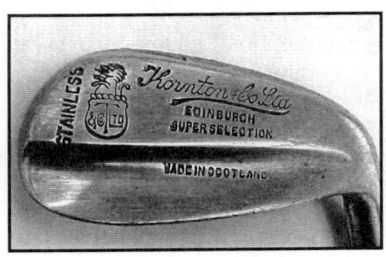

Jimmy Thomson "Limbershaft" driver.
                         Thornton & Company mashie.

[Edinburgh & Glasgow s and other cities]
    Brassie--(S) Beech head, marked for
       Willie Davis, Newport $850
    Driver--Short splice head $150
    Driver--Deep face socket head $125
    Brassie--Socket head, line name stamp $80
    Iron--Stainless, Brodie triangle/BS&A CM $50
*   Mashie--Stainless, dot face, lion on shield CM $50
    Mashie--Wonder series, dot face $40
    Niblick--Giant head $1,500
    Putter--Wonder series bent neck, dash face $50
    Putter--Iron blade, name in block letters $50

Tice Golf Company+

[Albany, NY]
        Driver--(U) Socket head, laminated hickory shaft $1,250

'Timperly'
        Driver--(A B) Baby model, small
        Schenectady style head $600
        Putter--(A B) Baby model, small Schenectady-type head .. $200
        Putter--(A B) Mallet head, very thick hosel $200

Tingey, Albert*
[St. Andrews; Brancaster and Watford e]
        Putter--(S) Beech splice head $1,000
        Putter--(S) Socket head $250

Tollifson, Arner C.
[Lake Geneva, WI, et al]
        Mashie--Pennant CM, Spalding hammer CM $50

Tolmie, J.
[Great Yarmouth e]
        Iron--Smooth face, large head, long blade $300

'Tom Thumb'
        Putter--Chromed blade $50

Toogood, Alfred*
[Chingford e, et al]
        Brassie--Socket head $60

Toogood, Walter*
[Ilkley e, et al]
        Brassie--Splice head $100

Tooley & Sons, A.*
[London and Forest Hill e]
        Driver--Small socket head $100
        Iron--Forest Brand, Maxwell pattern, stainless, trees CM .. $75
        Iron--(B) Two large hemispherical weights
        on back of blade $750
        Jigger--Smooth concave face, trees CM $85
*   Mid Iron--Powerful model, line face, trees CM $250

Wood Shafted Golf Club Value Guide

Putter--(B) Suitall model, Round sole, pointed top edge ... $400

A. Tooley & Sons "Powerful model 3-iron.
Jerry Travers model Schenectady putter.

Trapp, S.
[Wakefield e, et al]
    Driver--Socket head, romil face insert $60

Trapp, Tom
[Croydon e, et al]
    Spoon--Ideal model, socket head, face insert $60
    2-Iron--Dot face, Stewart pipe CM $40

Travers, Jerry+
[Amateur winner of US Open, 1915]
    Putter--Wood Schenectady style head $175
*   Putter--(A) Schenectady head, signature &
    Hartford address on back $200

Travers, T.
[Dublin I, et al]
    Brassie--Socket head $60
    Spoon--Marked "T T" on splice head, shaft stamp $150
    Putter--(B) The Fragile model, wood mallet head ,
    square wood handle $450
    Putter--Narrow scare wood head $300

Travis, Walter
[US & British Amateur Champion; designed many clubs most of which were made by Spalding or Wright & Ditson]
    Putter--Wood Schenectady-type, brass face plate w/

5 screws, marked "The Travis" $250
Putter- Extra long wood Schenectady-type, brass face plate w/
5 screws, marked "The Travis" $450

Tribble, A.
Brassie--Socket head $50

'Truhitol'
[London; brand of Rhys, Spencer & Co.]
Putter--(A) Rectangular head, shafted at heel,
sight line on top $275

'Tru-Line'
[Patent Engineering Company, Chicago]
Putter--(U) Removable aiming rod $2,500

'Tru-Put'
[Made by F.H. Ayers]
Putter--(A) Schenectady style with fiber face insert $250

Tryon Company, Edward K.+
[Philadelphia a]
Driver--Splice head, made by J. & D. Clark $250
Driver--Socket head, keystone CM $65
Iron--Smooth face, marked 'Made in Scotland' $100
Iron--Smooth face, oval marks for J & D Clark and Tryon $200
Mashie--The Imperial series, Wilson hammer CM $25
Mashie--M1 model, line face $40

J.H. Turner "Grampian Range series 1-iron. Each iron was named for a different Scottish mountain in the Grampian Range

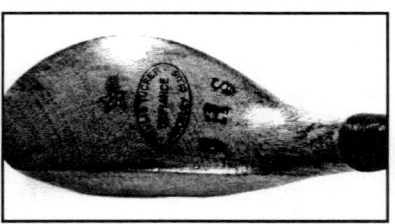

Willie Tucker "Defiance" brand splice head bulger wood.

Wood Shafted Golf Club Value Guide

    Mashie--Thistle model, line face $40
    Putter--Tip-Top model, iron blade, keystone CM $50

Tucker Brothers+
[Brothers Willie and Sam, New York]
    Driver--Defiance model, short splice head $200
    Driver--Defiance model, short socket head $125

Tucker, William+
[Ardsley and Binghamton, NY; Philadelphia, PA]
*   Driver--Defiance brand, Ardsley address, splice head $300
    Driver--(A S) Metal fairway club $300
    Brassie--Defiance brand, splice head $250
    Brassie--Defiance brand, socket head $150
    Approaching Mashie--Defiance brand, smooth face $125
    Driving Cleek--Defiance brand, smooth face $150
    Driving Mashie--Defiance brand, smooth face $100
    Jigger--Defiance brand, smooth face $150
    Lofting Iron--Defiance brand, smooth face $150
    Mashie--Defiance brand, Taylor's model,
    short blade, deep face $150
    Mashie Iron--Defiance brand, smooth face $125
    Mashie Jigger--Line face, name in script $100
    Mid Iron--Defiance brand, smooth face $100
    Niblick--Defiance brand, smooth face, medium head $150
    Putter--Defiance brand, gun metal blade $125
    Putter--Defiance brand, gooseneck $150
    Putting Cleek--Iron blade $100

Tulloch, J.
[Glasgow]
    Driving Iron--Oval name stamp, line face $45
    Mashie--Diamond face, Gourlay moon/star CM $50
    Putter--Made by D. Anderson, model 100, rounded back ... $80

Turnbull, Tom
    Driver--Splice head $90

Turner, John Henry*
[Abingdon e, et al]
    Driver--(B) Centre Balanced model, socket head,

  dowel plug in toe $150
  Driver--Socket head, stripe top $50
  Driving Iron--Smith style anti-shank,
  Sherlock Oxford CM $200
  Putter--(B) Combination wood/metal head, metal hosel $450
  Putter--(A) Block aluminum head like small Gassiat $200
*   Iron clubs--(B) Grampian Range series, mountains
  CM, each club having the name of a Scottish mountain
  in the range .... $100 each

Turpie, George+
[Edgewater, Chicago, et al]
  Mid Iron--Smooth face $60
  Mashie--Line face, MacGregor rose CM $45
  Mashie Niblick--Dot face, Stewart pipe CM $50

Turpie, Harry+
  Mashie--Line face, MacGregor rose CM $50

'Tuxedo'
[Wilson Co. store brand]
  Mashie--Stainless, line face $25

Twine, W.T.
  Driver--Splice head $100

Tyler, R.G. "Tug"+
[Bradford, PA and Muncie, IN]
100 Driver--(U) Ball to Ball model, aluminum and
  wood combination head, wood face plug $125
  Driver--(U) Rear Impact model, aluminum/wood
  combination head $150
  Driver--(U) Tyler Wood model, aluminum/wood
  combination head $150
  Niblick--(U) Center shafted, round face $3,000
  Putter--(U) Wood Schenectady-type, brass face
  w/ 4 screws $150
  Putter--(U) Schenectady-type, wood and aluminum
  combination head $300

U

U.D.S.
    Driver--(A) Ebony Finish model, wood face plugs $250

U.S. Golf Club Manufacturing Company+
[Albany, NY]
    Brassie--Model 139 splice head $350
    Iron--Smooth face, straight line name stamp,
    eagle shaft mark $300
*   Niblick--Oval head, smooth face, shaft stamp $350
    Putter--Gun metal blade, name and city in arc $250

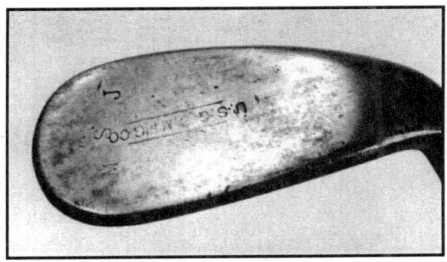

U.S. Golf Manufacturing Company (Albany) niblick.

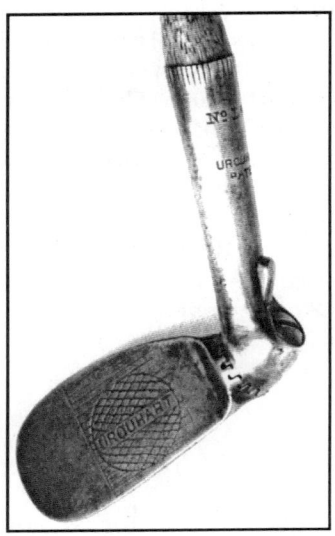

Urquhart Patent adjustable club.

U.S. Golf Manufacturing Company (Westfield) Gold Standard Driver

Thorobred model putter.

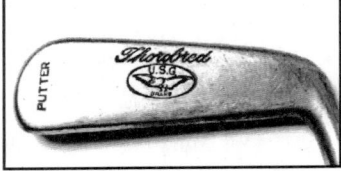

U.S. Golf Manufacturing Company+
[Westfield, MA]
* Driver--(U) Gold Standard series, combination bamboo, hickory and steel shaft, decal on crown $200
  Mid Iron--Holdfast series, line face $50
  Mid Iron--Ajax series, patent sewn grip, braided whipping .. $75
  Putter--Reliance series, eagle CM, flange back $60
* Putter--Thorobred series, stainless blade, eagle in oval CM $50

Underhill, Gardner F.
[New York]
Putter--(A) Mallet head $75
Putter--Model 20, gun metal blade, name in arc $100

Union Golf Company+
[Nashville, TN]
Driver--Shure Winner brand, stripe top,
jockey on horse CM $60
Mid Iron--Shur-Flite series, chromed $40
Niblick--Shure Winner brand, medium size head,
jockey on horse CM, dash face $40
Putter--Shur-Putt model, chromed blade $30

Urquhart, R.*
[Edinburgh; Robert Urquhart and his family worked at perfecting adjustable clubs for over 20 years. Several different adjustment mechanisms exist on Urquhart clubs]

*100   Iron--(B) Adjustable club, name in circle on face ...$1,200-2,500

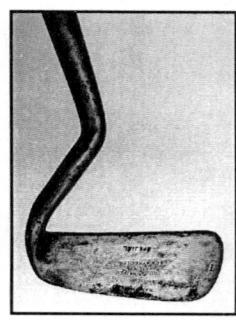

P.A. Vaile patent swan neck iron and swan neck socket head driver.

V

V.L. & A.
[Von Lengerke & Antoine, Chicago retailer]
    Driver--Stripe top socket head $45
    Brassie--Socket head $50
    Mashie--Centraject back, name in double oval $45
    Mashie--Perfect series, centraject back, dot face $45
    Putter--Velanay brand, lion & crown CM $40
    Putter--Blade, own brand $40

V.L. & D.
[Von Lengerke & Detmold, New York retailer]
    Driver--Yankee Dreadnought model, socket head $80
    Approaching Cleek--James Braid model, musselback $80
    Mashie Niblick--Vardon Autograph series,
    Stewart pipe CM, line face $75
    Niblick--Fairlie model, J.D. Dunn make,
    Maltese cross CM $200
    Pitcher-Gibson star CM, dot face $40

Vaile, P.A.
[New Zealand amateur; wrote the book How to Putt *and promoted swan neck clubs]*
    Driver--(B) Swan neck transitional shaped splice head $650
    Brassie--(B) Swan neck socket head $500
    Brassie--(B) Swan neck socket head, fancy face insert $550
*100   Iron--(B) Swan neck, made by Ayers $600
    Putter--(B) Swan neck hosel, gun metal blade $600

Valor Company, The*
[Smethwick e]
    Iron--Line face, benchwheel CM $75
    Niblick--Fairlie-type (anti-shank), dot face $175

Vardon, Harry*
[Worked several English clubs; he produced clubs in his shops at Ganton, and later Totteridge, but most clubs with his name were made by Burke, Spalding, Wilson or Stewart]

Driver--Short splice head, marked Ganton $350
Driver--Splice head, H. Vardon in big letters $300
Brassie--Small splice head $250
Niblick--Small head, smooth face, Anderson arrow CM ... $300
Named Irons--Harry Vardon autograph,
Stewart pipe CM, scored face .... $100 each

Vardon, Tom*
[Ilkley, Sandwich e; Harry Vardon's brother]
Brassie--Bulger splice head, marked "Ilkley" $350
Brassie--Splice head $150
Mashie--Autograph model, deep line face,
Nicoll hand CM $75
Named Irons--Tom Vardon autograph model,
Stewart pipe CM scored face .... $75 each

'Velometer'
[Made by Martin's Velometer Golf Clubs]*
Driver--(B) Socket head, slightly pointed $200-300

Venters, Jack
[Shinnecock Hills, NY]
Brassie--Splice head $400

Vickers, Limited*
[Sheffield e]
Jigger--Stainless, line face, VK CM $50
Mid Iron--Model 19, stainless, VK CM $40
Mashie--Model 6, stainless, VK CM $40
Mashie--Model 6 B, KK CM $40
Mashie--Model 23, rustless, flange sole, dot face $40
Niblick--Model 28, stainless, VK CM $50
Niblick--Mammoth-type, dot face $1,500
Spade Mashie--Stainless, VK CM $45
Putter--Model 20, stainless blade with thickened
sweet spot $75
Putter--Model 14, stainless blade, VK CM $55
Putter--Model 15, stainless straight blade, VK CM $50
Putter--Invicta model 20, gem style, VK CM $100

Victor+

Wood Shafted Golf Club Value Guide

[Chicopee and Boston, MA]
* Iron--Concentric back, smooth face $125
  Mashie--Smooth face, name in circle $125
  Putter--Iron blade $100

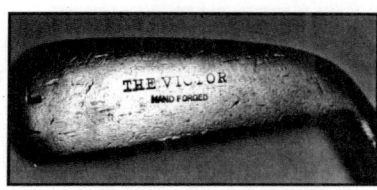

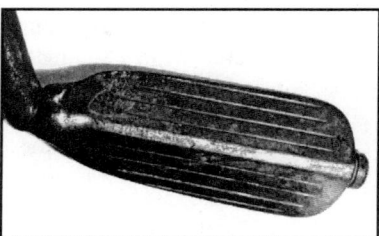

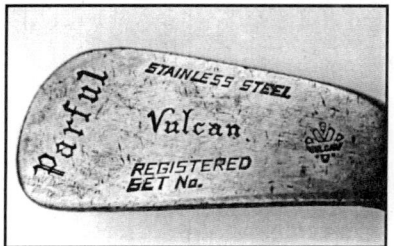

Victor Company iron.

Vories patent iron with selectable hitting lofts

Vulcan Golf Company "Parful" model mashie.

Victor-O.W.C.+
[also see Overman Wheel Co.]
      Cleek--Smooth face, round sole $150
      Niblick--Gun metal, small head, smooth face $2,200
      Putter--Gun metal blade $200

'Vim'
      Driving Iron--Greenfield series, line face, name in script $25
      Spade Mashie--Chrome, name in script $25
      Putter--Thick blade, name in script $30

Vories, I.H.
      Iron--Adjustable iron with 3 selectable hitting faces $2,500

Vulcan Golf Company+
[Portsmouth, OH]
      Driver--Model V-10, stripe top, socket head, face insert $45
      Driver--Socket head, green/white face insert $80
      Driver--Model V-12, socket head, fancy face insert $60
      Driving Iron--Stainless, line face $35

Jigger--Nipper model, long hosel $100
Jigger--"Chipper" 4 Loft $75
Mashie--Pirate series, stainless, line face $30
Mashie--Septem 5, stainless. Line face $30
Niblick--Septem 7, line face $30
Putter--Septem 8, stainless blade $50
Putter--Model 8, long thin blade and hosel $150
Putter--V-V model, 6" hosel $150
Putter--Burma model, sunset CM, dot face blade $35
Putter--Marked "Junior" in script $35
* Set--Parful series, registered set, dot face .... $30 each

W

W W P
[see Wilson Co.]

W W S
[Wilson Western Sports; the name of the Thomas Wilson Company after 1931. See Wilson Co.]

'W.S. Flite'
Niblick--Eagle CM, line face $40

Waggott, Thomas*
[Edinburgh s, et al]
Driver--(S) Splice head, dark stain $1,000
Driver--Short splice head $150

'Wales'
Putter--Line face, chromed blade $20

Walgreen Company
[Chicago]
Numbered Irons--Chromed head, line face .... $20 each

Walker, Cyril
Spoon--MacGregor model A733 .... $100

Wood Shafted Golf Club Value Guide

Walker, George
    Driver--Stripe top socket head $45

Walker, J.
    Playclub--Thick head, golden finish $5,000
    Putter--(L) Beech head, dark color $4,000

Walker, Thomas
    Driver--(S) Bulger splice head $400
    Long Spoon--(S) Well dished face $900

Wallace, S.B.
    2-Iron--Talisman model, large spade pip CM, line face $30

Wallis & Fulford
[Brough e]
    Driver--(B) Double V splice(2-axis) $750

Wallis, Willie
[Brough e]
    Niblick--Star Maxwell model, Gibson star CM,
    diamond/dot face $50
    Putter--Small steel mallet head (like Donaldson Bunny
    with no inserts) $150

Wanamaker Company, John D.
[New York-Philadelphia retailer]
    Driver--Taplow model, socket head $50

 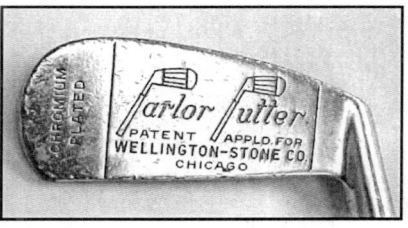

Way & Ross iron from the year the pair partnered in Detroit in 1916.
Parlor Putter club, which came with the "parlor Putter" smoking stand.

Brassie--Socket head, made by D. & W. Auchterlonie $60
Irons--Stewart pipe CM .... $45 each

Watt, James
[North Berwick s]
Driving Iron--Line face, Winton diamond CM $40

Watt, William*
[Perth, Edinburgh s, et al]
Spoon--Socket head, face insert $45
Mashie Niblick--Bobbie model, D&W Brodie CM $50

'Waverly'
[Vulcan Golf brand name]
Iron clubs--Line face .... $25 each

Way, W.H. (Bert)+
[Cleveland, OH]
Driver--Splice transitional head $250
Cleek--Smooth face, short blade, Condie rose CM $80
Niblick--Medium head, smooth face, Carruthers hosel $125

Way, Ernest
[Detroit, MI]
Mashie--Line face, Burke scales CM $45

Way & Ross
[Alec Ross & Ernest Way, Detroit, MI]
*   Mashie--Mussel back, dot face $100

Webb, W.H.*
[Frinton-on-Sea e]
Driver--(B) Own model one-piece $1,800
Niblick--(B) Fairlie model, Nicoll hand CM, line face $200

Weir, A.N.*
[Aberdeen s]
Driver--Socket head $60
Driver--(B) Short splice head, offset neck $300
Brassie--Short splice head $150

Wood Shafted Golf Club Value Guide

Putter--(A S) Marked Aberdeen $100

Joyce Wethered autograph 3-iron.
        Jack White long hosel "Suningdale" model putter.

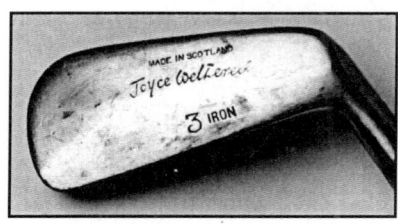
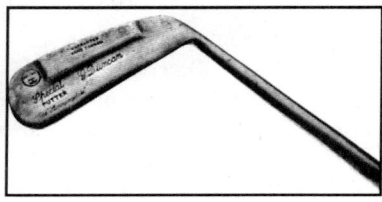

Wellington-Stone Company+
[Chicago; clubs were part of a golf motif smoking stand called the Parlor Putter]
*   Putter--Parlor Putter, line face, made without grip $200

'Westward Ho!'
       Mashie--Line face, marked 'Made in England" $40

'Joyce Wethered'
[The English ladies champion; an amateur, she allowed her name to be put on clubs after retirement from active competition]
*   Numbered Irons--Autograph series .... $80 each

Whitcomb, E.R.
       4-Iron--Dot face, Stewart pipe CM $35

White, Jack*

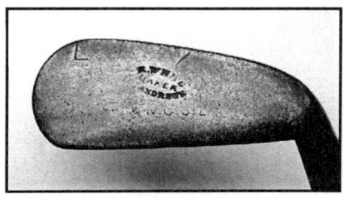
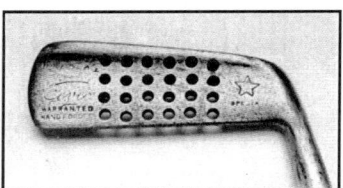

Robert White of St. Andrews mashie circa 1880-90.
        Jack White "Civic" model putter with drilled face.

[Sunningdale e, et al; Open Champion 1904]
        Driver--Stripe top, socket head, name in script $75-125
        Driver--(B) Sit-Rite model, concave sole, socket head $150
        Iron--Own Model, sun CM $45
        Iron--Autograph model, stainless, Palakona (bamboo) shaft $95
        Mid Iron--K 2, sun CM, stainless $45
*100   Putter--(B) Civic model, flange sole, holes drilled
        through face, Gibson star CM $400-600
        Putter--Boat shaped blade, pointed toe, convex face $250
*   Putter--The Sunningdale model, musselback-type
        weighted sole, 7" thin hosel, sun CM $200
        Putter--Super model, marked for Longniddry shop,
        W on face $125

        Numbered Irons--Stainless, flange sole, Gibson star CM $50 each

White, Robert*
[St. Andrews; blacksmith and pioneer iron club maker]
        Cleek--Smooth face $200-600
        Iron--Smooth face $200-500
        Lofter--Short blade, smooth face $200-500
        Lofter--Long blade $300-800
100 Mashie--Smooth face $200-800
        Niblick--Small head $350-1,200
        Niblick--Medium head $250-600
        Putter--long iron blade $300-500

White, Robert+
[Scottish immigrant working in Cincinnati, OH and several Chicago suburbs; head of P.G. Mfg. Co.; a founder of the American P.G.A. and early developer in the Myrtle Beach, SC area]
        Driving Iron--Dot face, name in diamond CM,
        marked Ravisloe CC $85
        Mashie--Smooth face, anvil CM $60
        Mashie--Smooth face, marked Cincinnati $80
        Mid Iron--Dot face, anvil CM, Homewood, IL $60

Whiting, Albert
[Folkstone]
        Spoon--(B) Wooden-iron model, socket head $200

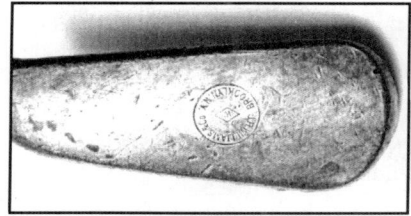 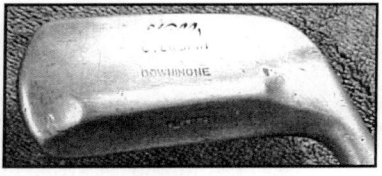

J.H. Williams mashie.   Wills "Overspin" model putter.

Whiting, S.
　　　Driver--Socket head $50

Whittet, William
[Falkirk s]
　　　Driver--(B) Dovetail/splice head $500

Williams Company, J.H.+
[Brooklyn, NY; maker of many iron heads for early U.S. club manufacturers. Their CM was a small W in diamond stamped into the hosel]
*　　　Mashie--Smooth face, Williams name stamped in circle ... $200
　　　Putter--"Metropolitan", straight blade small
　　　W in diamond CM $150

Williamson, Tom*
[Nottingham s]
　　　Brassie--Splice head $175
　　　Iron clubs--Smooth face, Stewart pipe CM .... $75 each
　　　Putter--Offset blade, Stadium anchor CM $60

'Wills'

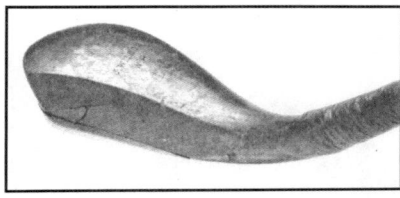 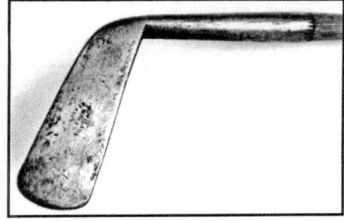

James Wilson spoon.   Robert Wilson cleek.

*   Putter--(U) Overspin model, gun metal, deep face blade, horizontal weight bar on back $300

Wilson Company, Harold A.+
[Toronto, ONT; sporting goods importer and retailer; also see Hawco]
    Iron--Smooth face, Forgan plume CM, Hawco mark in circle $200
    Mashie Niblick--Ace model 35, dash face $50

Wilson, James*
[St. Andrews; Hugh Philp's assistant for 7 years, he ran his own shop from 1852-1866]
*   Playclub--(L) Beech head $7,500-15,000

Wilson, Robert*
[St. Andrews; one of the earliest cleek makers in the home of golf]
*   Cleek--Smooth slightly concave face $400-800
    Iron--Smooth face $300-700
    Lofter--Smooth face $300-700

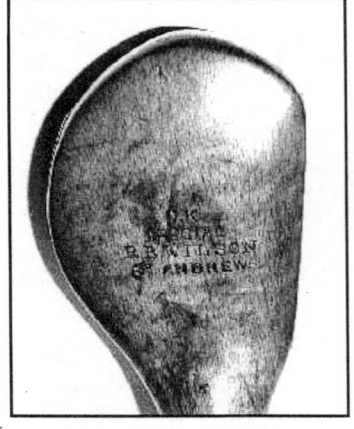

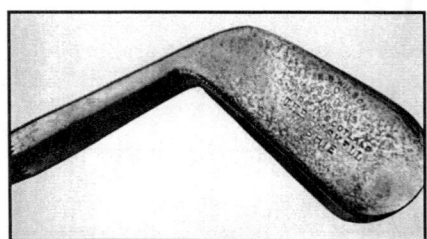

R.B. Wilson splice head driver.

R.B. Wilson mashie cleek.

R.B. Wilson "Haskell" patent hollow iron with leather damper.

Wood Shafted Golf Club Value Guide

    Lofter--Concave face $500-900
    Niblick--Small head, concave $800-2,000
    Putting Cleek--Long iron blade $400-800

Wilson, R.B.*+
[St. Andrews and US; pro and club maker to several English, American and German clubs. Most clubs also marked "O K Special"]

*   Driver--Small splice head $250
       Driver--Transitional splice head, leather face $250-450
       Brassie--Transitional splice head, leather face $250-450
       Cleek--Smooth face, "OK Special" $100
       Cleek--Guttie face insert, Stewart pipe CM $2,000
       Iron--Smooth face, Condie single fern CM $250
*   Mashie--The Haskell model, spring-face type face plate
       backed with gutta percha $1,250
       Mashie--Wide toe head, smooth face $200
       Mashie--Smooth face $90
*   Mashie Cleek--Smooth face, short blade $150
       Niblick--Small heavy head, smooth face $350
       Putter--Marked 'Rex Iron,' long shallow blade $250
       Putter--Short iron blade, deep face $150
       Putter--(B) 1000 model, iron blade, square hole cut in face $750
       Putter--(B) A 1 model, blade with no hosel $800
       Putter--Gun metal blade $80
       Putter--Accurate model, offset blade $75
       Putter--Oval convex faced blade $500
       Putter--Raised face (after Skinner), diamond face $250

Wilson, R.G.
[S. Croydon e, et al]

    Driver--Splice head, red face insert, aluminum
    backweights $250
    Brassie--Socket head $50
    Mashie Niblick--Long blade, line face $60

Wilson, R.
    Playclub--(L) C.1880, leather face insert $2,000

Wilson Company, Thomas E.+
[Chicago]

Pete Georgiady's

◇◇Early series and individual clubs
    Driver--Name in straight line, socket head $60
    Mashie--Line face, thick blade, large W' CM $40
    Mashie--(D) Baxpin model 1M, corrugated face $150
    Mashie--(D) Baxpin model 2A, corrugated face $150
    Mashie--Jock Hutchison autograph,

Thomas E. Wilson Company Tom Bendelow autograph mashie niblick.

Wilson Walker Cup series mashie.

Wilson Open Hearth Aim Rite series mashie.

 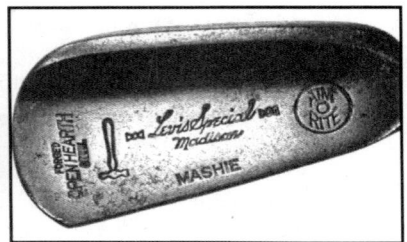

line face $75
    Mashie--(D) Wonder model, baxpin corrugated face $150
    Mashie--Open Hearth series, hammer CM,
    flange sole, line face $40
    Mashie--Carnoustie series with large W CM, line face $40
    Mashie--Wilsonian series, midget model $125
I   Mashie Niblick--Tom Bendelow autograph $75
    Mashie Niblick--(D) Baxpin model 1M, corrugated face .. $150
    Mashie Niblick--(D) Baxpin model 2A, corrugated face ... $150
    Mashie Niblick--(D) Baxpin model 2A1/2, ribangled face $175
    Mid Iron--Ashland Mfg. Co., line face, monogram CM $60
    Putter--Special 6 model, flange sole $60
    Putter--Amby-dex model, two-sided, wood head $350
    Putter--James Braid model 9, offset blade $45
    Putter--(A) Success model, mallet head $85
    Putter--(A) Mallet, Wilson in small script $75
    Putter--Kelly Club model $50
    Putter--Juvenile, straight line name $35
    Putter--(A) McNamara 3-way model, mallet head,

Wood Shafted Golf Club Value Guide

	three aiming lines on crown $100
	Putter--(A) Schenectady with patent date on back, large hollow W CM $175
	Putter--Wilsonian series, gun metal blade, lined ball face .. $100
100	Putter--XTA model, Sarazen autograph, extra long thin hosel $175
I	Putter--Model 2, extra long hosel $150

◇◇Sets of clubs

I	Aim Rite series, irons	$30 each
	Blue Ribbon series irons, stainless, line face	$30 each
	Carnoustie series woods	$35 each
	Carnoustie series irons	$25 each
	Archie Compston, champion series	$60 each
I	Crest Inter-related series irons, stainless	$50 each
	Cup Defender series irons, line face	$25 each
	Dixie series woods or irons	$25 each
	Fairview series irons	$60 each
I	Johnny Farrell autograph National Open series, chromium	$50 each
	Johnny Farrell model irons, stainless	$40 each
	Lady Lucky Stroke series irons, line face	$25 each
	Lincoln Park series clubs	$25 each
	Linkhurst series irons, stainless, line face	$25 each
	Ogg-mented, stainless, weighted toe	$60 each
	Open Hearth series irons, hammer CM	$25 each
	Plus Success series woods, socket head	$35 each

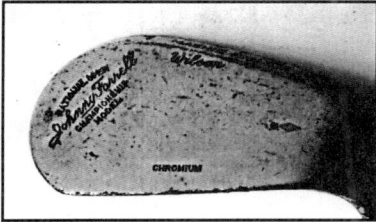

Wilson Championship model with Johnny Farrell autograph.

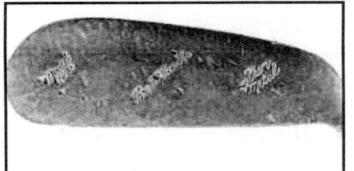

Wilson Model 2, long hosel putter.

Wilson Crest model putter from the set of irons.

Plus Success series irons (named) .... $35 each
Plus Success series irons (numbered) .... $30 each
Range series irons, stainless .... $25 each
Red Ribbon series irons, stainless, line face .... $30 each
Gene Sarazen series woods, splice head .... $200 each
Gene Sarazen series woods, plain or stripe top .... $50 each
Gene Sarazen series irons, stainless, line face .... $45 each
Gene Sarazen 6-9 series clubs, juvenile size .... $30 each
Gene Sarazen 11-13 series clubs, juvenile size .... $25 each
Sharpshooter series woods, socket head .... $30 each
Skokie series irons, stainless, line face .... $30 each
Streak series irons, stainless .... $25 each
Super Stroke series irons, chromed .... $30 each
Super Stroke series, Everbrite steel .... $50 each
Taplow series woods or irons .... $25 each
Ted Ray Seventy-Two series woods .... $50 each
Ted Ray Seventy-Two series irons,
stainless or chromed .... $40 each
Harry Vardon Seventy-Two series woods, green grip . $60 each
Harry Vardon Seventy-Two series irons, green grip .... $50 each
Vogue Set Irons--Green leather grips, line face .... $30 each
Vogue Set--4 irons (2,5,7,9) and putter $225
WWP irons, open face-beveled toe series, stainless,
dot face, WWP in circle CM .... $35 each
George Walker series woods .... $30 each
Walker Cup series woods, ivory inlay on crown .... $85 each
Walker Cup series woods, plain crown, face inserts ... $45 each
*   Walker Cup series irons, rainbow face grooves .... $125 each
Walker Cup series irons, dot face .... $35 each
Western Star series irons, dot face .... $45 each
Wilson Midget series clubs, toddler size .... $50 each
The Wilsonian series woods, socket head .... $35 each
The Wilsonian series irons, line or dot face .... $25 each
Wilsonian Junior series clubs, juvenile size .... $30 each

Wilson, William*
[St. Andrews; blacksmith and early maker of iron heads]

      Cleek--Long blade, smooth face $200-600
      Iron--Long blade, deep face $200-500
      Lofter--Long blade $200-500
      Lofter--(B) Anti-shank style, smooth face $650

Wood Shafted Golf Club Value Guide

Winchester iron supplied by Wilson.

Winchester Monel mashie niblick model 6832.

    Mashie--Thick heavy blade, St. Andrew CM $300-400
    Niblick--Small head $600-1,500
    Putter--Iron blade $150-250
    Putter--Gun metal blade, straight line name stamp $150-250
    Putter--Gun Metal blade, St. Andrew CM $300
    Putter--Iron blade, 'St. Andrew' CM $200

Wilson, William Christie*
[Hereford e]
    Iron clubs--Solwin model, rising sun CM, line face $75

Wilson, Kirkaldy & Lorimer
[St. Andrews]
    Iron clubs-Name in circle with O.K. Special, cross face $100

Winchester Arms Company+
[New York arms and hardware company selling its own branded clubs obtained from several makers]
    Driver--Jock Hutchison model, fiber face insert $160
    Driver--Model 6375, socket head $125
    Driver--Model 6358, socket head, insert $150
    Driving Iron--Model 6590, Vardon series, Monel,
    dash/line face $100
    Mashie--Model 6611 (Burke), flange sole. Dot face $100
    Mashie--Pickwick series model 6617 (Burke), dash face $75
    Mashie--Model 6716 (Burke), dot face, rounded back,
    Burke thistle CM $100
    Mashie--Model 61, St. Andrew Golf Co. stag CM $125
    Mashie--(D) Corrugated face $275
    Mashie--Jock Hutchison model, made by Wilson, dot face .. $85

Pete Georgiady's

```
Mashie--Model 6601, monel. Line face ............................... $100
Mashie Niblick--Model 6637, Monel, line face ................. $100
Mashie Niblick--Model 61, made by St. Andrew Golf Co.,
   Stag CM ........................................................................ $125
* Mashie Niblick--Jock Hutchison autograph ....................... $125
Mid Iron--Brae Burn, round sole ........................................... $75
Niblick--(D) Ribbed face, Gibson star CM ......................... $175
Niblick--Model 6718 (Burke), Monel ................................. $150
Rotary Iron--(D) Made by Burke for Winchester ............... $400
Putter--Brae Burn, blade ........................................................ $75
Putter--Pickwick series, blade, dot face ................................. $85
```

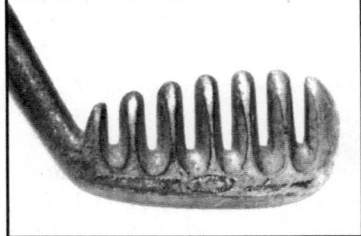 

Brown's patent perforated iron made by James Winton.
"Jumper" model iron from W. M. Winton & Son.

```
Putter--Model 6632, gun metal, flange sole ........................ $250
Putter--Model 6662 (Burke model 69), wide sole
   thistle CM .................................................................... $125
Putter--Model 6650, Jock Hutchison autograph series,
   Monel, Burke thistle CM ............................................. $120
Putter--(A) Model 6671, 1915 Braid-Mills, stamped
   for Winchester ............................................................. $200
Putter--(U) P.A. Vaile model, double bent neck,
   dash face, Burke thistle CM ........................................ $350
Putter--Model 6660, Brown-Vardon style .......................... $250
Putter--Mills AK model, marked Winchester ..................... $250
```

Winckworth-Scott, E.H.
[see Lillywhite's]
```
         Putter--(B) Winckworth-Scott model, autograph name stamp,
            square solid steel shaft ..................................................... $750
```

Wood Shafted Golf Club Value Guide

Winders, N.
    Brassie--Socket head $45

Winfield Special
    Putter--Iron blade $40

Wingate, S.
    Brassie--Socket head $45

Winton, J.
[Montrose s]
    Brassie-Short splice head, face insert $200
    Brassie--Socket head $90
    Lofter--Smooth face $70
    Putter--(S) Transitional splice head $250

◇◇Brown patent series irons
    Cleek--(B) Horizontally slotted face $2,000-3,500
    Driving Mashie--(B) Horizontally slotted face $2,000-4,000
    Mashie--(B) Horizontally slotted face $2,000-4,000
    Mashie--(B) Thistle model, vertically slotted face . $2,000-4,000
    Mashie Niblick--(B) The General model,
    vertically slotted face $2,000-4,500
*100   Mashie Niblick--(B) The Major model,
    vertically slotted face $2,000-4,000
    Mashie Niblick--(B) Roger Brown model, vertical
    slots in top edge and sole $3,000-5,000
    Mid Iron--(B) Horizontally slotted face $2,000-4,000
    Niblick--(B) The Major model, vertically
    slotted face $2,000-4,000
    Putter--(B) Straight neck, horizontally slotted face $2,000-4,000
    Putter--(B) Bent neck, horizontally slotted face $2,000-4,000

Winton Company, W.M.*
[Montrose & London, used the diamond cleek mark]
    Driver--Socket head, stripe top $80
    Brassie--Socket head, stripe top $80
    Cleek--Model 86, "Bogie" groove in bottom center of back $90
    Cleek--Model 97, dot face $50
    Driving Iron--Model 1, line face $45
    Driving Iron--Model 4, dot face $45

Driving Iron--Model 26, standard blade $50
Iron--Model A5, Harry Vardon series, standard blade $75
Jigger--Model 5, dot face $50
Jigger--Ted Ray own model, line face $50
Jigger--Totteridge-Vardon model, line face, diamond CM .. $50
* Jigger--The Jumper model, shallow face,
pointed toe, line face $100
Mashie--Model 1, line face $40
Mashie--Model 4, dot face $40
Mashie--Model 20, flange sole, line face $50
Mashie--Model 41, dot face $45
Mashie--Model 42, Smith model (anti-shank) $175
Mashie--Model 43, slightly rounded back $45
Mashie--Model 82, groove in bottom center of back $90
Mashie--Model 92, Ted Ray own, line face $75
Mashie--Model 143, standard blade $50
Mashie--Model AM, line face $40
Mashie--The Cert model, concave face $80
Mashie--(D) The Cert model, ribbed face $150
Mashie--Model C5-Vardon, musselback, line face $85
Mashie Niblick--Model B4, thick blade $50
Mashie Niblick--Model M18, standard blade $50
Mashie Niblick--Model P4, dot face $50
Mashie Niblick--(B) Smith model (anti-shank), dot face ... $150
Mashie Niblick--(D) The Cert model, corrugated face $150
Mashie Niblick--Model Z, stainless, diamond CM $60
Mid Iron--Model 3, line face $40
Mid Iron--Model 5, dot face $40
Mid Iron--Model 66, line face $40
Mid Iron--Model 72, dot face $40
Mid Iron--Model 83, groove in bottom center of back $90
Mid Iron--Model 89, slightly concave dot face $50
Mid Iron--Model H, straight back $40
Mid Iron--Model P3, centraject back $60
Mid Iron--Alex Herd own model $60
Niblick--Model 7, large head $50
Niblick--Model 12, dot face $50
Niblick--Model 17, dreadnought head, line face $50
Niblick--Model 24, Fairlie model (anti-shank) $175
Niblick--Model 77, dot face $50
Niblick--Model 106, dot face $50

Wood Shafted Golf Club Value Guide

Niblick--Ted Ray own model, diamond back, pointed toe ... $85
Niblick--Giant model, super large head, dot face $1,500
Niblick--The Last Word model, super large head,
dot face $1,500-1,800
Niblick--Win-On model, smooth face sand iron $100
Niblick--Bogie model, cavity back, smooth face $250
Sammy--Line face, shallow blade $65
Sammy Niblick--Line face $85
Spade Mashie--Model 6, line face $50
Putter--Model 11, bent neck $60
Putter--Model 33, 2 level back $75
Putter--Model 35, long face $50
Putter--Model 64, dot face $50
Putter-Model 103, blade $50
Putter--Model A6-Vardon, iron blade $60
Putter--Model A7-Vardon, iron blade $60
Putter--Model M, gem style $80
Putter--The Spieler model $90
Putter--Calamity Jane model, stainless, replica C.1960s $75
Putter--Harris model, long teardrop hosel $125
Putter--Square wood head, weight in toe $250
Putter--Miracle model, splice wood head, brass sole,
lead face $250
Putter--Mascot model, oval hosel, dot face blade,
pointed toe $250
Putting Cleek--Model 22, iron blade $50

Irons--The Spieler series, notched hosel joint .... $60 each

Wisden & Company, J.*
[London sporting goods house]
Mashie--Royal series, smooth face $75
Putter--Gun metal blade $125
Putter--(A) Royal series, mallet head $125
Putter--Wisden's Royal model, bent blade style,
2 lions CM $100

'Wood-Wand'
Putter--Iron blade $35

Woolley, Ted

6-Iron--Wilson Red Ribbon model, stainless, dot face $35

Worthington Company+
[Elyria, OH; largely a ball manufacturer, also produced clubs]
 Driver--Socket head, W. Anderson autograph $225
 Driver--Socket head, made by Worthington Mfg. Co. $150
 Putter--Iron blade $60

Wright & Ditson Company+
[Boston, MA sporting goods manufacturer and retailer]
 Driver--Model A, socket head, deep face $50
 Driver--Model AV, circular ivorine face, 5 plugs $100
 Driver--Model C, narrow head, plain face $60
 Driver--Model F, small head, plain face $50
 Driver--Model HV, circular ivorine face, 5 plugs $100
 Driver--Model IV, circular ivorine face, 5 plugs $100
 Driver--Model M, small head, plain face $50
 Driver--Model N, socket head, plain face $50
 Driver--Model O, ivory 2-screw face insert $150
 Driver--Model P, plain face $50
 Driver--(U) Model R, Rigden brass backweight $75
 Driver--Model RD, plain face $60
 Driver--(U) Model RJ, Rigden backweight,
 3 dowel plugs in face $250
 Driver--(U) Model RN, Rigden brass backweight $75
 Driver--(U) Model RNC, brass one piece sole
 plate/backweight $100
 Driver--(U) Model RNJ, Rigden backweight,
 3 dowel plugs in face $250
 Driver--Model X, socket head, plain face $50
 Driver--Model XBE, socket head, ivorine insert
 with 9 plugs $125
 Driver--Model 1, socket head, steel face $150
 Driver--Model 1, socket head, plain face $60
 Driver--Model 2, socket head, plain face $60
 Driver--Model 3, socket head, plain face $60
 Driver--Model 6, socket head, plain face $60
 Driver--Model 7, socket head, plain face $60
 Driver--Model 53C, socket head, black fiber
 insert with 5 plugs $75
 Driver--Model 53C, socket head, ivorine face insert $90

Wood Shafted Golf Club Value Guide

Driver--Model 56C, splice head, brass backweight $100
Driver--Dreadnought model, large socket head, plain face $100
Driver--Model 71, socket head, plain face $50
Driver--Socket head, Bamfar laminated bamboo shaft $150
Driver--(A) Square wood plug in back $200
Driver--Splice head, name in block letters $150
Driver--(B) One piece, leather face insert $1,500-2,000
Brassie--Model A, plain face $50
Brassie--Model AV, circular ivorine face, 5 plugs $100
Brassie--Model C, narrow head, plain face $60
Brassie--(U) EM model, triple splice head $400
Brassie--Model F, plain face $50
Brassie--Model H, plain face $50
Brassie--Model HV, circular ivorine face, 5 plugs $100
Brassie--Model IV, circular ivorine face, 5 plugs $100
Brassie--Model N, socket head, plain face $50
Brassie--Model O, ivory 2-screw face insert $150
Brassie--Model P, plain face $50
Brassie--(U) Model RN, Rigden brass backweight $75
Brassie--(U) Model RNC, brass one piece sole
plate/backweight $100
Brassie--(U) Model RNJ, Rigden backweight,
3 dowel plugs in face $225
Brassie--Model X, socket head, plain face $50
Brassie--Model XBE, socket head, ivorine insert
with 9 plugs $100
Brassie--Model 1, socket head, plain face $50
Brassie--Model 2, socket head, plain face $50
Brassie--Model 3, socket head, plain face $50
Brassie--Model 6, socket head, plain face $50
Brassie--Model 7, socket head, plain face $50
Brassie--Model 73, socket head, plain face $50
Brassie--Dreadnought model, large socket head, plain face $125
Brassie--Model 53C, socket head, black fiber
insert with 5 plugs $75
Brassie--Model 53C, socket head, ivorine face insert $90
Brassie--Model 56C, splice head, brass backweight $140
Brassie--(A) Square brass plugs in back $200
Brassie--(U) Skooter model, brass sole edge plate $250
Spoon--(A S) Long head, checkered face $250
Spoon--Model CS, socket head, plain face $60

Spoon--Model LS, long face $60
Spoon--Model 6, socket head, fiber face $60
Spoon--(U) Model 52C, fiber face insert, 5 plugs $80
Baffy Spoon--Model RS, long face $75
Wood Cleek--Model WC, long narrow socket head $150
Approaching Cleek--Dysart Fife model, made in Scotland, musselback, anvil CM $75
Approaching Cleek--Model 9, straight name stamp, smooth face $75
Cleek--(U) Cran model, wood face $700-900
Cleek--(U) Spring face model $700-900
Niblick--Name in arc at toe, small head, smooth face, hosel knurling $650
Iron--Model 5, straight name stamp, smooth face $75
Iron--Model Y-5, youth club $35
Mashie--(U) Spring face model $750-1,000
Mashie--(B) Vertical slotted face ('rake iron' type), open on bottom, Roger patent $8,000
Mashie--Junior model, stainless, dot face $25
Mid Iron--(U) Spring face model $750-1,000
Mid Iron--Kro-Flite model, line face $30
Mid Iron--Kro-Flite F 2 model, bottom half of face line scored $40
Mid Iron--Kro-Flite model, marked "Wright & Ditson, Licensees" $50
Niblic--Smooth face, concave face, small head $600
Niblic--Flange sole, dot face, lion CM $75
Mid Iron--Kro-Flite model 29, marked "Wright & Ditson, Licensees," oversize head $75
Pitcher--Kro-Flite F 7, ribbed face $100
Putter--T-shaped pendulum style head $1,200
Putter--(A) BM model, mallet head $75
Putter--Spring face model $1,000-1,200
Putter--(A) HH Model, Schenectady style $150
Putter--Travis model, square wood head, brass face $300
Putter--Rainbow model, dot face $50
Putter--(A U) Schenectady, marked in double circle Wright & Ditson outside, BGI inside $300
Putter--Model 10, wood Schenectady style, brass face $200
Putter--Model LW, oval hosel, broad flange sole $100
Putter--Model C94, oval hosel, round sole, blade $75

Wood Shafted Golf Club Value Guide

Putter--ARF model, long hosel, offset blade $50
Putter--Model CH (Chicopee), ... $200
Putter--Model HB, oval hosel, hollow back $200
Putter--(A) Model NH, Schenectady style with
ridge on top $150
Putter--(A) Model MR, mallet head after Ray model $75

Winton "Jumper" utility club.

Wright & Ditson socket driver in the A. H. Findley series.

Putter--Model RL, wood mallet head, large brass
backweight $200
Putter--Fownes model, wood mallet head with heel,
paddle handle long face $500
Putter--George Wright Autograph, stainless blade $50
Putter--Super gooseneck, gun metal $250

◇◇Early clubs with script stamp
    Driver--Splice head, bulger face $200
    Cleek--Selected model, smooth face $100
    Iron--Smooth face $100
    Niblic--Smooth concave face $500
    Putter--Gun metal blade $100
    Putter--(A,S) $250

◇◇A.H. Findlay series
*   Driver--Short splice head $175
    Driver--Socket head $75
    Driver--(A) $225
    Brassie--(A) $225

Brassie--Stem shaped neck on short socket club head $350
Cleek--Smooth face $75
Mashie--Smooth face $75
Mid Iron--Smooth face $75
Niblic--Smooth face, medium head $125
Niblick--Fairlie-type (anti-shank) smooth face $225
Putter--Thick, T-shaped gun metal head $1,200
Putter--Wood Schenectady style $250

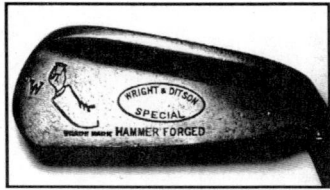 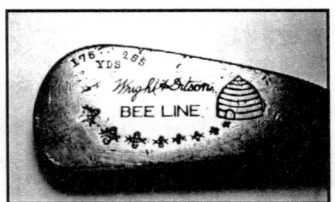

Wright & Ditson mashie from the "One Shot" series.

Wright & Ditson mashie from the Bee Line series.

◇◇St. Andrews series (earlier clubs have no CM, later clubs have hammer & roses CMs)
Driver--Socket head $40
Brassie--Socket head $40
Cleek--Line face $35
Driving Iron--Line face $35
Driving Mashie--Dot face $35
Jigger--Dash face $45
Mashie--Dot face, hammer & roses CMs $25
Mashie--St. Andrews, convex dot-dash face $200
Mashie Iron--Dot face $35
Mashie Niblic--Dash face $35
Mashie Niblic--Hammer & roses CMs, dot face $25
Mid Iron--Dot face, hammer & roses CMs $25
Niblick--Dot face $35
Niblick--Hammer & roses CMs, dot face $25
Putter--Blade, dot face $40
Putter--Gooseneck blade $50
Putter--Blade, hammer & roses CMs, dot face $30
Putting Cleek--Long blade $50

Wood Shafted Golf Club Value Guide

◇◇Juvenile clubs
    Driver--Socket head $30
    Brassie--Socket head $30
    Cleek--Smooth face $35
    Mashie--Smooth face $30
    Mid Iron--Smooth face $30
    Putter--Blade $35

◇◇One Shot series (arm holding shot glass CM)
    Approach Cleek--Model 8, musselback, dot face $60
    Approach Iron--Model 1, circular dot face $60
    Cleek--Model 2, line face $45
    Cleek--Model 3, convex back, circular dot face $60
    Cleek--Model 4, Carruthers hosel, dot face $60
    Cleek--Model 6, diamond/dot face $50
    Cleek--Model 7, smooth face $60
    Cleek--Model G9, gooseneck, beveled sole, dash face $45
    Driving Iron--Model WDI, line face $50
    Driving Iron--Model 1, smooth face $60
    Driving Iron--Model 2, circular dot face $60
    Driving Mashie--Model 1, dot face $50
    Jigger--Model 1, dot face $50
    Jigger--Model G4, gooseneck, dash face $50
    Lofting Mashie--Model 6, diamond/dot face $50
    Lofting Mashie--Model 10, dash/dot face $50
    Mashie--Model 2, short head $45
*   Mashie--Model 3, short hosel, circular dot face $60
    Mashie--Model 7, Taylor's model, deep face $60
    Mashie--Model 8, diamond/dot face $45
    Mashie--Model 10, convex face with lines $100
    Mashie--Model G11, gooseneck, beveled sole, dash face ... $45
    Mashie--(D) Dedstop DS6, corrugated face $125
    Mashie Iron--Model 1, dot face $45
    Mashie Iron--Model 2, circular dot face $60
    Mashie Iron--Model 3, line face $45
    Mashie Jigger--Model 3, long narrow blade $50
    Mashie Niblic--(U) Model 3, Foulis model, concave face . $150
    Mashie Niblic--Model 6, deep face, line face $45
    Mashie Niblic--(D) Model C51, corrugated face $125
    Mashie Niblic--(D) Model C92, slotted face $125
    Mashie Niblic--Model C51, circular dot face $60

Mashie Niblic--Model G11, gooseneck, beveled sole,
dash face $45
Mashie Niblic--Model M, dot face $45
Mid Iron--Model WM, line face $45
Mid Iron--Model 2, smooth face $50
Mid Iron--Model 3, short head $45
Mid Iron--Model 5, diamond back, diamond/dot face $60
Mid Iron--Model 6, dot face $45
Mid Iron--Model 7, diamond/dot face $45
Niblic--Model 4, random dot face $60
Niblic--Model 6, smooth face $60
Niblic--Model 9, cross/dash face $50
Niblic--Model G5, gooseneck, dash face $50
Niblic--(D) Model C98, corrugated face $150
Niblic--Model M, dot face $45
Push Iron--Model G8, gooseneck, beveled sole, dash face .. $45
Sammy--Model WY, smooth face $60
Putter--Straight face, iron blade, dot face $50
Putter--Flange sole, dot face $60
Putter--Gem style, dot face $100
Putter--Model 1, gooseneck $50
Putter--Model 2, gooseneck $50
Putter--Model 5, half gooseneck $50
Putter--Model 9, Maxwell pattern, cross/dash face $60
Putter--(A) Model BM, mallet head after Braid-Mills $60
Putter--Model BV, shallow face, rounded back $250
Putter--Model F, narrow blade, line face $50
Putter--Model H. heavy offset head, diamond face $60
Putter--(A) Model RM, Ray style $70
Putting Cleek--Model 8, circular dot face $60

◇◇Bee Line series
    Driving Iron--B 1, line face $35
    Jigger--B 8, line face, bee CM $60
*   Mashie--B 5, line face, bee CM $35
    Mashie Iron--B 4, line face, bee CM $35
    Mashie Niblic--B 6, line face, bee CM $35
    Mashie Niblic--(D) B 6, double waterfall face $3,500
    Mid Iron--B 2, line face $35
    Mid Mashie--B 3, line face $35
    Niblic--B 9, line face, bee CM $35

Wood Shafted Golf Club Value Guide

    Pitcher--B 7, line face, bee CM $40
    Pitcher--(D) B 7, grooved face $150
    Pitcher--(D) B 17, waterfall face, bee CM $300-400

    Pitcher--(D) B 17, double waterfall face $3,500
    Putter--B 10, line face, bee CM $40
    Putter--B 15, line face, bee CM $50

Wynne, Philip*
[Chingford, London, et al]
    Driver--Socket head $75
    Spade Mashie--Line face, pipe CM $45

Y

Yeoman, William+
[Chicago]
    Brassie--Short splice head $150
    Driver--Splice head, marked "Formerly Herd & Yeoman" $250
    Named Irons--William Yeoman model, Stewart pipe CM,
    scored face .... $60 each
    Numbered Irons--William Yeoman model,
    Stewart pipe CM, scored face .... $50 each
    Numbered Irons--Stewart RTJ/FO model, line face .. $125 each

Yonkers Sporting Goods Co.
[New York City]
    Niblick--Dash face $65

Youds, J.*
[Chislehurst and Hoylake e]
    Driver--Short splice head $125
    Driver--Socket head, face insert $60
    Mashie--(B) Smith model (anti-shank), Stewart pipe CM . $175
    Named Irons--J. Youds model, Stewart pipe
    CM scored face .... $60 each
100   Putter--(A B) Mallet head, lead face $300

[Detroit, MI; sole manufacturer of Walter Hagen brand golf clubs from 1926 onward. Also see Hagen, Walter]
    Sand Iron--(U) Walter Hagen model, stainless, concave face, flange sole $350-500

Z

Zappe, S.A.
[Springfield, OH]
    Driver--Socket head $75

Wood Shafted Golf Club Value Guide

Modern Wood Shafted Putters

The following clubs made with wood shafts were produced a decade or more after the discontinuance of the general use of hickory shafts in golf clubs. These specialty putters have become collectible in recent years and are not included with the original wood shafted club entries because of their more modern manufacture.

There are also a large number of 'replica' and 'souvenir' putters with wood shafts in circulation. Many of these are made in Scotland and none are included here because they are considered more novelty than clubs for serious golf play.

'Craftsman'
   Putter-Bronze blade, long square hosel 'Bench Made' $40

Crisman, Otey
[Selma, AL; Founded in 1946, Otey Crisman Jr. and his son, Otey III have made clubs, primarily putters under their own name as well as for a number of other companies, notably, First Flight, Scoggins, and King, all of which are stamped with the "Otey Crisman" mark in script. COLT Golf Co., N.Y. putters were made by Otey Crisman but without cleek mark attribution. Best known for his hickory shafted putters, most models were also offered in a variety of shafts inc. steel, aluminum, bamboo or fiberglass]
Dates generally run as follows:
- *1946-1964 Clubs stamped both "Selma, Al." and the letter "C" surrounded by the letter "O" on the hitting face.*
- *1964-1977 "Selma, Al" stamp dropped but O.C. in face remains.*
- *1977 to Present - O.C. in face dropped.*

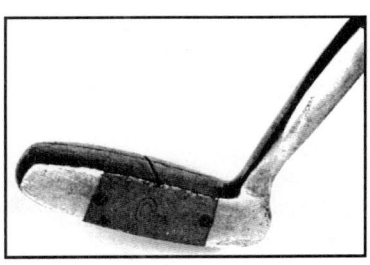

◇◇Non-"Selma" marked clubs.
    Putter--(A) FLM-1, mallet head, brass insert for First Flight $25
    Putter--AH, made for Scoggins $20
    Putter--31H, George DeLuca Memorial Pro-Am $30
    Putter--38G, brass blade, fiberglass shaft) $25
    Putter--Otey Original, 40th Anniv. Ltd. Ed.(1986) $100
    Putter--Model 55, Colt Golf $55
    Putter--(A) 82H, Colt Golf, mallet head $55

◇◇"Selma" stamped clubs
    Sand Wedge--Model 99 .... $45
*   Putter--(A) 12H, mallet head $30
    Putter--15H, brass blade $30
    Putter--(A) 18HB, mallet head, brass face insert $30
    Putter--23X, brass blade, bamboo shaft $45
    Putter--34H, stainless steel blade $30
    Putter--Silver Touch model, nickel silver blade $40
    Putter--(A) 70B, mallet, brass face insert $30
    Putter--NN1, brass blade $30
    Putter--Bell S model, similar to Ping (rings like a bell) $45
    Putter--(A) Croc H, croquet style head $200
    Putter--(A) 111H, "bassackwards" $175

Gradidge
*   Putter--Bobby Locke autograph model,
    stag head CM $75

Hogan, Ben
◇◇Macdougall-Carnoustie series putters
    Model P-200, brass blade $200
    Model P-202, semi mallet $200
    Model P-204, thick blade $200
    Model P-206, mallet $200
    Model P-208, streamliner $200
    Model P-210, adjustable weight mallet $200

Wood Shafted Golf Club Value Guide

MacGregor+
    Putter--Model 102GH, Mighty Mite, Bob Toski autograph, brass Bull'seye-type head $45

Nicoll, George*
    Putter--Gem model, chromed finish, modern hand mark $35
    Putter--White heather model, blade $30
    Putter--Splice wood head, perforated leather grip $30

Northwestern Golf
    Putter--Forward Thrust model, shaft with offset bend 6" above hosel $25

Spalding+
    Putter--Blue Chip model, flanged blade $100
    [the Blue Chip also was made in a steel shaft model]
    Putter--Calamity Jane, cartoon lettering $100
    Putter--Calamity Jane model, anvil CM, markings painted colors $50-75
    Putter--Calamity Jane model, Winton/Condie replica $50
    Putter--Chicopee model-1960s replica $100

Wilson, Thomas E.+
[Chicago]
    Putter--Perfect Balance model, iron blade with brass face ... $45
*   Putter--283 model, standard blade, Gene Sarazen autograph $75

ABOUT PETE GEORGIADY

Pete is, without doubt, the most scholarly collector I have yet come upon. He has an unabated love for British golf, especially the formative years in Scotland. In addition to obtaining two degrees from Miami University in Oxford, Ohio he attended law school at Dundee University in Scotland. It was there his interest in golf collecting actually began.

He was befriended by an elderly resident of the city who, after recognizing Pete's love for the game, gave him his first wood shafted golf club, a 1915 Braid-Mills aluminum mallet head putter. Pete laughs as he says, "I thought it was valuable beyond all consideration because it was old and unusual. I came to find out that it was very common." His father gave him two more wood shafted clubs the following Christmas, and thus the malady of golf collecting had claimed another victim. He started scouting around Salvation Army stores and thrift shops to "collect anything and everything with wood shafts. My love for Scotland made me especially interested in clubs of Scottish origin."

Pete quickly developed a burning desire to know who made the various clubs he acquired. The thing that sets him apart from most collectors is the voluminous research he does. He has spent countless hours pouring over golf handbooks, trade publications, patent journals and advertisements. Over the years he has undertaken and successfully completed some extensive research projects including those on deep groove irons and aluminum headed clubs. Pete has also identified more than 200 different cleek marks. As he got more and more into this process he wanted to learn all he could about the club makers. On trips to Scotland he spent much time with the late Eric Auchterlonie from whom he learned so much about early Scottish club makers. Pete's Compendium of British Club Makers is the authoritative work on the subject.

During the rare hours that Pete is not involved in golf research, golf collecting or golf writing, he is probably watching tapes and reading newspaper reports of his beloved Manchester United Football Club. He is an avid fan of English and Scottish Premier League soccer. His son Bryan has inherited his father's love of golf and has begun his own collection with a special interested in Old Tom Morris. Pete also enjoys playing golf and antiquing with his lovely wife Kay. Their home is a pleasant mixture of antique items and golf memorabilia.

For me, one incident accurately reflects Pete's expertise on golf history. At a recent Annual Meeting of the Golf Collectors Society, the after dinner speaker cancelled at the last moment. The Committee turned to Pete and, with little notice, he gave n informative and entertaining speech. He is able to combine an encyclopedic knowledge of old golf clubs with a modest personality and an effusive sense of humor. I have learned more about the history of the game of golf from Pete than any other person and perhaps that is the highest compliment of all.

Dan Bagdade
West Bloomfield, Michigan

Pete Georgiady, playing 19th century 'goff' in the National Hickory Championship, August 2002

Pete Georgiady's

Buying, Selling and Learning More

Included below is a list of people engaged in the business of golf memorabilia. Some handle a full range of golf artifacts, some specialize in only clubs, books or in other items. Several of these people have catalogs or mail price lists, some maintain shops and others sell at golf and antique shows.

Golf Collectors' Society
PO Box 241042
Cleveland, OH

(440) 460-3979
(440) 460-3980 fax

**British Golf
  Collectors' Society**
PO Box 13704
North Berwick, E. Lothian
EH39 4ZB
bgcs@globalnet.co.uk

William Reed's Antique Golf
1245 37th Street
Des Moines, IA 50311-2706
(515) 277-6592

Heritage Hickories
Allen Wallach
300 Edge Hill Rd.
Glenside, PA 19038
(215) 886-8875
bo@membrane.com

Bob Lucas
A Different Drummer
309 Hamilton Street
Geneva, IL 60134
(630) 262-0432
antqgolf@aol.com

John Sherwood
Canterbury, England
sherwoodgolf@btinternet.com
01227 765849

Jack Rutherford's
Golf Collectors Gallery
704-1555 Finch Avenue E.
Toronto, ONT M2J 4X9
Canada
416 493-4653

Chuck Furjanic's
Golf Collectibles
PO Box 165892
Irving, TX 75016
1 800 882-4825
furjanic@directlink.com

Classic Golf
Randy Jensen
4617 Dodge Street
Omaha, NE 68132
1 800 728-0566
www.classicgolfinc.com

Wood Shafted Golf Club Value Guide

Golfiana
George & Susan Lewis
PO Box 291
Mamaroneck, NY 10543
27 Purdy Street
Harrison, NY 10528
914 835-5100
www.golfiana.com

Cambridge Golf Antiquities
A Shop at the Lodge
17 Mile Drive
Pebble Beach, CA 93953
(831) 626-3334

Greg & Barbara Hall
Cleveland, OH
(440) 871-9319
bnggolf@mediaone.net

Mike Gallagher
506 Addison Street
Philadelphia, PA 19147
(215) 922-6139
mikegallagher@worldnet.att.net

Golf Collectibles & Antiques
Peter Helweg
3225 W. Grace Street
Richmond, VA 23221
(804) 355-6425
phelweg@gateway.net

Antique Golf
Iain Walker
10 Glasgow Road
Paisley, PA1 3QG
Scotland
0141 889 1860
info@antiquegolf.com

Kev Murray
Sheridan Collectibles
Suite 151, 24-28 St. Leonard's Rd.
Windsor, Berks. SL4 3BB
England
01628-661972
golf.collector@btinternet.com

Peter Dunn
The Golf Addict
2975 Dundas Street W.
Toronto, ONT M6P 1Z2
416 766-2101

Golfhounds
Jim Dryer
8040 Plantation Lakes Drive
Port St. Lucie, FL 34986
(772) 429-0066
Golf.hounds@att.net

Brendan Casey
Wot-A-Racket
250 Shepherds Lane
Dartford, Kent
DA1 2PN England
wot-a-racket@talk21.net

Golf's Golden Years
David Berkowitz
PO Box 842
Palatine, IL 60067
(847) 934-4108
antiquegolf@mediaone.net

Table Rock Golf Club
Jim Butler
3005 Wilson Rd.
Centerburg, OH 43011
1 800 688-6859
www.tablerock.com

Tom Mitchell
Golf and Other Sports Antiques
90 Norman Drive
Ramsey, NJ 07446
201 825-3464
golftique@att.net

Bob Georgiade
3013 Ridge Road
Durham, NC 27705
(919) 489-5876
snowhill@earthlink.net

Guttysnhix Golf Collectibles
Tom Johnson
3170 Rte. 43
Mogadore, OH 44260
(330) 677-8997
sales@guttysnhix.com

Eric O. Wolke
84-21 60th Drive
Elmhurst, NY 11373
(718) 898-5479
Acaseric@aol.com